EARLY HISTORY

PATRON

Dato' Seri Dr Mahathir Mohamad

SPONSORS

The Encyclopedia of Malaysia was made possible thanks to the generous and enlightened support of the following organizations:

DRB-HICOM GROUP

GEC-MARCONI PROJECTS (MALAYSIA) SDN BHD

MALAYAN UNITED INDUSTRIES BERHAD

MALAYSIA NATIONAL INSURANCE BERHAD

PERNAS INTERNATIONAL HOLDINGS BERHAD

PETRONAS BERHAD

RENONG BERHAD

SUNGEIWAY GROUP

TENAGA NASIONAL BERHAD

UNITED OVERSEAS BANK GROUP

YAYASAN ALBUKHARY

YTL CORPORATION BERHAD

© **Editions Didier Millet, 1998**
Published by Archipelago Press *an imprint of* Editions Didier Millet Pte Ltd
121, Telok Ayer Street, #03–01, Singapore 068590
Tel: 65-324 9260 Fax: 65-324 9261 E-mail: edm@edmbooks.com.sg

Kuala Lumpur Office:
25, Jalan Pudu Lama, 50200 Kuala Lumpur, Malaysia
Tel: 03-2031 3805 Fax: 03-2031 6298 E-mail: edmbooks@edmbooks.com.my
Websites: www.edmbooks.com
www.encyclopedia.com.my

First published 1998
Reprinted 1999, 2004, 2006

Colour separation by Overseas Colourscan Sdn Bhd (236702-T)
Printed by Tien Wah Press (Pte) Limited
ISBN 981-3018-42-9

ACKNOWLEDGMENT

The Encyclopedia of Malaysia was first conceived by Editions Didier Millet and Datin Paduka Marina Mahathir. The Editorial Advisory Board, made up of distinguished figures drawn from academic and public life, was constituted in March 1994. The project was publicly announced in October that year, and eight months later the first sponsors were in place. By 1996, the structure of the content was agreed; later that year the appointment of Volume Editors and the commissioning of authors were substantially complete, and materials for the work were beginning to flow in. By late 1998, five volumes were completed for publication, and the remaining ten volumes fully commissioned and well under way.

The Publishers are grateful to the following for their contribution during the preparation of the first five volumes:
Dato' Seri Anwar Ibrahim,
who acted as Chairman of the Editorial Advisory Board;
and the following members of the Board:
Tan Sri Dato' Dr Ahmad Mustaffa Babjee
Prof. Dato' Dr Asmah Haji Omar
Puan Azah Aziz
Dr Peter M. Kedit
Dato' Dr T. Marimuthu
Tan Sri Dato' Dr Noordin Sopiee
Tan Sri Datuk Augustine S. H. Ong
Ms Patricia Regis
the late Tan Sri Zain Azraai
Datuk Datin Paduka Zakiah Hanum bt Abdul Hamid

SERIES EDITORIAL TEAM

PUBLISHER
Didier Millet

GENERAL MANAGER
Charles Orwin

PROJECT COORDINATOR
Marina Mahathir

EDITORIAL DIRECTOR
Timothy Auger

PROJECT MANAGER
Noor Azlina Yunus

EDITORIAL CONSULTANT
Peter Schoppert

EDITORS
Alice Chee
Chuah Guat Eng
Elaine Ee
Irene Khng
Sharaad Kuttan
Jacinth Lee-Chan
Nolly Lim
Kay Lyons
Premilla Mohanlall
Wendy (Khadijah) Moore
Alysoun Owen
Amita Sarwal
Tan Hwee Koon
Philip Tatham
Sumitra Visvanathan

DESIGN DIRECTOR
Tan Seok Lui

DESIGNERS
Ahmad Puad bin Aziz
Lee Woon Hong
Theivanai A/P Nadaraju
Felicia Wong
Yong Yoke Lian

PRODUCTION MANAGER
Sin Kam Cheong

VOLUME EDITORIAL TEAM

EDITOR
Wendy (Kahdijah) Moore

DESIGNER
Ahmad Puad bin Aziz

ILLUSTRATORS
Anuar bin Abdul Rahim
Chai Kah Yune
Cheong Hoi Chan
Stephen Dew
Kerry Elias-Moore
Ishak bin Hashim
Tan Hong Yew
Yeap Kok Chien

CONTRIBUTORS

Prof. Dr Barbara Watson Andaya
University of Hawaii at Manoa

Asyaari Muhamad
Universiti Kebangsaan Malaysia

Baszley Bee Basra Bee
Universiti Kebangsaan Malaysia

Dr Peter Bellwood
Australian National University

Prof. James T. Collins
Universiti Kebangsaan Malaysia

Ipoi Datan
Muzium Sarawak

Kamaludin bin Hassan
Geological Survey Department

Assoc. Prof. Leong Sau Heng
Universiti Malaya

Dr John Miksic
National University of Singapore

Mohd Kamarulzaman A. Rahman
Universiti Kebangsaan Malaysia

Mohd Kassim Haji Ali
Muzium Negara (retired)

**Prof. Dato' Dr Nik Hassan Shuhaimi
Nik Abdul Rahman**
Universiti Kebangsaan Malaysia

Assoc. Prof. Dr Othman Yatim
Museum of Asian Art, Universiti Malaya

Zulkifli Jaafar
Muzium Negara

THE ENCYCLOPEDIA OF
MALAYSIA

Volume 4

EARLY HISTORY

Volume Editor
Prof. Dato' Dr Nik Hassan Shuhaimi
Nik Abdul Rahman

ARCHIPELAGO PRESS

Contents

Introduction

Malaysia's prehistory begins with the earliest known traces of human habitation around 40 millenniums ago, and extends through the protohistoric period to the founding of the Melaka Sultanate in 1400 CE, the date commonly used as the starting point of the historic era. Because so much has been written about Melaka and its significance in Malaysian history, the long period preceding it has been overshadowed, and outside of academic circles little is known about the rich archaeological heritage of prehistoric Malaysia. This book seeks to redress this imbalance.

Cast in brass moulds, tin coin 'trees', known as *pohon pitis*, were used as early currency in Kelantan.

TOP RIGHT: This gold ear ornament, perhaps of Malaysian origin, was found by the archaeologist I. H. N. Evans at Kuala Selinsing in Perak. It is believed to date to the 8th or 9th century CE.

The archaeologist Alastair Lamb (left) explains the restoration of a Bujang Valley temple site to Malaysia's first prime minister, Tunku Abdul Rahman (right), while the archaeologist Tom Harrisson (centre below) oversees excavations at the prehistoric sites in Sarawak's Niah Caves.

Digging up the past

Malaysia comprises the Malay Peninsula, the southernmost tip of the Asian mainland, located midway along the ancient East–West trade routes, and the states of Sabah and Sarawak, situated 530 kilometres further east across the South China Sea in northern Borneo. Situated between 2 and 6 degrees north of the equator, Malaysia is characterized by a hot, wet, equatorial climate. Both the fractured political geography and the climate have affected the study of early history. Scholars have tended to concentrate their research on either the Peninsula or the Bornean states, resulting in an incomplete view, while the torrid climate and the dense rainforests have meant that few artefacts other than earthenware and stone and metal tools remain from the earlier periods. Most of these, including early burials, have been found in the protected environment of caves. The only surviving architectural remnants are stone foundations of 5th–13th century buildings from the early kingdom period in Kedah and from Santubong in Sarawak.

Despite these drawbacks, Malaysia pioneered archaeological excavations in the Southeast Asian region. The first site report was published by G. W. Earl in 1863, but even though amateur archaeologists were busy collecting artefacts and digging up sites, it was not until I. H. N. Evans joined the Museums Department in 1912 that proper archaeological research began. Other pioneering archaeologists included H. D. Collings (1930s) who excavated on the west coast, M. W. F. Tweedie (1940s–1950s) who published a summary of the Malayan Stone Age, G. de G. Sieveking (1960s) whose work at Gua Cha set new standards of research, and Alastair Lamb (1950s–1960s) who excavated in the Bujang Valley. In Sarawak, the most prominent archaeologist was Tom Harrisson, the curator of the Sarawak Museum from 1947 to 1967. B. A. V. Peacock introduced archaeological training after Independence in 1957, and after the National Archaeological Survey and Research Unit was set up in 1969, local archaeologists took charge of excavations. Since then, significant discoveries have been made by the Malaysian archaeologists Nik Hassan Shuhaimi, Zuraina Majid, Adi Haji Taha, Ipoi Datan and Leong Sau Heng and the Australian archaeologist Peter Bellwood. Even as this book goes to print, new excavations and advanced research methods are pushing back dates and rewriting theories. Many cultural interpretations from the colonial era are now considered outdated. However, there are still considerable differences of opinion, particularly regarding theories on the dating and origin of Peninsular Malaysia's earliest inhabitants.

This large carnelian bead was found at the protohistoric site of Kuala Selinsing in Perak.

Prehistoric Malaysia

The earliest evidence of human occupation in Sarawak is a 38,000-year-old skull from the Niah Caves, although this date is currently under revision. The earliest from the Peninsula is an 11,000-year-old skeleton from Gua Gunung Runtuh in Perak. The oldest artefacts are Palaeolithic stone tools from Kota Tampan, Perak, dated to 34,000 years ago, while the earliest Bornean artefacts are stone tools from Tingkayu, Sabah, produced between 28,000 and 18,000 years ago. Around 5,000 years ago, hunter-gatherer lifestyles changed dramatically when the population acquired the knowledge of producing polished stone tools and earthenware. Evidence of this Neolithic culture can be found either on its own, or at Mesolithic sites, including the Niah Caves in Sarawak, Gua Cha in Kelantan and Gua Kechil in Pahang. Some academics believe that the cultural change in Peninsular Malaysia was the result of trade between communities in the north of the Peninsula and central and southern Thailand.

Apart from the discovery of a bronze bell in Muar, Johor, Peninsular Metal Age sites are also concentrated in the north. East coast discoveries were often situated near gold sources, while those on the west coast were near tin sources, which perhaps provided the ore needed for the production of bronzeware. Metal Age culture is also represented by iron items, including long-shafted tools known to the Malays as *tulang mawas,* or 'ape's bones', which have only been found in Peninsular Malaysia.

Villagers at Kampung Pencu near Muar, Johor, unearthed this Dongson-type bronze bell (dated 150 CE) while levelling a mound for a house site.

The presence of bronzeware from North Vietnam provides the first tangible

evidence of long-distance seafaring and the establishment of maritime trade links with mainland Southeast Asia, while Indian beads found at Metal Age sites, such as Kuala Selinsing (200 BCE–900 CE) and Changkat Menteri (1–800 CE), both in Perak, are proof of trade ties with South Asia.

Protohistoric Malaysia

The earliest confirmed kingdom in Kedah's Bujang Valley dates from the 5th century CE, while a polity was established at Santubong, Sarawak, and another at Chi tu in Kelantan in the 7th century. During the 8th–14th centuries, settlements were established in Johor, Perak, Pahang, Kelantan and Terengganu. During this early kingdom period, diplomatic ties were established with China, and trade was conducted with that

Part of the Thai pottery cargo recovered from the 14th–15th century 'Nanyang' shipwreck.

country, India and other governments in Southeast Asia. Up to the 14th century, Hindu–Buddhist influences had a major impact on Malaysian culture. This is evidenced by relics found in the Bujang Valley, the Kinta Valley of Perak, and at Santubong. At the same time, megalithic culture was evident in the Bernam Valley of Perak and in Sabah and Sarawak, while Dongson style existed where bronze drums were found. In remote areas, communities still practised Stone Age culture. The first confirmed evidence of a polity which had embraced Islam comes from an inscribed stone found in Terengganu, dated 1303 CE.

Although Malaysia's early history cannot boast of ruins on the scale of Angkor Wat, the many phases and variety of cultures which have existed over the millenniums have yielded an abundance of fascinating archaeological remains. The opinions expressed in the following pages are the authors' own, and although they have endeavoured to select the most important and reliable information available, some theories and dates are still the subject of debate. Ongoing research will no doubt resolve some of the unanswered questions. Much of the information in this book has never been published outside academic journals, and it is hoped that the reader will acquire a new understanding of the early historical background which has left its legacy in the rich cultural traditions of today's Malaysia.

Dated 1028 CE, this footstone from a grave near Pekan, Pahang, could be the oldest evidence of Islam in Malaysia. However, it remains unconfirmed because the style of the script dates to the 1470s. It has been suggested that the stone may have been made then to replace an earlier one.

Chronology

PALAEOLITHIC & HOABINHIAN (MESOLITHIC) c. 40000–2500 BCE

NEOLITHIC c. 2800–500 BCE

TECHNOLOGY

From 32000 BCE (or earlier) Palaeolithic pebble tools produced at stone tool workshop at Kota Tampan, Perak. Pebble tools found at Niah Caves, Sarawak, dated to 23000 BCE. More sophisticated bifacial flake tools made at Tingkayu, Sabah, between 26000 and 16000 BCE. From 12000 BCE Hoabinhian bifacial stone tools found at over 30 Peninsular Malaysian sites.

Polished stone tools and earthenware appear at cave and open sites in Peninsular Malaysia 2800–2000 BCE. Artefacts from open sites, including tripod vessels from Jenderam Hilir, Selangor, show similarities to those from rice-producing sites of Thailand, perhaps indicating agricultural lifestyles. Pottery appears in Sarawak and Sabah around 1500 BCE, coinciding with Austronesian expansion.

ARCHITECTURE

No surviving examples. The prototype of basic Negrito temporary shelters built of saplings and palm leaf thatch may have been used since the Hoabinhian period. Peninsular caves and rock shelters were used as habitation sites during the Hoabihian period.

No surviving examples. Austronesian expansion in Sabah and Sarawak may have introduced the pile house. Houses of the Orang Asli Senoi from Peninsular Malaysia, constructed with poles, bamboo, palm thatch and rattan, may have been introduced during the Neolithic period. Some polished stone tools may have been used for timber house construction.

LITERATURE

No available information.

No available information.

POLITICS AND SOCIAL CONDITIONS

Based on ethnographic reports of the Negritos, probably no social units larger than bands of about 30–40 individuals. Leadership based largely on seniority. No differentiation of social groups.

Probable evolution of leadership positions based on prowess of individuals.

ART

No surviving examples.

Haematite cave paintings of human, animal and abstract motifs found at Gua Tambun, Perak, may date from Neolithic times.

ENVIRONMENT

Volcanic eruption in Sumatra which created Lake Toba 32000 BCE probably devastated Peninsular Malaysia. Palaeolithic stone tool making site at Kota Tampan abandoned due to ash falls (date under revision, may be 73000 BCE). Land bridges connected Borneo with Peninsular Malaysia during Ice Ages, c. 16 000 and 9 000 BCE. Sea levels rose, severing land bridges 8000 BCE.

From 8000 BCE sea levels rose and may have peaked 5 metres higher than present levels around 3000 BCE. Warmer climates encouraged a larger population. Early prehistoric coastal sites would have been flooded. High sea levels may have facilitated early Austronesian sea migrations, enabling deeper riverine penetration into the interior.

ECONOMICS

The entire band of 30–40 people probably formed the basic subsistence unit. Possibility of minor product exchanges and social information between inland and coastal peoples beginning from the Hoabinhian period. A seashell found at Gua Sagu, Pahang, may be evidence of these exchanges. Encouragement of plant resources—early horticulturalism—began.

No actual remains found in Peninsular Malaysia, but possible field agriculture of rice and foxtail millet. Open settlement sites suggest agriculture. Rice remains from 2500 BCE in Gua Sireh, Sarawak, could be evidence of rice production. Overland trade exchanges between communities in Peninsular Malaysia and Thailand may have begun. Sea nomad economy began in Sabah.

RELIGION

The 8000–9000 BCE Perak Man found at Gua Gunung Runtuh, Perak, was buried with grave goods and food offerings, indicating a belief in the afterlife. Hoabinhian flexed burials from Gua Cha, Kelantan, and Niah Caves, Sarawak, as well as a fragmentary burial from the midden site of Guar Kepah, Seberang Perai, were treated with haematite, indicating burial rituals.

Extended burials appear in Gua Cha, Kelantan (1000 BCE), and Niah Caves, Sarawak (1750–500 BCE). Pottery, polished stone tools and stone bangles were used as grave goods. Log coffin burials, lustration rites and ritual haematite treatment found at Gua Cha. Religious beliefs may have centred on ancestor worship and animism.

METAL AGE
c. 500 BCE–500 CE

Bronze drums and bells of Dongson style (North Vietnam) found at Peninsular Malaysian sites (c. 580 BCE–150 CE). Bronze celts at Peninsular sites may date from 1300 BCE; those from Sabah c. 500 CE; and a bronze knife from Niah Caves, Sarawak, to 100 CE. Iron implements, including adzes, axes, and the long-shafted *tulang mawas* found at Peninsular sites, date from 100 CE.

Cist graves constructed from granite slabs found in the Bernam Valley of southern Perak/northern Selangor date between 100 and 800 CE. Megalithic traditions of Sabah and Sarawak, including menhirs and dolmens, may date from the Metal Age. No surviving examples of domestic architecture but stumps from Kuala Selinsing indicate pile dwellings made of wood and thatch.

No available information.

More elaborate and wealthier cist grave burials indicate status differentiation, some of which may have been inherited. By the end of the Metal Age, societies may have been consolidating into divisions of nobility and commoners. Wealth from trade becomes an important tool of aspiring rulers. The display of wealth in the cist graves indicates a successful economy.

Extensive haematite cave murals at Gua Kain Hitam (Painted Cave) in the Niah Caves complex, Sarawak, may date from the 1st century CE. The tradition of charcoal cave drawings from Gua Sireh, Sarawak, Baturong Caves, Sabah, and some Peninsular cave sites may have evolved during the Metal Age.

Environmental conditions approximate those of the present day. The settlement sites of Kuala Selinsing, Perak (began c. 200 BCE), were re-sited as the river changed course or silted up and were permanently abandoned around 1000 CE.

The port site of Kuala Selinsing, Perak (began c. 200 BCE), and the inland sites of the Bernam Valley (100–800 CE) connected by trade routes to the east coast. By 200 BCE long-distance sea trade in bronzeware, beads, pottery and iron tools began with mainland Southeast Asia, India and China. A motivation for trade may have been the acquisition of rare goods.as status symbols.

Increasingly elaborate cult of the dead. Dongson drums probably used as cult objects in burial rites for high-status persons. Canoe burials practised at Kuala Selinsing and secondary boat burials and murals, possibly depicting these boats, found in Gua Kain Hitam, Sarawak, where ceremonial dancing may have taken place. Cist graves in Bernam Valley furnished with highly valued imported objects.

EARLY KINGDOMS
500–1300 CE

Increasing use of iron for agricultural tools. Iron production at Santubong, Sarawak. Bronze casting, silver and gold working, pottery making and probably bead making at the sites of Kuala Selinsing and the Bujang Valley of South Kedah. Organizational and technical skills evolve for construction of stone architecture.

Permanent architecture in brick, stone and laterite blocks appear in the Bujang Valley, South Kedah, and at Santubong, Sarawak. Only the bases survive; the upper parts were probably of wood. Most of these were *candi*, or religious shrines. Best known is Candi Bukit Batu Pahat (Temple on the Hill of Cut Stone). Domestic architecture continued to be built in perishable materials.

Oldest Malaysian stone inscriptions dating from 400 CE found in South Kedah and Seberang Perai. These include Sanskrit Buddhist texts, names of rulers and kingdoms, engravings of stupas, and prayers for a sea captain.

Earliest Malay kingdom appears in the Bujang Valley, Kedah, from the 5th century CE. Polities appear at Santubong in Sarawak and Chi tu in Kelantan in the 7th century. Rulers functioned as the fulcrum for rituals and trade networks. Kingdoms often had an Old King—the father in semi-retirement—and a Young King—who conducted daily affairs of the state.

Hindu–Buddhist sculptures in stone, terracotta and bronze found in the Bujang Valley of Kedah; Santubong in Sarawak and the Kinta Valley of Perak date from the 5th century CE. Rock engravings of human figures (c.1100) found near Santubong, and megaliths in Sabah, Sarawak, Negeri Sembilan and Melaka.

Rice-producing areas established in river valleys upstream from port kingdoms. Inland rainforest clearance probably confined to slash-and-burn agriculture practised by Orang Asli groups. Early kingdom sites may have been lost due to changes in coastal contours or river courses.

Early port kingdoms evolve into entrepôts. From the 5th century, kingdoms conducted trade with China, India, West Asia and Southeast Asia. Rainforest products exchanged for imported goods. Mangrove areas exploited for resources by Orang Laut. Small-scale tin and gold mining begins. Tributary relations with China established with some kingdoms. Srivijayan overlordship from 7th to 11th century.

Introduced through trade contacts at coastal ports, Hindu–Buddhist beliefs were incorporated into existing beliefs, including reverence for ancestors and mountains. Buddhist shrines in Bujang Valley date from 500 CE; Hindu shrines after the 11th-century Cola attacks. Megalithic and indigenous beliefs continue with log coffin burials in Sabah and jar burials in Sarawak.

EARLY ISLAMIC
1300–1600 CE

Advances in mass production of metalware and pottery. Metal workers and craftsmen attached to royal courts. Technological advancements in metallurgy required for production of ritual objects for rulers, including kris and spears. Early use of firearms. Probably imported from the Near East.

Chinese accounts of wooden palaces, watch towers and palisades, but no surviving examples. The *Sejarah Melayu* (Malay Annals) describes the 15th-century wooden palace of Sultan Mansur Shah. Portuguese accounts of a stone mosque in Melaka. Port towns organized according to the various ethnic communities of the traders. Carved Islamic gravestones used for important people.

The inscribed Terengganu Stone, dated 1303 CE, the earliest confirmed evidence of Islam in Malaysia. It is the oldest Malay text in the Arabic script in existence. Other early Batu Aceh gravestones in numerous Peninsular Malaysian sites are inscribed with rulers' names, dates, and Qur'anic verses. The *Sejarah Melayu* describes the 15th-century court of the Melaka Sultanate.

The arrival of Islam in early 14th century greatly influenced Malay culture and lifestyle. Rulers took the title of 'sultan'. The Terengganu Stone records Islamic laws prohibiting the people from stealing, fornication and rebellion. Sultanates would have functioned in much the same way as the kingdoms, with the court operating as a ceremonial centre and a locus for economic activity.

Carved and inscribed gravestones, known as Batu Aceh, found in many Peninsular Malaysia sites, date from the 15th century. The date of a Pahang gravestone from the 13th century is still unverified. The carved megaliths from Pengkalan Kempas are probably from pre-Islamic times but one is inscribed with the word 'Allah'.

Malay polities were three-tiered with the capital located near a river estuary; an agricultural area upstream; beyond that the hinterlands were still untouched. Small-scale tin and gold-mining would have silted some rivers.

Influential Muslim traders enhanced trade and contributed to the rise of Islamic ports such as Melaka. Coinage is introduced from Pasai, Sumatra, and the first known indigenous coins are minted in Melaka. The *kancil* coin is introduced to Kelantan in the 15th century. Merchants also used gold dust and silver bars as coinage. Tin was exhanged for foreign goods.

The acceptance of Islam by the Melaka Sultanate in the early 15th century is well documented, but Islam arrived in Terengganu a century earlier. By the 16th century it was firmly established throughout the Malay World. Away from the coastal Peninsular regions, and throughout much of Sabah and Sarawak, ethnic groups continued to practise indigenous religious beliefs.

LEFT: Measuring 10 centimetres in length, this highly polished Neolithic stone axe was found in Upper Perak. The Neolithic period is characterized by sophisticated stone tools and pottery showing a level of skill far in advance of the earlier Hoabinhian technology.

BELOW CENTRE: Animals, human figures and abstract designs painted in haematite adorn the walls of the rock shelter of Gua Tambun near Ipoh in Perak. Neolithic artefacts were also found in the cave, but it is not known whether the paintings date from the same time.

BELOW: The floor of this archaeological excavation at Gua Peraling in Ulu Kelantan reveals an array of stone tools dating from the Hoabinhian period. Settlement in this interior region may have begun around 12,000 years ago when sea levels rose after the last Ice Age.

RIGHT: Boat-shaped coffins were found in Gua Kain Hitam, also known as the Painted Cave, in the Niah Caves complex of Sarawak. Two archaeologists standing by a rock (centre left) are dwarfed by this cave which is also famous for its haematite paintings. The paintings depict similar 'boats of the dead', believed to have carried the souls of the deceased to the afterworld.

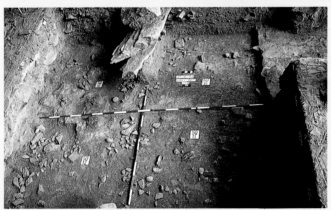

PREHISTORY

Because of Malaysia's political geography, its prehistory has two separate trajectories: the Malay Peninsula forms the southeastern tip of the Asian mainland, while Sabah and Sarawak are part of the island of Borneo, which was at certain times part of continental Asia.

Fossil remains from Java show that early humans (*Homo erectus*) first entered the region more than one million years ago. Evidence suggests they were replaced by the incoming ancestors of modern humans less than 150,000 years ago. Traces of *H. erectus* have not yet been found in Malaysia where the record of humanity, according to radiocarbon dating methods, begins about 40,000 years ago. These early humans had to cope with many environmental changes. When sea levels were low during the Pleistocene, they could have used the land bridges connecting mainland Asia to Sumatra, Java and Borneo, or they may have crossed the sea using rafts.

The initial peopling of Malaysia is both a story of great fascination and a source of heated debate. The first modern human occupants were quite closely related to the first Australo-Melanesian colonists of western Melanesia and Australia. Excavations in the Niah Caves of Sarawak have produced numerous remains of these people, dating from possibly 40,000 years ago and onwards, while Peninsular Malaysian rock shelters with evidence of Hoabinhian occupation, such as Gua Cha, also have skeletal remains of a related population who first penetrated the interior rainforests about 12,000 years ago.

Opinions differ as to whether present-day Malaysians descend entirely from Pleistocene founder populations or from subsequent migrations. It is this author's view that 3,000–4,000 years ago Austronesian-speaking peoples from Taiwan dispersed through the islands of Southeast Asia fundamentally altering the human shape of Malaysia. All the indigenous Borneans today are Austronesians, who perhaps first colonized Borneo 3,500 years ago, as evidenced by finds in Sabah at the Madai Caves and at Bukit Tengkorak, and in the Niah and Mulu Caves of Sarawak.

This limestone adze, dating from Neolithic times, measures 23 centimetres in length.

Peninsular Malaysia is quite different, and much more diverse ethnically. Among the Orang Asli, the Negritos probably descend from the tool-makers of the Hoabinhian cultural period, whereas the ancestry of the Senoi agriculturalists may derive from people practising a mixed Hoabinhian and Neolithic culture, the latter involving migrations from Thailand 4,000 years ago. Both groups speak Austroasiatic languages unrelated to Austronesian. The Malays are Austronesians, but it is not sure when they first settled in the Malay Peninsula. Archaeology suggests that the Peninsula was still mainly occupied by Semang hunters and Senoi agriculturalists as recently as 2,000 years ago. The first major

This hollow-footed Neolithic vessel discovered in Peninsular Malaysia is of unknown use. It may have been used as a potter's turntable or as a pot stand.

spread of the Malay language might have occurred during the period of Srivijaya after 670 CE. At a similar date, Malay perhaps first spread to Borneo as a trade language.

Investigating past environments

The term palaeoenvironment, used to denote the external conditions of past ages, takes into account all aspects of previous climates, the physical and chemical conditions of the soil, and life forms that have affected and influenced the survival of organisms or ecological communities, particularly humans. Palaeoenvironmental studies concentrate on the Quaternary period, the most recent period of geological time, which covers approximately the last 1.6 million years.

Fossilized remains, like this animal skeleton preserved in a limestone cave near Ipoh, Perak, provide valuable information for palaeoenvironmental reconstruction.

Peat cores reveal past environments

At Pekan Nenas, a pineapple-growing district of Johor, geologists use an auger to extract a peat core. By analysing the stratigraphy of the core and its preserved pollen remains, researchers can reconstruct past climates and vegetation changes due to rising and falling sea levels.

A core sample (above) obtained at Pengelayan, Sarawak, shows a clear distinction between the darker peat layer and that of the greenish gray marine clay. The latter indicates that 5,000 years ago, during high sea levels, the area was covered by sea, while the peat sequence shows that thick swamp forests have covered the region ever since.

At Sungai Mas in the Bujang Valley of South Kedah, an archaeologist sorts shards discovered among the remains of what is believed to be an early port kingdom. In the absence of written material, ceramics provide valuable clues to the technological and cultural development of a society. Shards discovered at Sungai Mas include those of Chinese and Middle Eastern wares dating from the 7th century CE, which indicates that international trade was conducted at this site.

Clues from sedimentary deposits

Valuable information on former climate and environmental conditions is deduced from sedimentary deposits. Their thickness, orientation, stratigraphic relation and fossil content are all important in explaining the environment where they were deposited, and for cross-correlation to other environments. Sediment accumulation is an ongoing process, occurring in lakes, valleys, river channels, estuaries, deltas, beaches, marine basins and deep oceanic troughs. The rate of accumulation, in combination with the existing climate and other factors, provides data on past climatic conditions.

Peat is commonly used in palaeoenvironmental and palaeoclimatic reconstructions. Made from semi-carbonized plant remains that have accumulated in waterlogged environments, peat forms in enclosed basins and flood plains, or in areas of high moisture content. Peat thickness varies according to the subsoil topography. In the Rajang and Baram deltas of Sarawak, for example, it is common to find peat deposits from 5 to 10 metres thick, but in Peninsular Malaysia, near Sabak Bernam in Selangor, and at Pekan in Pahang, it seldom exceeds a depth of 6 metres.

Peat deposits represent valuable records of climatic change as they form an ideal medium for pollen preservation, and their development is closely related to climatic conditions. In Malaysia, peat sites investigated include Marudi in Sarawak, Pekan Nenas in Johor, and Pantai Remis in Perak.

Sediments from lake basins provide a record of palaeoenvironmental changes in the surrounding areas. Lithological changes—variations in the colour, composition and texture of rocks—reflect sedimentation processes. Alternation of cold and warm phases produces sediments higher in mineral matter or organic constituents. Pollen grains and other fossils preserve well in lake sediments and are widely used in palaeoenvironmental reconstruction.

Human occupation around lakes often results in increased sediment because of soil erosion due to land clearing. In Perak, deposits indicate that the palaeolithic inhabitants of Kota Tampan had settled around a former lake area which occupied an area of 68 square kilometres, three times the size of the present Chenderoh Reservoir on the Perak River.

Caves contain sediments that originated from within, like cave earth, rock rubble and speleothems (secondary mineral deposits in stalagtites and stalagmites), and sediments that accumulate from outside influences like rivers, wind and animals. All these are used for reconstructing the cave conditions of the past. The popularity of caves as shelters for early humans is known from many sites in Malaysia. These include the Niah Caves in Sarawak where Malaysia's earliest known prehistoric human remains (about 38,000 years old) were found, and Gua Gunung Runtuh near Lenggong where Perak Man (11,000 years old) was discovered.

Alluvial and marine deposits

Sediments which accumulate from the action of running water are known as alluvial deposits. These are found in deltas, flood and coastal plains, river valleys, river channels and alluvial fans. The nature of the deposits, in association with the age of their formation, provides information on past hydrological conditions, including changes in river patterns over time.

Quaternary sedimentary deposits in Malaysia indicate that very active fluvial processes operated during the Pleistocene (the first epoch of the Quaternary period). In lowland Peninsular Malaysia, these sediments are known as the 'Old Alluvium'. Studies done at Pantai Remis in Perak date the age of the 'Old Alluvium' from 28,000 to more than 55,000 years ago.

Many global continental shelves feature geomorphic indications of past lower sea levels, and deposits such as peat and terrestrial fauna preserved in sediments below present sea levels offer further proof. In the Strait of Melaka and the South China Sea, peats have been recorded below the sea bottom, indicating lower sea levels in the past. Similarly, erosional features found at altitudes higher than present-day sea levels show evidence of past high sea positions. These features occur in many coastal regions and include abrasion flats and oyster relics at Gertak Sanggul, Penang; sea level notches at Bukit Kodiang, Kedah; notches in coastal rocks at Bukit Keluang, Terengganu; and inland beach ridges at Seberang Perai, Penang, and at Beruas, Perak.

In the deep sea, sedimentation proceeds uninterrupted, unaffected by sea level changes. Deep-sea research has yielded information on the global climate going back more than a million years. This data is gleaned from investigating sediments and their fossil contents, particularly Foraminifera (marine protozoans), which preserve in their skeletal remains a record of the ocean's isotopic composition at the time they were alive.

Methods for estimating dates

Age dating is the term used to determine the age of a sedimentary sequence which enables a correlation based on a similar time event to be established. Evidence of environmental changes can then be correlated between different areas. The age of the Kota Tampan Palaeolithic site in Perak was determined in this way by correlating the volcanic ash layer overlaying the gravel deposits in which the stone tools were found, to dated similar ash deposits found at Serdang in Selangor.

Other dating techniques include radiometric dating methods; incremental dating, which uses the study of tree rings (dendrochronology) and lichens (lichenometry); and artefact dating, which assesses archaeological periods from artefacts such as stone tools, metal objects and ceramics.

Information from fossils

Various types of fossils provide information on past environments. Plant macrofossils, such as seeds, leaves, fruits and wood, provide limited information on the local ecology, but analyses of the pollen and spores present in these enable the reconstruction of past vegetation, the interpretation of vegetation migration patterns, and shifts in the altitudinal limits of the tree line. Using these methods, archaeologists have been able to suggest, from the finding of a non-native, pine-dominated sample at Subang near Kuala Lumpur, that the Malay Peninsula experienced a seasonal climate during the Middle Pleistocene period. Foraminifera provide information on salinity variations and past water temperatures, while deep-sea samples facilitate the reconstruction of the Quaternary global climate.

Radiometric dating

Different radiometric dating methods are used according to the type of material to be dated, and its expected time span. The table below outlines the various methods, their isotope value, the time span they are effective for and the various materials used to obtain dates by each method. The most popular method used in Malaysia is radiocarbon because materials containing carbons are readily available.

METHOD	ISOTOPE	RANGE (YEARS)	MATERIAL
Radiocarbon	^{14}C	0–70,000	peat, wood, charcoal, organic mud, shell
Uranium series	^{234}U	50,000–1,000,000	coral, molluscs, marine carbonate
	^{230}Th	0–400,000	coral, molluscs, deep sea cores
	^{231}Pa	5,000–120,000	coral, molluscs
Fission track	^{238}U	0–100,000,000	volcanic tuff, volcanic ash
Thermoluminescence		0–1,000,000	loess, dune sand, pottery, flints

Pleistocene wood resins found in the 'Old Alluvium' at Pantai Mine in Perak were preserved in the basal part of the peat layers.

The 'Old Alluvium'

Occurring in the Malaysian lowlands, the 'Old Alluvium', also known as the Simpang Formation, is a Quaternary alluvial deposit forming a series of terraces made up of gravel, sand, silt and clay together with peat. Stratigraphic studies and dating using radiocarbon and thermoluminescence methods done at Pantai Mine, an open-pit tin mine in Perak, revealed that the exposed terraces date from 28,000 to more than 55,000 years BP (before the present). Lower units beyond the range of these dating techniques could be even much older.

Location of the study area

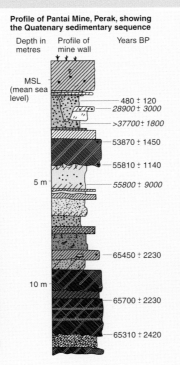

Profile of Pantai Mine, Perak, showing the Quatenary sedimentary sequence

Depth in metres | Profile of mine wall | Years BP

MSL (mean sea level)

480 ± 120
28900 ± 3000
>37700 ± 1800
53870 ± 1450
55810 ± 1140
55800 ± 9000

5 m

65450 ± 2230

10 m

65700 ± 2230

65310 ± 2420

Gravel — Crossbedding — *55800 ± 9000* Thermoluminescence date
Sand — Shells, shell fragments — 55810 ± 1140 Radiocarbon date
Clay — Wood
Peat — Plant remains — Pottery shards
— Tree stumps — Seed remains
— Roots — Scour base

BELOW LEFT: This cross section of Pantai Mine showing the exposed face of the mine pit corresponds to the stratigraphic diagram on the left.

BELOW RIGHT: Tin mining activities have exposed the Pleistocene deposits of sands and gravels interbedded with woody peat known to geologists as the 'Old Alluvium'.

Source: After Kamaluddin Hassan (1992)

The Pleistocene or Ice Age period

The epoch from about 1.6 million years ago to about 10,000 years ago is known as the Pleistocene. Also referred to as the Ice Age, it is characterized by extended cold periods known as glacials, alternating with warmer stages, or interglacials. Pleistocene climatic changes in Malaysia are documented from both local and global studies using sedimentary evidence, fossils, and oxygen isotope records.

The granite summit plateau of Sabah's Mount Kinabalu, Southeast Asia's highest peak, shows the characteristic scarring produced by glaciation which occurred during the Pleistocene.

Microscopic protozoaic shellfish, known as foraminifers (above), and microscopic pollen grains and spores are used to determine past environments. However, there are not many continuous pollen records that span the entire Pleistocene, since sediment accumulation relies on geological factors and constraints, such as tectonic activities and climate. Most palynological studies concentrate on the period since the last interglacial, from 120,000 years ago.

The 34,000-year-old site of Kota Tampan where this stone tool was found was much further from the sea than at present as the sea level then was at least 80 metres lower than at present.

Pollen records as climatic indicators

Palynology, the study of living and fossil pollen grains and plant spores, is widely applied in the reconstruction of Malaysia's past environmental conditions. This is because the sedimentary distribution of the pollens and spores shows the types of vegetation which prevailed during the time they were deposited.

Pollen records from lowland Peninsular Malaysia and from the South China Sea reveal low sea levels during Ice Ages. Peat deposits found in the Melaka Strait and the South China Sea, showing an abundance of pollens characteristic of mangrove forests, have been recorded at depths of 4.3 metres, 14.6 metres and 68 metres below mean sea level, corresponding to the respective ages of 55,800, c. 80,000, and c. 11,100 years ago. When these data are correlated to oceanic oxygen isotope records of the same period an interrelated global pattern of large-scale sea level changes is revealed. These worldwide fluctuations were caused by the abstraction of sea water into ice sheets during the glacial cycle, and the reverse effect when these melted during the interglacial or warm cycle.

Evidence that Malaysia experienced a cooler, more seasonal climate during the middle Pleistocene is indicated by pollen records from Subang near Kuala Lumpur which are dominated by pine and grass pollens, suggestive of the pine woodlands of Thailand and Luzon in the Philippines. As these species are not currently indigenous to Malaysia, it is probable that during this cooler period the rainforests were pushed further south, with correspondingly lower sea levels. Pollen records worldwide show similar climatic fluctuations, as do glacial studies.

During the last interglacial period, indications are that the Malaysian climate was even slightly warmer than at the present time.

Sea level records as glacial indicators

Evidence of changing sea levels during the Pleistocene is known from many parts of the world including Malaysia. During the Quaternary (the last 1.6 million years), successive glacial–interglacial cycles resulted in the alternate retreat and advance of continental ice sheets causing repeated sea level oscillations. The lowest worldwide sea level of the last glacial period (c. 18,000 years ago), which correlates with that of Malaysia, is estimated at 100–180 metres below the present level, although it is currently accepted as being around 100 metres.

Even though

The Pleistocene global climate

The world's oldest continental pollen record, cored from the Colombian highlands, shows how glacial/interglacial cycles affected the tropical mountain vegetation throughout the Pleistocene. The lowering of vegetation belts from 1,600 metres to 1,000 metres in altitude indicated glacial periods when mean temperatures fell about 8 °C. When these findings were correlated with oxygen isotope records from the eastern Pacific Ocean, remarkable climatic similarities were revealed, showing a global pattern.

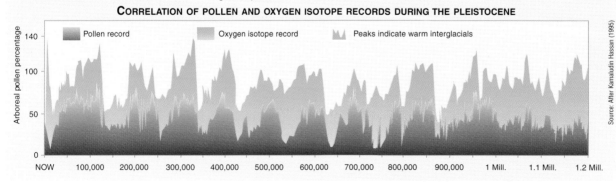

CORRELATION OF POLLEN AND OXYGEN ISOTOPE RECORDS DURING THE PLEISTOCENE

Pollen record   Oxygen isotope record   Peaks indicate warm interglacials

Arboreal pollen percentage: 140, 100, 50, 0

NOW 100,000 200,000 300,000 400,000 500,000 600,000 700,000 800,000 900,000 1 Mill. 1.1 Mill. 1.2 Mill.

Source: After Kamaludin Hassan (1995)

RIGHT: During Pleistocene Ice ages, when lower sea levels were a global phenomenon, Malaysia's coastline extended much further out into the Melaka Strait than at present, and islands like Penang and Pangkor were joined to the mainland. The map (below right), of the coastal regions of Penang and Perak, shows present and past shorelines up to 80,000 years ago. The satellite image (above right) shows the present coastline of Penang and Perak.

Continental ice sheets are a rich source of information on past global atmospheric conditions and climate. An Antarctic ice core, which yielded climatic records of the last 160,000 years, showed a remarkable correlation between past glacial and interglacial temperature changes and the atmospheric concentration of gases such as carbon dioxide and methane.

The last glacial period is indicated by three minima, around 20,000, 60,000 and 110,000 years ago, when the global mean temperature was 6 °C colder than at present. The last interglacial was significantly warmer than that of the Holocene period (the last 10,000 years), while the end of the previous glacial was quite similar to the last glacial maximum. These records also compare well with deep sea oxygen isotope records.

Meanwhile, in Greenland, data from an 250,000-year-old ice core indicate abrupt climatic shifts during the last interglacial. Ice core records, in combination with deep sea data, provide useful proxy reference for prevailing global climatic conditions. These data also provide the means for correlating sea level behaviour and factors affecting tropical sedimentation patterns, particularly with regard to the Malaysian environment.

glacially derived sediments are rather scarce in the tropical region, the presence of earlier glacial activity is not unknown. Morphological features on Mount Kinabalu in Sabah show smooth surfaces, limited U-shaped valleys, crescentic cracks, crescentic gouges, glacial grooves and striae—all products of glacial action. It has been suggested that Mount Kinabalu was glaciated more than once during the Pleistocene.

Climate evidence in the deep sea

Due to the fragmentary nature of terrestrial records, it is difficult to reconstruct a long-term and continuous interpretation of environmental change spanning the Pleistocene. Deep sea sediments provide a better alternative, since a more complete record of deposition is preserved in the world's oceans.

The oxygen isotopic analyses on plankton from a deep sea core located in the Solomon Plateau of the Pacific Ocean recorded 22 marine stages. These stages represent records of the last 800,000 years and provide evidence of cold periods when ice sheets were extensive, and warm periods when ice sheets were correspondingly small. Studies indicate that the warm peaks were of similar levels, suggesting that global ice volumes and sea surface temperatures during peak interglacials were similar to or slightly higher than those of the present day. The duration of the interglacials was around 10,000 years, while a full glacial cycle seems to have lasted around 100,000 years.

Present-day shoreline

Extent of land area about 55,800 years BP

Extent of land area about 80,000 years BP

Land above 100 metres

Depth of sea

Strait pf Melaka

Penang · Butterworth

Taiping

South China Sea

PENINSULAR MALAYSIA

Strait of Melaka

Pulau Pangkor   Lumut

10   0   10   20 km

Source: After Kamaludin Hassan (1995)

Pleistocene sea levels

In this diagram, sea level records from the Huon Peninsula in New Guinea, which correspond to those worldwide, show the huge fluctuations in sea levels brought about by the subsequent freezing and melting of oceans over the last 140,000 years. In Malaysia, sea levels during the last glacial maximum about 18,000 years ago have been estimated at between 100 and 120 metres lower than at present. During low sea levels, when the land surface of Malaysia was much larger than at present, human and animal populations moved across land bridges connecting Borneo to the Malay Peninsula.

Researchers from the Sabah Museum excavate at Tingkayu, East Sabah, which was once a lake in Pleistocene times between 28,000 and 18,000 years ago. Stone tools found there are evidence of human occupation during that period.

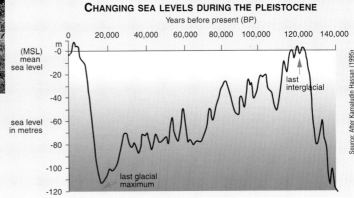

CHANGING SEA LEVELS DURING THE PLEISTOCENE

Years before present (BP)

Source: After Kamaludin Hassan (1995)

The postglacial and Holocene periods

The epoch after the last Ice Age, about 18,000 years ago, when the ice cover began to retreat, is known as the postglacial period, while the Holocene, also known as Recent, covers approximately the last 10,000 years of this period. Throughout this time, both high and low sea level changes occurred on a global scale. In Malaysia, low sea levels created land bridges which facilitated the migration of animals and humans between the Malay Peninsula and Borneo, while high sea levels inundated much of the lowlands of the Peninsular west coast.

Fishermen at Pantai Sri Tujuh, Kelantan, make use of the shallow seas to net fish. As water depths along much of the east coast do not exceed 100 metres, relatively minor fluctuations of sea level result in substantial shoreline shifts. The last major drop in sea level occurred during the postglacial period (see box below).

Geological evidence of changing sea levels

The rise of seas over land areas, known as transgression, their subsequent retreat, or regression, and the highest, lowest and relatively stationary sea level conditions all leave records in the form of sediments and fossil assemblages. The relation of this data to the known dates of various sea levels provides useful indicators for reconstructing Malaysia's palaeoenvironment.

Sea level records from the Strait of Melaka, the South China Sea and the Karimata Strait (between Sumatra and Kalimantan) indicate that the Sunda Continental Shelf, embracing Malaysia, Borneo, Sumatra, Java and other mainland Southeast Asian countries, has experienced many episodes of

Mid-Holocene high sea levels

The effect of the mid-Holocene high sea level on coastal areas is indicated from Perak where 5,000-year-old shorelines have been found 26 kilometres inland. Extra proof that the present coastal plain was inundated by the sea during the Holocene comes from beach rocks (right) found in soil from a Perak tin mine.

submergence and exposure. In response to glacial and interglacial climatic changes, which are effected by the melting and freezing of ice sheets, sea levels worldwide, including the Sunda Continental Shelf, have fluctuated up and down.

The latest dramatic episode of the emergence of the Sunda Continental Shelf occurred 11,100 years ago, around the beginning of the Holocene. Evidence of this comes from records from offshore Terengganu, on the east coast of Peninsular Malaysia, which show that the sea level then was about 68 metres below the present-day level. This is indicated by the occurrence of peat deposits at various levels in cores of sediments taken from the South China Sea bed. From the palynological analyses of these peats it was revealed that they accumulated in an environment of mangroves, brackish lagoons and freshwater swamps. Aside from the peats, many of the sediment cores sampled from locations ranging from hundreds of metres to hundreds of kilometres apart, revealed the presence of laterites. As the formation of laterites only occurs when oxide deposits are exposed to the air and are subsequently weathered, the presence of these laterites, together with the peat deposits, indicates not only shallow sea conditions in the past, but even the emergence of the sea bed, which at present lies more than 160 kilometres offshore.

The peat accumulation shows that this low sea level remained stationary for perhaps a millennium (a very brief geological period), until around 10,000 years ago. After that, the sea level rose sharply at a rate of around 1.8 centimetres a year, until about the mid-Holocene, around 5,000 years ago, when it may have peaked about 5 metres higher than the present level. From the mid-Holocene onwards, the sea level gradually descended to its present position.

Postglacial low sea levels on the east coast

Offshore locations showing past shorelines

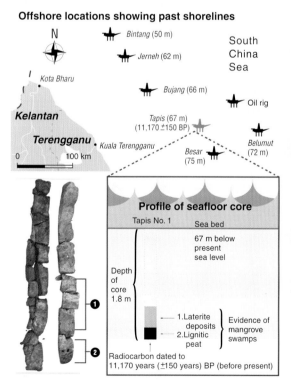

In 1973, geologists took seafloor cores from oil rigs off the Terengganu coast in the South China Sea (top left). These showed evidence of lateritized surfaces (1) and mangrove swamps (2) 50–70 metres below present-day sea levels. Radiocarbon dating of the mangrove-peat level (2) from a seafloor core from Tapis No.1 oil rig (left) gave a date of c. 11,170 years ago. This suggests that the present-day coastline of Kelantan and Terengganu was perhaps 160 kilometres inland during the postglacial period, and that vast areas of the South China Sea were then exposed land surfaces, the marginal areas covered by mangrove forests.

Geographic and demographic effects of sea level changes

When the sea level was 68 metres lower than at present, the land masses of the Sunda Continental Shelf emerged from the sea connecting the islands of Sumatra, Java, Borneo and Palawan (southwest Philippines) with mainland Asia. This extension exposed a large tract of Southeast Asian land areas and permitted free migratory routes for animals as well as humans between mainland Asia and the present-day islands of the Malay Archipelago. This land connection was also in existence during earlier Pleistocene glacial phases as the sea levels then were correspondingly low.

The high sea level recorded during the mid-Holocene produced a contrasting picture as the sea inundated a large area of Southeast Asia which had been previously exposed. As a result, the land surface area was reduced and was slightly smaller than its present-day size.

The re-exposure of many present-day coastal landforms, in particular the Peninsular coastal plains, only took place fairly recently (in geological terms) after the regression of the mid-Holocene high sea level began about 5,000 years ago.

Climate and vegetation changes

The large land surface area exposed during the low sea levels at the beginning of the postglacial period influenced the climatic conditions and vegetation patterns of the Southeast Asian hinterland. Low sea level contours of the Sunda Continental Shelf at 68 metres (11,100 years ago) and at about 100 metres (c. 18,000 years ago, the last glacial maximum) show some similarities in the exposed land area. This suggests that climatic conditions during both periods were similar. There would have been seasonal variations and slightly drier conditions than today, especially in the interior.

During the last glacial maximum, the palynological record from the Bandung basin, west Java, 665 metres above sea level, indicates that the boundary of the lower montane forest was 1200 metres lower than at present. This suggests distinctly cooler conditions with an estimated temperature lowering of 7 °C, and drier and more seasonal climatic conditions. Other similar studies conducted in the Java highlands and Sumatra also indicate that the lower montane forest boundary was 400–800 metres lower. These records suggest that around 11,100 years ago, Malaysia was also slightly drier and cooler, compared to present-day climatic conditions.

At about the beginning of the Holocene, for the duration of approximately 1,000 years, there was a return to near glacial conditions. Termed the Younger Dryas Stadial, this episode of climatic cooling, from about 10,000 to 11,000 years ago,

Holocene sea level

The huge fluctuation of Malaysia's sea levels during the Holocene is indicated in the above graph.

interrupted the general trend of postglacial climatic improvement. This short-term climatic change was a global phenomenon as worldwide evidence from pollen records, deep sea oxygen-isotope data and ice cores from Greenland and Antarctica recorded equivalent temperature changes.

The Younger Dryas record in Southeast Asia is indicated from samples taken in the Sulu Sea from water depths of over 4000 metres. The oxygen-isotope variations in the foraminifera, as well as radiocarbon dates, showed that the event occurred synchronously in the surface and deep waters of the Sulu Sea and the northern Atlantic Ocean. The temperature of the South China Sea during this period was about 5 °C lower than today.

During the Younger Dryas, the climatic cooling probably exerted influence on Mount Kinabalu in Sabah, the highest peak in Southeast Asia. Its summit plateau shows evidence of various glaciations during the Pleistocene. Dates of organic material from a pool at the summit show that the last deglaciation of Mount Kinabalu occurred about 9,200 years ago, which suggests that the short glacial activity of the Younger Dryas was presumably also experienced at Mount Kinabalu.

Limestone flaked tools (above) found at Gua Peraling, Ulu Kelantan (above top), are evidence of human habitation in the interior of the east coast during the Hoabinhian period from about 10,000 years ago when the Peninsular land area was vastly different from its present-day size.

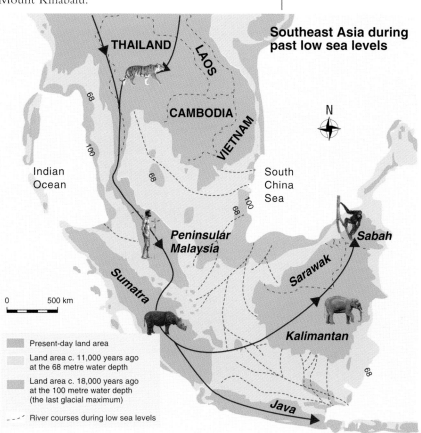

Southeast Asia during past low sea levels

Present-day land area

Land area c. 11,000 years ago at the 68 metre water depth

Land area c. 18,000 years ago at the 100 metre water depth (the last glacial maximum)

River courses during low sea levels

The impact of the palaeoenvironment

Geological records indicate that ever since the earliest known human habitation of Malaysia—38,000 years ago in Sarawak's Niah Caves—the region has experienced large-scale episodes of environmental change. How humans reacted to these changes is difficult to gauge. However, environmental conditions are believed to have been the main factor in the abandonment of two early Perak communities: the Palaeolithic settlement of Kota Tampan and the protohistoric settlements of Kuala Selinsing.

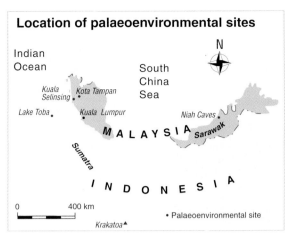

Location of palaeoenvironmental sites

Indian Ocean

South China Sea

Kuala Selinsing · Kota Tampan

Lake Toba · Kuala Lumpur

Niah Caves ·

MALAYSIA Sarawak

Sumatra

INDONESIA

0 400 km

Krakatoa ▲

· Palaeoenvironmental site

Sumatra's Lake Toba, the largest lake in Southeast Asia, was formed as a result of a huge volcanic explosion which some scientists believe may have triggered the onset of the last Ice Age. Dust and ash fallout over Malaysia are thought to have caused the abandonment of the Palaeolithic settlement at Kota Tampan.

The archaeological site at Kota Tampan, Perak, is presently situated in the midst of an oil palm plantation. However, during the settlement period it was on the shores of a palaeo-lake which was five times larger than the present artificial Lake Chenderoh, formed by a dam on the Perak River.

Dense mangrove forests now completely surround the protohistoric settlement sites of Kuala Selinsing which were originally located close to the river bank.

Early human responses

How humans in the past responded to environmental change depended on the timescale of the change. If it occurred over hundreds or even thousands of years, people would have been unaware of the overall trajectory of change. But events such as volcanic eruptions or earthquakes, which reoccurred within a person's lifetime, would have provided justification for moving away from the affected environment. However, over time, when human communities who had put down roots were faced with environmental stress or natural hazards, they preferred to change the environment rather than move away. They began burning, irrigating and building dikes, all of which ultimately produced a cultural landscape.

Environmental changes affecting human settlement

The most significant environmental changes which have occurred in Malaysia since the last glacial period concerned the distribution of land and sea. During glacials, sea levels dropped, exposing large land areas presently covered by sea, while mild phases produced surges of high sea levels, which, in turn, produced variations in the distribution of land and sea. The lower than present-day sea levels recorded from the last glacial period imply that if there was human habitation in the marginal areas during this time, these would now be under water.

Environmental conditions are believed to have been a major factor in the re-siting and later abandonment of the protohistoric settlements of Pulau Kelumpang, a mangrove forested island in the Kuala Selinsing estuary of Perak. Radiocarbon datings indicate that the settlements began about 2,000 years ago and were repeatedly occupied until they were permanently abandoned in the 11th century CE. Although the sites are presently surrounded by mangrove swamps, surveys show that the settlements started along the banks of the river mouth and the estuary. The most likely reason for

This earthenware pot, believed to be of local manufacture, was discovered at the protohistoric site of Kuala Selinsing.

the total abandonment of the site is the major morphological change which occurred in the estuarine area. The increasing siltation of the river banks and the river mouth (which continues today) probably hindered the inhabitants' access to the river and the sea. As the main trade routes were along rivers and waterways, this environmental change would have been sufficient justification for abandoning the settlement sites.

Volcanic effects on the early environment

Even though volcanic activity ceased in Peninsular Malaysia about one million years ago, the surrounding region is one of the most volcanically active areas of the world. Volcanic eruptions can wreak havoc on the environment, and ash clouds can affect even distant human communities. Eruptions can also create tsunami (seismic sea waves), such as those produced by the eruption of Krakatoa in 1883 which destroyed the nearby coastal areas of Java and Sumatra, killing an estimated 36,000 people.

Although Malaysia is part of stable Sundaland, it is still affected by volcanic action. Volcanic ash deposits have been found in many areas of Kedah, Perak, Selangor and Pahang. These are believed to have most likely derived from the volcanic explosion which created Lake Toba in northern Sumatra. A recent example is the 1991 eruption of Mount Pinatubo in the Philippines, when large quantities of ejected ash material left their impact even in Kuala Lumpur, more than 2500 kilometres away. For a number of days, sunlight was not as bright as normal and visibility was reduced because of the suspended volcanic ash and dust particles in the atmosphere.

Volcanic activity is believed to have caused the demise of the earliest known site of human habitation in Peninsular Malaysia, at Kota Tampan, Perak, which dates around 30,000–34,000 years ago. Because of numerous stone tools found at the site in various working stages, as well as dense accumulations of quartzite flakes and small boulders used as stone anvils, Kota Tampan is believed to have been a workshop for making stone tools.

The status of Kota Tampan as a Palaeolithic site was debated for many years after its initial discovery by H. D. Collings in 1938. Then, in 1987, Zuraina Majid rediscovered the site to resolve the doubts and to confirm the validity of its Palaeolithic history. In doing so, she reaffirmed its importance not only in the Malaysian but also the Southeast Asian context.

The stone tools which were excavated from gravel beds underlying volcanic ash deposits have been scientifically matched to the volcanic ash from the eruption at Lake Toba. Similar ash found at Ampang, Selangor, has been radiocarbon dated to around 34,000 years ago, and ash deposits also from Lake Toba have been identified at Bentong and Raub, Pahang. It is reported that in the Lenggong area (near Kota Tampan), ash deposits are up to

9 metres thick. However, this is considered to be too thick for direct-fall accumulation as Lake Toba is about 320 kilometres away. It is assumed that these thick deposits probably accumulated as a result of running water.

Scholars postulate that the Palaeolithic settlement and stone tool workshop at Kota Tampan was evacuated because of ash cover from the volcanic eruption of Lake Toba. The site was probably abandoned immediately after the event as unfinished stone tools were left *in situ*. Kota Tampan, therefore, is not only the oldest Peninsular site of human habitation yet confirmed, but is also the earliest recorded example of the impact of the palaeoenvironment on such a site.

These crude stone tools from the Palaeolithic settlement at Kota Tampan were buried under layers of ash produced by the volcanic explosion of Lake Toba, Sumatra, in the late Pleistocene.

The evacuation of Kota Tampan

In this artist's impression, based on scientific evidence, a huge ash and dust cloud advances on the stone tool-making workshop at Kota Tampan, Perak. The cloud was produced by the eruption of the Sumatran volcano which created Lake Toba. As stone tools were found abandoned in various stage of workmanship under the dated ash cover, archaeologists believe that the fallout was the reason for the workshop's hasty abandonment. The site, now in an oil palm plantation, was located on the shores of a former lake which could have been formed by a landslide which dammed the Perak River. The suggested age of 34,000 years ago for the Toba eruption is currently undergoing evaluation. Research suggests that the last major eruption occurred 74,000 years ago, and as this much earlier date is backed up by fission-track dating on volcanic ash samples from Serdang, Selangor, this evidence will undoubtedly have very strong implications for Malaysian prehistory.

ABOVE: Archaeologists excavating in the cave mouth of Lubang Angin (Wind Cave), part of the huge Mulu Caves complex in Sarawak's Gunung Mulu National Park, used gaslights even in daylight hours as national park restrictions prohibited the trimming of trees which shaded the site even at noon. During the 1989 excavation, extended burials with associated burial items, similar to those found in the Niah Caves (bottom left), were discovered. The burials of Lubang Angin were dated between about 1000 BCE and 500 CE, which correlates with the Niah dates.

FAR LEFT: This turn of the century photograph shows a large rainforest tree being felled by Senoi tribesmen whose ancestors may have been the first agriculturalists of Peninsular Malaysia.

NEAR LEFT: An Orang Asli uses a blowpipe to fell game at Bukit Prai, Selangor, in this photograph taken around 1906. At his left side is the open quiver with darts.

NEAR RIGHT: A human mandible is revealed in this archaeological trench at the rock shelter of Gua Peraling, Kelantan, which has large Hoabinhian deposits dating from the early to middle Holocene.

BELOW: Neolithic artefacts were first discovered at the open site of Jenderam Hilir, Selangor, by tin mining operations, and subsequent archaeological excavations revealed a large cache of stone tools and earthenware, including a complete vessel (bottom right) and many hollow legs of tripod vessels (below right) which are also found in Neolithic sites in Thailand.

PREHISTORIC
SETTLEMENT PATTERNS

To reconstruct the settlement patterns of ancient societies, archaeologists use what they term as 'the known site distribution'—that which is recovered by archaeological research—as well as 'the total settlement pattern'—that which existed at the time the ancient society was in existence. These two patterns can obviously be very different in regions where archaeological survival is problematic.

In Malaysia, the known patterns indicate that Hoabinhians and early Borneo hunter-gatherers camped in caves, near lakes, and laid down coastal shell middens, while the sites of Neolithic people tended to focus on river valleys, reflecting the need for fertile soils for cultivation. Early historical sites tend to be found in coastal locations from which their inhabitants could trade with outsiders for commodities such as rice, glass beads and metals. From around 1,500 years ago, such coastal settlements also lubricated the flow of foreign ideas into Malaysia, especially those associated with the Hindu–Buddhist and Islamic religions.

In the hot and wet environment of Malaysia, few sites survive to be identified and excavated. The visible distribution is thus only a very small part of the former total pattern. Therefore, in order to reconstruct a total settlement pattern for a given time period, archaeologists use ethnography and history as a guide. These show that foragers, such as the Negritos and Punan, live in small, temporary camps which leave few traces unless they are located in caves. Agriculturalists tend to live in villages, but also use minor camps for other activities. Villages leave identifiable archaeological traces, but are not universal as many agriculturalists of the Asia–Pacific region today still live in scattered, single family homesteads.

However, one important generalization can be made from both archaeology and ethnography. As past societies became more complex—as they moved towards statehood and urban life—their settlement sizes increased. In Thailand and Vietnam, large villages appeared with agriculture from the 3rd millennium BCE. Towns developed during the Iron Age (after 500 BCE), as rice agriculture with iron tools became more intensive and capable of supporting much denser populations. But lesser settlement types continued; both farmers and town dwellers used hunting camps on occasion, and throughout Malaysian prehistory, foragers continued to live side by side with agriculturalists and urban people, as they decreasingly do today.

Reconstruction of a total prehistoric settlement pattern can be a very difficult undertaking. In regions where villages and cities were made of brick, as in the Middle East, survival can of course be excellent and it is possible to trace the growth of a settlement hierarchy—a patterning of settlements where a few large centres come to dominate many smaller settlements, as in today's Malaysia. In Iraq, settlement hierarchies were developing by 4000 BCE, while in northeastern Thailand and Vietnam, these developments began during the Iron Age, about 500 BCE. In Peninsular Malaysia, it is likely that a similar settlement hierarchy was also in formation during the Iron Age, perhaps dominated by coastal trading settlements such as Kuala Selinsing. But in Malaysia, ancient sites do not project high above the ground as they do in zones further north. This does not mean that data are not there to be discovered, but it does mean that they will be harder to discover.

ABOVE TOP: **This photo of a group of agriculturalist Orang Asli from Ulu Batu, Selangor, appeared in Skeat and Blagden's** *Pagan Races of the Malay Peninsula* **(1906).**

ABOVE: **Raising orphaned animals as pets is a common practice of the Penan of Sarawak who are the last of Borneo's peoples to still maintain a hunter-gatherer lifestyle.**

ABOVE RIGHT: **This illustration, entitled 'Orang-Bukkit from Amontai,' is from Carl Bock's** *The Head-hunters of Borneo* **(1881). These hill people were described by Bock as being the 'only tribe of Dyaks who do not practise head-hunting'. They wore baskets on their backs 'containing all their wordly goods' and used blowpipes for hunting game.**

BELOW RIGHT: **This illustration dated 25 October, 1885, entitled 'Semang Quivers', is by J. De Morgan. Negrito tradition ascribes the origin of the various patterns incised on the bamboo quivers to directions given by supernatural beings. These magical patterns assist in procuring game and keep evil spirits at bay.**

Adaptation to cave environments

Limestone massifs pitted with caves and rock shelters are scattered throughout the Malaysian rainforests. Findings have revealed that people have frequented them from as early as 40,000 years ago until comparatively recently. The bulk of Malaysian archaeological evidence has been found in these cave sites as they offer a much more conducive environment for preservation than do open sites which are exposed to the degradations of the equatorial climate.

In this 1950s photo a Negrito group occupy a Perak rock shelter. Their ancestors may have been the cave dwellers of the Hoabinhian period whose remains have been found in many Peninsular Malaysian cave sites.

At Gua Cha, Kelantan, cave-dwelling Hoabinhians buried their dead by partially covering the corpse with stone slabs or lumps of tufa (soft, porous rock). The skull of this young male adult skeleton rests on a stone 'pillow'.

At Gua Harimau in Perak, grave goods from burials dating from 2,000 to 5,000 years ago included jewellery, pottery and bronze axes with their moulds for casting. The last find indicates the possibility of a much earlier emergence for the Peninsular Malaysian Bronze Age than had been previously thought, and the deceased may have been a bronzeworker as grave goods often denoted occupation.

Peninsular Malaysian cave sites

The earliest Peninsular Malaysian cave sites date from the Hoabinhian cultural period which appeared around 13,000 years ago. To date, there is no evidence in Peninsular Malaysia to indicate human occupation between the period of Kota Tampan (c. 30,000–34,000 years ago) and the Hoabinhian. However, the rock shelter site of Lang Rongrien in southern Thailand has yielded stone tools dated from 28,000 to 38,000 years ago, which slightly resemble those from Tingkayu in Sabah, and more tools dated to 26,000 years ago have been found further north at the Moh Khiew Cave.

Among the oldest cave sites in eastern Peninsular Malaysia are Gua Sagu and Gua Tenggek, both in Pahang. Gua Sagu was occupied from 14,000 years ago until 1,000 years ago, thus covering the Palaeolithic and Neolithic periods, while Gua Tenggek was used from about 10,000 years ago.

At the important site of Gua Kechil in Pahang, three phases of human occupation have been recorded. The first yielded Hoabinhian stone tools and cord-impressed pottery. These materials persisted into the second phase, accompanied by plain pottery, polished adzes, shells and animal bones. In the last phase, bones and shells declined while pottery increased with the introduction of red-slipped ware, and Hoabinhian tools gave way to polished ones. The beginning of this third phase, dated to 4,800 years ago, is regarded as the commencement of the Neolithic as well as showing indirect evidence for the practice of horticulture. A similar sequence and assemblage was also recorded at Kota Tongkat in Pahang.

The best-known rock shelter site in Peninsular Malaysia is Gua Cha in Kelantan. Datings from burials indicate human occupation from 10,000 to 2,000 years ago. During the Hoabinhian phase, hunters and gatherers probably lived there and subsisted on pigs, primates, wild cattle and possibly taro. Neolithic culture appeared with the introduction of pottery and signs of horticulture about 3,000 years ago, but during this period the rock shelter was mainly used for burials. Much of the pottery was probably grave goods, while the

Shards of cord-marked pottery from Gua Kechil, Pahang.

presence of a marine shell spoon denotes contacts with coastal areas or people.

Gua Peraling, another rock shelter in Kelantan, provides evidence of dense Hoabinhian occupation with abundant bifacial stone tools, fragmented burials and massive amounts of food remains underlying some Neolithic burials. Further south, at Gua Cawas, Hoabinhian occupation dates to around 12,000 years ago. Banana, rattan and bamboo species have been identified from layers between 12,000 to 5,000 years ago, but whether these are connected with horticulture is yet to be determined.

In Terengganu, Gua Taat was occupied between 8,920 and 2,630 years ago with strong Hoabinhian evidence but none for the Neolithic. The cave dwellers here were probably related to the pre-Neolithic occupants of Gua Cha as the local Semaq Beri (Orang Asli) still travel to Kelantan and back using an ancient route which passes near to Gua Cha.

Another important site is Gua Gunung Runtuh, near Lenggong in Perak, where there is evidence of occupation from about 13,000 years ago. The cave was used for cooking, stone tool making and the occasional burial. During the late Pleistocene, the occupants hunted monkeys, tapir and turtles, collected shells and utilized stone tools similar to those at Kota Tampan. During the Holocene, pigs, deer, lizards and monkeys were hunted and numerous shells were collected. A major discovery at this cave was the 10,000-year-old 'Perak Man', the oldest complete skeleton yet found in Malaysia. Nearby, Gua Teluk Kelawar yielded similar artefactual evidence of occupation from 9,000 years ago, while at Gua Harimau, further north, seven burials dating from 5,000 to 2,000 years ago were unearthed.

Evidence of continuous occupation since the Hoabinhian has been found at Gua Kelawar, near Sungai Siput in Perak, where stone tools, shells, animal bones, bone implements and pottery were found. An iron spear head and 19th-century ceramic finds indicate recent usage, probably by the Orang Asli who also produced the cave's charcoal drawings (see 'Cave drawings').

Cave sites in Sarawak

The renowned Niah Caves in northern Sarawak contain the longest record of human occupation in island Southeast Asia. It may have begun around 40,000 years ago, although the date of the skull formerly believed to be from this period is undergoing evaluation. The skull is of Australo-Melanesian affinity, which implies that Borneo was formerly populated by this group before being totally replaced by Austronesians.

During the last Ice Age, Niah was probably 200 kilometres further inland and might have had a drier and more seasonal climate which resulted in the predominance of large mammal remains such as rhinoceroses, tapirs and the giant pangolin. During the Holocene, these species declined, while the tapir and pangolin became extinct as the forests grew denser. With the rise in sea level and the encroachment of the coastline, shellfish became an important part of the cave dwellers' diet.

Apart from being used as a habitation site, West Mouth was used as a cemetery area from 14,000 to 3,500 years ago. Neolithic assemblages appeared around 2000 BCE with the emergence of pottery and adzes. Other finds include bronze bangles, beads and metal implements, heralding the arrival of the Metal Age.

Another Sarawak cave, Gua Sireh, may have been occupied from 20,000 years ago, during the last glacial maximum when the site was 500 kilometres inland. The Neolithic phase began around 4,500 years ago with the appearance of pottery. Rice grains from a shard dated to 4,500 years ago are the oldest evidence of domesticated rice in Malaysia (see 'Rice production'). Gua Sireh was also used for burial purposes and has charcoal drawings on its walls (see 'Cave drawings').

At Lubang Angin in Gunung Mulu National Park in northeastern Sarawak, several burials were found ranging between 700 BCE and 500 CE. The main materials found were pottery grave goods, similar to those from the Niah Caves, together with some glass beads and iron fragments.

Cave sites in Sabah

The rock shelter of Hagop Bilo is located in the Baturong limestone massif in southeastern Sabah on the shoreline of the extinct Tingkayu lake. When the lake dried up, people moved from the open Tingkayu sites into Hagop Bilo where midden deposits date from 18,000 to 12,000 years ago. Finds of stone tools include some reminiscent of the Tingkayu lanceolates. During the Metal Age, the

cave was used by the Orang Sungai, as wooden coffins, shards and cave drawings have been found.

Hagop Bilo was abandoned 12,000 years ago when the cave dwellers moved to the Madai Caves which were closer to the sea. The largest of these, Agop Atas, is still seasonally occupied by Idahan who collect birds' nests. The smaller Agop Sarapad lies above Agop Atas. Both caves were occupied 10,000 to 7,000 years ago. But due to the acidic guano deposit in Agop Atas few materials, apart from stone tools, were preserved there, unlike in the alkaline shell midden at Agop Sarapad where stone tools and food remains, including those of orang utan, cattle, the Sumatran rhinoceros, wild dogs and possibly the Javan rhinoceros and tigers, were recovered. The Madai Caves were abandoned 7,000 years ago, but around 1000 BCE and up to the recent past the caves were again occupied. During the Atas period (c. 800 BCE–500 CE), the frequency of stone tools declined as iron and copper-bronze became available. The Idahan period commenced with their occupation of Agop Atas around the 16th century.

Location of cave sites

Gua Senyum, Pahang

Gua Cha, Kelantan

Gua Taat, Terengganu

The West Mouth, Niah Caves, Sarawak

Gua Cawan, Kelantan

Madai Caves, Sabah

Hagop Bilo, Sabah

During the archaeological excavations between the Idahan houses in Agop Atas, Sabah, in 1980, an imported ceramic jar was found under a wooden coffin dated to 1000 CE.

23

Adaptation to open environments

During the last Ice Age when the climate forced Europeans to live in caves, Malaysia experienced a much milder climate. Thus, the traditional notion of early humans as cave dwellers may not be correct for this region as many Palaeolithic sites are located in open areas. However, towards the end of the Pleistocene and into early Holocene times, caves became the preferred habitation. Only later, during the Neolithic when agricultural lifestyles began, did populations return to open environments.

Kota Tampan: A palaeo-lakeside site
At Kota Tampan in Perak, a stone tool workshop dating to 30,000 years ago (above right), which manufactured pebble and flake tools (below), was originally sited on the shores of a palaeo-lake believed to have been six times larger than the present nearby Lake Chenderoh (above left) formed by a dam on the Perak River.

Unique stone tools of Tingkayu
An oil palm plantation (below top) spreads across the former bed of Lake Tingkayu in southeastern Sabah which formed when a lava flow dammed the Tingkayu River 28,000 years ago, and then drained around 18,000 years ago. Bifacial stone tools found around the lake (above) are indicative of a high level of skill—unique if they are from that time period. They were found buried in clay (below bottom) which is difficult to date as it contains no charcoal or bone.

Palaeolithic open sites

In Malaysia, stone tool workshop sites of late Pleistocene times have been found on the shores of palaeo-lakes (extinct lakes) at Tingkayu in southeastern Sabah, at the Peninsular sites of Kota Tampan and Bukit Jawa in Perak, as well as at a recently reported site at Kubang Pasu in Perlis. Finds from these Palaeolithic sites indicate that the settlements probably comprised only a few families. These lush environments, which provided a year-round source of protein in the form of fish, abundant game and plant life, could easily have supported larger populations, but at that time humans had apparently not yet developed a social system to enable them to live in larger groups.

It is possible that people living in these resource-rich environments were already leading a less mobile life than hunter-gatherer groups from other regions. This adaptation to life in the open would have required the construction of more lasting shelters. However, these assumptions are difficult to prove since no traces remain of their dwellings which would have been made from organic materials. Future research into their lithic tools may reveal if some of these were suitable for wood-working tasks, particularly the skilfully made bifacial lanceolates from Tingkayu which suggest that some Palaeolithic groups in resource-rich environments probably already had the technological skills to construct simple dwellings.

During this early adaptation to life in the open, Malaysians were very close to evolving a more sedentary settlement pattern. However, this did not happen. One possible cultural reason might have been because humans had not yet learned to live in larger groups which would have enhanced their domination of a particular area. For instance, in the Tingkayu Valley and the entire region of east Sabah, archaeological evidences have shown that towards the end of the Pleistocene period, and for the entire early Holocene period, habitation sites moved from open sites back to caves and rock shelters again.

Hoabinhian shell middens

In Peninsular Malaysia, the shell middens of Guar Kepah in Seberang Perai, and Seberang Perak near Teluk Intan in Perak represent the only two rare instances of open sites known from the early to early mid-Holocene period. They are associated with Hoabinhian hunter-gatherers as stone tools found in the middens are similar to those found among Hoabinhian assemblages from at least 30 inland caves and rock shelters. These were used as habitation and burial sites by early Holocene hunter-gatherers who apparently sheltered in caves because of the wetter climate established in the region since the post-glacial period.

The shell middens comprise accumulated food refuse left by Hoabinhian groups who frequented these coastal sites for their exploitation of shellfish. An enormous quantity of mollusc shells are found in these middens. However, this is not conclusive evidence for a sedentary community as molluscs are a seasonally predictable food source, and this would have been common knowledge to the region's hunter-gatherers. At the Guar Kepah shell middens, stone tools as well as fragments of human skeletal remains have also been found. Some of these were treated with haematite, a mineral pigment often used by prehistoric groups in their burial rituals, which strongly suggests that the middens were not just refuse dumps but were also sacred places.

Neolithic evidence from open sites

Although adaptation to open sites had begun fairly early in Malaysia, this process did not lead to innovations in the economy of the late Pleistocene and early Holocene groups who continued to live by hunting and foraging. The major cultural change in the Malaysian archaeological record—as reflected in the finds of new artefacts such as pottery, ground and polished stone tools, as well as new burial modes—did not take place until the late mid-Holocene period. In mainland Southeast Asia, fully sedentary farming villages had emerged 5,000 years ago, including the important sites of Non Nok Tha and Ban Chiang in northeast Thailand, as well as sites in the Red River Delta in North Vietnam.

Evidence for the establishment of Neolithic farming villages in Malaysia is scanty, due in part to the hot and wet equatorial climate. Once a settlement was abandoned the rainforest would soon take over, while river bank settlements would have been lost by erosion. However, judging by the large quantity of stray finds and hoards (comprising four or more objects) recovered from locations all over the country, Neolithic Malaysians were well adapted to life in the open river valleys. Finds included polished stone adzes, many of which were retrieved from present-day paddy fields and from the banks of rivers, especially the Kelantan and Tembeling rivers. Hoards of polished stone artefacts have been found at Tanjung Malim and Batu Gajah in Perak, at Gelugor in Penang, and near Kuala Pilah in Negeri Sembilan, and have been retrieved during mining activities, for example, in the Tui Gold Mine in Pahang and the Kenaboi Mine in Negeri Sembilan. Neolithic assemblages have also been recovered from caves and rock shelters, including Gua Cha in Kelantan and the Niah Caves in Sarawak. However, these were special burial places rather than habitation sites. Communities who used the caves may have lived in nearby open sites, or further afield if the cave had river access, as the bodies could have been brought there by raft.

Neolithic farming communities

In 1930, another Neolithic settlement was discovered beside the Tembeling River at Nyong in Pahang. This was the first time a large amount of pottery had been found outside a cave site. Other finds included polished stone implements, such as quadrangular adzes and some unusual stone knives known thereafter as 'Tembeling knives' (see 'Rice production'). Stone slabs used for grinding and sharpening stone tools, and stone anvils used in the manufacture of pottery were also found indicating that pottery and stone tool production was carried out at the settlement. Because much of the river bank site had been disturbed by river erosion, it was not possible to conduct a more detailed study. This open site has been ascribed to the Neolithic period by means of relative dating based on the polished stone tools and cord-marked pottery. There are no radiocarbon dates for this site as this dating method was unknown at that time.

In 1977, a Neolithic settlement site was discovered at Jenderam Hilir near the Langat River, not far from the confluence of its main tributary, the Semenyih River. The choice of this location must have been based on several considerations, including the availability of water, aquatic food and

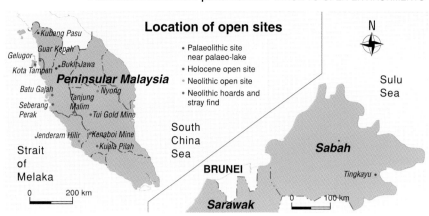

Location of open sites

- Palaeolithic site near palaeo-lake
- Holocene open site
- Neolithic open site
- Neolithic hoards and stray find

Kubang Pasu
Guar Kepah
Gelugor
Bukit Jawa
Kota Tampan
Peninsular Malaysia
Batu Gajah
Nyong
Tanjung Malim
Seberang Perak
Tui Gold Mine
Jenderam Hilir
Kenaboi Mine
Kuala Pilah
Strait of Melaka
South China Sea
BRUNEI
Sarawak
Sulu Sea
Sabah
Tingkayu
0 200 km
0 100 km
N

resources and fertile alluvial soil. It was also strategically sited to exercise control of these inland river routes to the foothills of the Main Range, the source of raw materials suitable for the manufacturing of tools and other artefacts. Although neither human skeletal remains nor faunal remains were found, studies of site materials clearly show that the settlement belonged to a sedentary community. Finds of an adze blank, stone slabs used for grinding and sharpening stone adzes, and anvil stones suggest that stone tools and pottery were manufactured at the settlement. This is backed up by an x-ray fluorescence study of pottery samples which showed that local clay was used. Among the numerous earthenware finds were tripod vessels similar to those from the famous Neolithic site of Ban Kao in central Thailand.

Radiocarbon dates have been obtained from the Jenderam Hilir open site. A charred tripod leg revealed a date between 2183 and 1935 BCE which was very close to the date obtained from a charcoal fragment excavated from this site. The radiocarbon date of Jenderam Hilir is 60 years later than that obtained from the Ban Kao site.

Stone bangles
A stone disc discarded before perforation was complete (above: front, side and back views), found in the Tui Gold Mine, Pahang, shows how it was produced by rotary grinding on a stone using a section of bamboo with wet river sand as an abrasive. When finished it would have resembled this Neolithic stone bangle (left) found near Tembeling, Pahang.

Tripod vessels
Among the pottery finds at the open Neolithic site of Jenderam Hilir were the remains of at least 45 tripod vessels (below left and right). The legs of these pots have ventilation holes for the heat to escape during firing (above left). The presence of these vessels indicates a sedentary lifestyle as they are difficult to stack and transport. Although no direct evidence for farming was found at the site, pollen analysis on soil trapped in a tripod leg has revealed a high percentage of fern spores (left inset). This suggests that the community was living in an open environment rather than a forested one, which leads to the inference that the land was cleared for cultivation.

Adaptation to rainforest environments

The prehistoric record in Malaysia enshrines the ancestry of two major rainforest hunting and gathering groups: the Negritos of the Malay Peninsula and the Punan/Penan of inland Sarawak. These two groups are quite different in biological ancestry and language, and they seem to indicate how quite varied trajectories in the past can give rise to very similar adaptations in the present.

Face decoration
Charcoal, red ochre, turmeric and lime are used for Negrito face decorations. In the 1950s photo above, a girl from Ulu Kelantan wears similar designs as those on Negrito women drawn by De Morgan in Skeat and Blagden's *Pagan Races of the Malay Peninsula* (1906).

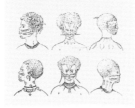

Decorative symbols incised on bamboo hair combs worn by Negrito women serve as charms to protect against venomous reptiles and insects. The illustration is from the book above.

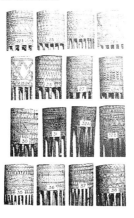

The Peninsular Hoabinhian economy

Both the Negritos (including the Semang) and the Punan/Penan (hereafter referred to as the Punan) live in small family bands in the rainforest, hunting, collecting, and sometimes trading forest products with nearby agricultural populations. Both groups have the trapping and blowpipe technology which allows them to hunt in the rainforest—a difficult environment because of the absence of large herds of ground-dwelling animals, a lack of visibility compared to grasslands, the elusiveness of arboreal animals, as well as the problems involved in harvesting tree top resources such as fruits.

The major archaeological record of Peninsular Malaysian hunting and gathering comes from the Hoabinhian pebble tool industry which occupied the northern and central regions from about 12,000 to 4,000 years ago. Most of these sites are caves and rock shelters, but Holocene shell middens also occur on the west coast and in northern Sumatra. Within the Hoabinhian economy, hunting of forest mammals, including rhinoceros, wild cattle, pigs and deer, together with shellfishing and river fishing, are all attested. Caves recently excavated in the interior of Kelantan have yielded phytoliths (silica bodies derived from plant cell structure) of rattan, bamboo, various banana species, palms, and the *ipoh* tree (*Antiaris toxicaria*) used for making bark cloth and for poisoning blowpipe darts or arrows. No Hoabinhian sites have ever yielded agricultural crop remains in secure association, and claims for Hoabinhian agriculture remain without foundation. However, plant resource management with techniques akin to 'proto-cultivation'—small-scale clearance, replanting and protection—were probably necessary. In addition, some degree of hunting specialization was probably practised, as attested by the predominance of immature wild pig remains in the refuse deposits at the rock shelter of Gua Cha in Kelantan. Recorded instances from both the Peninsula and Borneo describe how bearded pigs were killed in great numbers by hunters during seasonal migrations. Aboriginal hunters ambushed the pigs at river crossings where 30–300 animals have been known to swim across en masse.

Rainforest habitation theories

There has recently been a debate amongst anthropologists and prehistorians about whether or not hunters and gatherers were ever able to occupy equatorial rainforest environments independently, without access to agricultural populations with whom they could trade for carbohydrate foods such as rice. This may sound strange to those accustomed to thinking of the rainforest as a cornucopia of resources, but the reality is different; rainforests are not easy environments for human occupation. Even so, some opinions in favour of a total absence of pre-agricultural humans in rainforests have been expressed too strongly. The Hoabinhian record from Malaysia is one of the best in the world for showing that hunters and gatherers were able to penetrate the interior of the Peninsula at the end of the Pleistocene when wet rainforests had replaced the drier vegetation formations of the last glacial maximum. It appears that the early Hoabinhians actually colonized the rainforests purposefully. Paradoxically, though, no human occupation is in evidence in the Peninsula during the last glacial maximum (about 20,000 years ago), perhaps because the coastline was so far away and rivers

A Negrito from the Bateq subgroup demonstrates the use of a blowpipe.

at that time were too shallow to be easily navigable by raft or bark canoe. In order to inhabit the rainforested interior of the Malay Peninsula, the Hoabinhians used a network of large limestone caves for shelter. In some interior riverine caves, such as Gua Cha and Gua Peraling in Kelantan, they left archaeological deposits of considerable thickness and artefact density. Although there is no direct evidence, one must presume a developed form of animal trapping technology, as well as a projectile technology of some kind, perhaps involving the bow and arrow and the blowpipe with vegetable poisons used on the projectile tips.

The poisonous Ipoh tree

One of the most important tree resources of the Malaysian rainforests is the *ipoh* or upas tree which yields a lethal sap used for poisoning blowpipe darts, as well as arrows which were formerly used by the Negritos. The hand-coloured engraving (left) entitled 'The Upas, or Poison Tree of Java' is from *The Gallery of Nature and Art* (1814). It shows a highly dramatized tableau of a variety of stunned prey beneath 'this evil plant'. The map (top right) from Skeat and Blagden's *Pagan Races of the Malay Peninsula* (1906) shows the distribution of *ipoh* and the blowpipe throughout Southeast Asia, while the photograph below the map from the same book is captioned 'Padang the Semang collecting poisonous sap from the Upas Tree. Ulu Siong, Kedah'. The pen and ink drawings by De Morgan, also from this book, (far right) show the following blowpipe apparatus: Negrito blowpipes (1 and 2), dart (3), poison spatula (4), section of the mouth end of a blowpipe, showing the dart in position in the inner tube, with a wad behind the butt end of the dart (5), also showing the arrangement for splicing the inner tube and that for joining the mouthpiece end on to the inner tube (6, 7), and a Semang dart quiver (8).

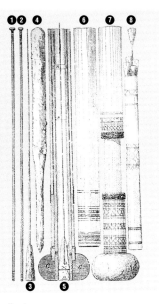

Bornean rainforest habitations

In Borneo, the archaeological record is different from the Hoabinhian. It emphasizes flake rather than pebble tools, but there are long sequences here extending back for 20,000 years or more in the Niah Caves in Sarawak and in the Baturong Caves in southeastern Sabah. These regions would have been quite far inland about 20,000 years ago when glacial sea levels were very low, so again there is evidence for rainforest penetration. However, no such evidence for human occupation before agriculture is yet known from the deep interior of Borneo. Perhaps Austronesian-speaking agriculturalists were the first permanent inhabitants to penetrate this region between 4,000 and 3,000 years ago, a conclusion supported by the observation that no Negrito populations have ever been recorded in Borneo.

At the Baturong Caves of Sabah, finds attest to human occupation from 18,000 to 12,000 years ago when the caves were perhaps 150 kilometres further inland.

Today, apart from the Punan of Sarawak and Kalimantan, hunter-gatherer groups are virtually absent in island Southeast Asia (excluding Irian Jaya and northern Halmahera) owing to the size and density of the cultivator population. Linguistically, the Punan groups all speak Austronesian languages, and thus belong to a language family with a very convincing vocabulary for an agricultural lifestyle at the proto-Austronesian level (perhaps located in Taiwan about c. 5,000 years ago). Therefore, it is speculated that if these equatorial groups, like the Peninsular Negritos, are relatively indigenous to the region, could the Punan's current Austronesian language affiliation be the product of an ancient language shift? The answer appears to be in the negative from a biological perspective as the Punan are members of the same Mongoloid grouping as the mainstream agricultural populations of Indonesia and the Philippines. A more likely origin involves a move from a lowland and coastal agricultural economy, perhaps as long ago as 3,500

years during the initial Austronesian colonization of Borneo, into an interior rainforest hunting and gathering economy in restricted regions (mostly in the island's northern centre).

The proto-Austronesian economy was doubtless not totally agricultural. Like all farmers in regions of sparse population, the early Austronesians also had thriving hunting, collecting and maritime economies, well attested by the widespread archaeological record of coastal shell middens and hunted wild animal bones in sites. Thus, specializations towards hunting and gathering, when economic conditions made such lifestyles worthwhile, as in the interior Borneo rainforests, need cause no surprise. The Punan live in regions where agriculture is a difficult activity (wet rainforest, clayey and stony soils), and for societies with traditions of exchange, such economic tendencies are to be expected. This conclusion, however, does not turn the Punan into purely commercial foragers; they are clearly genuine hunter-gatherers just like the Negritos, albeit with a totally different historical trajectory.

In this photograph taken in 1971, a Punan from the Punan Busang subgroup returns from a successful hunt with a barking deer he has bagged with a blowpipe dart.

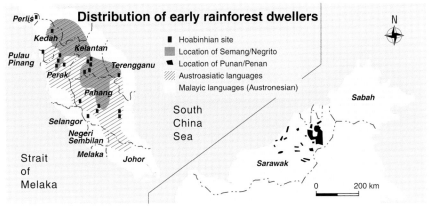

Distribution of early rainforest dwellers

Perlis
Kedah
Pulau Pinang
Kelantan
Perak
Terengganu
Pahang
Selangor
Negeri Sembilan
Melaka
Johor
Strait of Melaka
South China Sea
Sabah
Sarawak

- ■ Hoabinhian site
- Location of Semang/Negrito
- ◄ Location of Punan/Penan
- Austroasiatic languages
- Malayic languages (Austronesian)

0   200 km

N

ABOVE: This megalithic alignment, of unknown antiquity, was reconstructed at the Petronas Megalith Park in Kuala Lumpur after the stones were excavated from a Negeri Sembilan site which was in the way of a gas pipeline.

LEFT: Incised tubes of bamboo which were traditional grave goods of the Negritos are illustrated in Skeat and Blagden's *Pagan Races of the Malay Peninsula* (1906). The symbolic pattern (far left) signifies a burial bamboo of a chief, while the pattern (near left) belongs to a married woman.

RIGHT: Stone grinding stones found in the Hoabinhian cave site of Gua Senyum in Pahang.

ABOVE RIGHT: This illustration of the exterior and interior of a Senoi blowpipe is also from *The Pagan Races of the Malay Peninsula* (1906).

RIGHT: A prehistoric stone sculpture discovered in western Sarawak is of unknown origin.

These prehistoric charcoal cave drawings at Gua Sireh, Sarawak, may depict a wrestling match watched by a crowd of onlookers. The two participants are clearly shown in the centre of the panel in opposing positions with their arms locked in a wrestling embrace.

The legendary Tom Harrisson (far right), who spearheaded the Sarawak Museum excavations at the Niah Caves for two decades from the late 1950s, is shown working in the West Mouth of the Niah Great Cave, where Malaysia's oldest skull, dating from perhaps 35,000 years ago, was found.

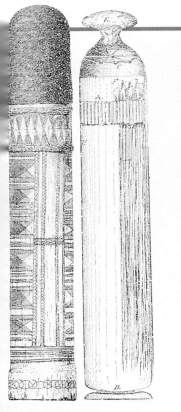

PREHISTORIC TECHNOLOGY AND ART

Malaysia's technological development during prehistoric times is evidenced by stone and metal tools, earthenware, bronze drums and bells, and body ornaments such as beads. About 30,000–40,000 years ago, or earlier, pebble tools were being manufactured at Kota Tampan, Perak, and at Sarawak's Niah Caves. These tools were simple, but more sophisticated technologies existed, as revealed by finds of bifacial tools in southern Thailand and Sabah.

This polished stone ring, dating from Neolithic times, was found at Gelugor, Perak.

Between 14,000 and 8,000 years ago, when the climate warmed after the last Ice Age, human societies flourished. This era marks the Hoabinhian cultural period of the Malay Peninsula. During this time, technological differences were more apparent between the Peninsular and Bornean sites than they had been 30,000 years ago. The Hoabinhian stone tools of Kelantan's Gua Cha are quite different from the pebble and flake industries of Sabah and Sarawak. This could reflect the beginning of an 'agricultural' economy during the Hoabinhian period, but no such developments can yet be suggested for Borneo.

By at least 4,000 years ago in the Peninsula, and 500 years later in Borneo, in the period known as the Neolithic, the hunter-gatherer world began to face its greatest challenge—the agricultural lifestyle. Systematic crop cultivation began and technology underwent major changes. Pottery and ground-stone tools made a dramatic appearance. However, the hunters and gatherers did not disappear. Indeed, they live on today as the Peninsular Orang Asli group, the Negritos, and also, perhaps, the Punan of Sarawak. Malaysian Neolithic industries reflect different influences. Those of the Peninsula belong to Neolithic cultures found from southern Thailand to Pahang, Sabah's are aligned with the Philippines and Taiwan, while Sarawak sites may combine Peninsular and Philippine influences.

By perhaps 200 BCE, both the Malay Peninsula and Borneo were coming within the orbit of cultures capable of manufacturing items of bronze and iron. At about the same time, contact with India and China began. The period between about 200 BCE and 200 CE, which coincides with the Roman Empire in the West and the Qin/Han Empire in China, was one of remarkable linkages in world trade. Malaysia played its part in all of this because of its strategic location between the Indian Ocean and the South China Sea. The result was a kind of revolution in Malaysia's archaeological affairs. Bronze drums, beads, fine pottery and iron tools turned the course of cultural evolution from tribal village towards protohistoric civilization. The roots of Srivijayan domination of the region were laid, together with the roots of domination of the whole region today by the Malay language. Yet, throughout all of this, Malaysian technology has developed as a kind of palimpsest. The new came in, but the old often lived on side by side with the new to contribute to the richness which characterizes Malaysian culture today.

Measuring 20 centimetres in height, this Neolithic stone adze, of a 'beaked' variety found only in Peninsular Malaysia, was discovered in Upper Perak.

The manufacture of stone tools

Stone tools were essential items in prehistoric Malaysian societies. The shape and design of these tools evolved from crude Palaeolithic chopping stones, dating from about 35,000 years ago, into sophisticated polished stone tools during the Neolithic, about 2,000 BCE, when agriculture and more sedentary lifestyles began making inroads into the hunter-gatherer economy.

How a flaked stone tool is made

The flaked stone tools found at Tingkayu, east Sabah, particularly the lanceolate knives, are the most sophisticated of Malaysia's Palaeolithic implements. This artist's interpretation, although not conclusive, illustrates the various steps in the production of a bifacial stone tool.

Using a stone anvil as support, a hammer stone was used to strike off a large flake.

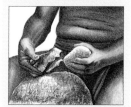

The head of the tool was shaped by striking off smaller flakes with the hammer stone.

Pressure flaking with a wood or bone point produced a thin, well-shaped tip.

The sharp-edged lanceolate point was lashed, or glued with resin, to a wooden haft.

Palaeolithic stone tools

As the Stone Age lifestyle revolved around the use of stone tools, the study of these artefacts reveals much about the ability of early Malaysians to survive, as well as their level of technology.

During the Palaeolithic, stone tools were used for hunting and gathering activities and as weapons. Important Palaeolithic sites where stone tools have been found include the Niah Caves of Sarawak, Kota Tampan in Perak, and Tingkayu in Sabah.

In 1987, the archaeologist Zuraina Majid discovered a Palaeolithic stone tool-making workshop at Kota Tampan, near Lenggong, Perak. The site was found intact as it had been abandoned when it was covered by ash from the huge volcanic eruption in Sumatra which produced Lake Toba about 34,000 years ago. The dense array of quartzite remnants included stone anvils and hammer stones (the equipment for making stone tools), stone cores (the raw material for the tools), finished and unfinished stone tools, together with flakes and chips, the waste from stone tool production.

The most typical of these tools are large choppers manufactured by striking flakes off one edge of a pebble (unifacial). Despite their crude appearance, these chopping tools were very versatile. They were probably used to kill animals, crush animal skulls and bones, chop down trees and as fighting weapons. Sharper-edged hand adzes were probably used to carve up prey, while smaller flake tools would have been used to slice up the meat.

Indications are that the Palaeolithic site excavated by Zuraina Majid in 1996 at Bukit Jawa, Lenggong, Perak, could be anywhere from 50,000 to 100,000 years old. This would make the stone tools from that site the oldest ever found in Malaysia. Prior to this discovery, the oldest stone tools found, believed to be 35,000 years old, were from Sarawak's Niah Caves.

The most sophisticated tools from the Palaeolithic are bifaces found around what was formerly the shoreline of a lake at Tingkayu in Sabah. The lake was formed 28,000 years ago by a lava flow and drained around 15,000 years ago. The tools are believed to date to sometime during this

Bark cloth beaters

Found at various Peninsular sites, these Neolithic tools are made from a cylindrical block of stone, about 6–8 centimetres in diameter, with one face incised with a grooved, crosshatched pattern. They are believed to have been used to pound bark to produce cloth for clothing, similar to the waist cloth worn by the Orang Asli (left), although the Orang Asli used wooden beaters.

period, although the finding of similar bifacial tools at Lang Rongrien in southern Thailand, which are dated to 27,000 years ago, is evidence that the technology was in existence during that time. The Tingkayu stone tools, which show a level of skill unique for their time period in Southeast Asia, were manufactured on site. The stone tool industry at Tingkayu has revealed a range of flakes, large bifaces, and smaller and quite remarkable lanceolate points and knives. These knives do not occur elsewhere in Southeast Asia, except for one apparent lanceolate found in a tin mine in Kedah in the 1930s.

Mesolithic tool evolution

The period from about 10,000 years ago until the appearance of agricultural communities about 4,000 years ago is known to archaeologists as either the Mesolithic or the Hoabinhian (a term derived from a culture in North Vietnam). Stone tools from this time have been found at limestone rock shelters and cave sites throughout Malaysia. The most typical Hoabinhian tool, found at most Malaysian cave sites, is a pebble flaked on both sides (bifacial) which creates a continuous cutting edge around the periphery. A variant of this tool is known as a Sumatralith, an elongated unifacial pebble tool which takes its name from a similar implement found in Sumatra. These tools, which are noticeably different from those of the Palaeolithic, are evidence that during the Hoabinhian period there was an improvement in the thinking and creative ability of the population in developing tools suitable for their desired tasks.

Based on stone remnants which bear traces of haematite, it is believed that grinding stones were used to crush haematite into powdered form. This powder was used in burial ceremonies, as proven by

This stone tool recovered from Kota Tampan, Perak, dates from around 31,000 years ago.

the discovery of haematite-covered skulls in Seberang Perai, and it was probably also used for body decoration.

Excavated food remains show that the people of the Hoabinhian period were expert hunters who used stone tools to kill a variety of prey, including seladang (wild cattle), deer, serow (antelope goats), pigs, monkeys, sun bears and rodents.

Although the evidence is not conclusive, many scholars believe that the ancestors of the present-day Orang Asli group known as the Semang or Negritos were inhabiting the Peninsula during the Hoabinhian cultural period.

Neolithic tools reveal changing lifestyles

By 2,000 BCE, important economic changes had begun in Malaysia, including the introduction of agriculture and a move to more settled lifestyles in sedentary villages. Known as the Neolithic, this era produced the first Malaysian pottery as well as new types of stone tools which were technologically more advanced.

Neolithic stone tools were roughly shaped by flaking on all the stone's surfaces, then were ground or polished until smooth. The most characteristic of the Neolithic tools is the quadrangular adze, many of which have been found in river valleys where the early agricultural communities were probably sited. Neolithic tools have also been found in buried land surfaces: one was revealed 6 metres deep in the Tui Gold Mine in Pahang. Some have been found in caves, and were probably used for burial purposes.

In contrast to Hoabinhian tools, those of the Neolithic are diverse in both size (40–500 millimetres) and form, and comprise a large variety

This polished Neolithic adze, measuring 17 centimetres in length, was found in a cave in the limestone massif of Bukit Changkul in Perlis. It could have been a grave artefact as it shows no sign of use despite being perhaps 3,000 years old.

of polished axes, chisels and different types of adzes.

Neolithic stone implements were used to cut down trees for agricultural purposes, to shape timbers, and for other carpentry uses in the construction of homes and boats. It has been suggested that the larger unfinished chisels could have been used for ploughshares, but the majority of the polished smaller chisels and adzes were carpenter's tools.

Other Neolithic stone artefacts include bark cloth beaters and the so-called 'Tembeling knives'. The latter have mainly been unearthed along the Tembeling River valley of Pahang, where other Neolithic artefacts are common. They could have been used for reaping, or for skinning and cutting up carcasses.

At Gua Cha in Kelantan, as well as at some other Peninsular Malaysian rock shelters, both Hoabinhian and Neolithic tools have been found during archaeological excavations. Although it is generally believed that the Neolithic people succeeded the Hoabinhian, there is no break in the stratigraphy suggesting different occupations, but nor is there convincing evidence of a local evolution from Hoabinhian to Neolithic.

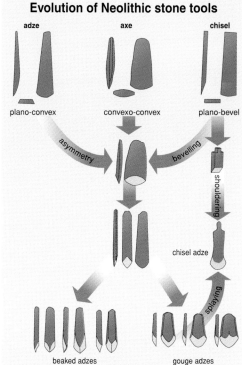

Evolution of Neolithic stone tools

This hypothetical diagram of how polished stone tools developed in Malaysia was devised by the ethnographer H. D. Noone in 1941. It shows how the different forms and techniques used to produce the common adze, axe and chisel acted upon each other to evolve into the distinctive gouge and beaked adzes which have only been found in the Malay Peninsula. The fine workmanship, choice of quality stone, and hollow grinding technique show the high standard of Neolithic tool-makers. The use of these tools is yet to be confirmed.

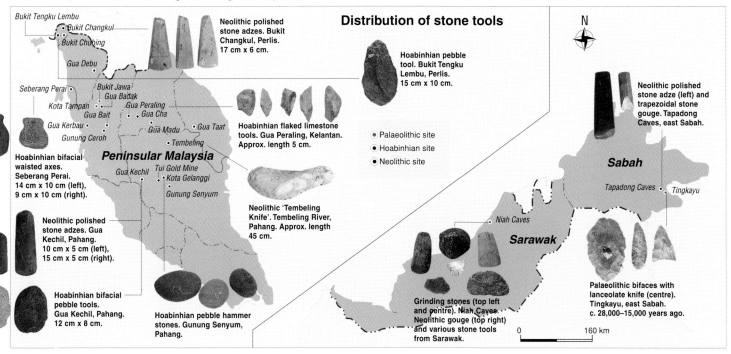

Distribution of stone tools

Earthenware

In the development of human culture, the discovery of how to produce earthenware from clay was one of humanity's first major artistic and scientific innovations. Earthenware appeared in prehistoric Malaysia when Neolithic cave dwellers began the shift from a hunting and gathering lifestyle to one based more on agriculture. Pottery vessels were not only needed to store and carry food and liquids, but were also utilized in religious rituals and beliefs. In prehistoric burials, earthenware was used as both grave goods and as jars in secondary burials.

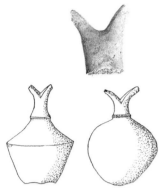

Double-spouted vessels from Sarawak
Scholars have yet to agree on the function and use of the mysterious double-spouted vessels which were part of the grave furniture in the Sarawak archaeological sites of Lubang Angin (above top (detail)) and at Niah Caves (above middle). However, Tom Harrisson, who headed the major Niah excavations in the 1960s, believed that the double spout could have been symbolic of the hornbill's beak and casque, and that this was related in Kenyah and Kayan culture with the human head. A beaded baby carrier from the Sarawak Museum (above) depicts this design of a human head spouting hornbill casques. It is likely that the vessels played an important role in the religious rituals of early Sarawak.

Distribution of earthenware

The usefulness of clay was discovered in Europe during the Palaeolithic period when humans began to shape figurines out of lumps of clay. The earliest shards found in Malaysia may belong to the Mesolithic or Hoabinhian period, but the majority of earthenware finds are from the Neolithic period, around 2500 BCE. During this time, when agriculture developed and coastal trade began, the functional use of earthenware rapidly evolved into an important requisite in the social, economic and religious life of prehistoric communities.

Because clay was readily available, inexpensive and easy to mould, its usefulness was quickly apparent. The basic principle of producing earthenware has remained practically unchanged since the prehistoric period. When organic clay is shaped into objects and fired, they then become inorganic and, therefore, non-perishable.

In Malaysia, most of the prehistoric earthenware which has been found is from the Neolithic period, and by studying the evolution of its features and traditions, archaeologists can, indirectly, discover much about the Neolithic society which produced these wares. In Peninsular Malaysia, prehistoric pottery has been found at various archaeological sites, including Bukit Tengku Lembu in Perlis; Kodiang in Kedah; Gua Harimau, Gua Badak, Gua Kajang, Gua Teluk Kelawar, Gua Kerbau and Gol Bait in Perak; Gua Cha and Gua Musang in Kelantan; Gua Kecil, Gunung Senyum and Gua Sagu in Pahang; and Jenderam Hilir in Selangor. Early pottery has also been found in abundance at sites in Sarawak, including Gua Bungoh near Bau; Gua Sireh near Serian; Gua Sarang at Tatau outside Bintulu; the famed Niah Caves, site of Malaysia's earliest human habitation; and Lubang Angin in the Gunung Mulu National Park. In Sabah, prehistoric vessels occur at the Tapadong Caves on the Segama River; at Hagop Bilo in the Baturong Caves, at Agop Atas in the Madai Caves, and at the important rock shelter site of Bukit Tengkorak near Semporna.

Of the prehistoric earthenware yet found in Malaysia, 90 per cent has been discovered in or near cave mouths, the vast majority comprising shards. Other artefacts discovered together with the shards consist of food wastes, polished stone tools and shell remains. However, pottery discovered in grave areas, together with human burials, differs from that found in other areas because the vessels are usually complete. This type of earthenware has been found at Gua Cha, Bukit Tengku Lembu, Gua Harimau and the Niah Caves.

Shapes and designs

There are many differences in the shapes of Neolithic vessels discovered in Peninsular Malaysia compared with those from Sabah and Sarawak. The peculiar single- and double-spouted vessels from the Niah Caves and Lubang Angin, Sarawak, have not been found in Peninsular Malaysia or Sabah. Similarly, the shapes of flasks and jars from Sarawak and Sabah differ from those found in Peninsular Malaysia. Furthermore, the footed pot stands, goblets and trumpet-shaped vessels from Gua Cha, Bukit Tengku Lembu and Gua Harimau in Peninsular Malaysia do not occur in Sabah and Sarawak.

An early potter's 'wheel'
Found at Gua Musang, Kelantan, this footed and perforated Neolithic vessel of red ware—shown from the front and tilted to show the hollow foot—could have been a censor, a pot stand, or an early type of turntable. It is similar in design to turntables used by potters in Aceh, Sumatra (see diagram). The roughly shaped clay is put on the dish and the potter turns the 'wheel' with his left hand while modelling the clay with his right. The hollow centre could have been used for inserting a stick to turn the 'wheel'.

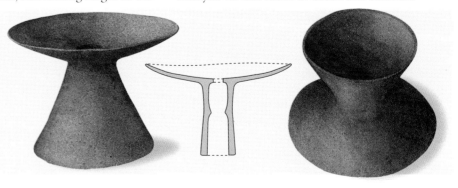

Three-colour wares
Found in a burial site at the Niah Caves, this striking three-colour urn (left) was the only earthenware vessel of this type found in Malaysia until the 1989 excavation of Lubang Angin in Gunung Mulu National Park revealed shards of similar colour and design (above). The patterns on these wares include impressed circles and incised geometric designs coloured with red pigment. The distance between the two sites is about 130 kilometres, but it is now believed that they shared a common cultural origin.

Various techniques were used to decorate the vessels. Designs were impressed into the clay using cord-bound and carved paddles, woven mats, shells and combs. Impressed cord prints dominate the designs of prehistoric earthenware from Peninsular Malaysia where more than 90 per cent of pottery finds display these markings. In contrast, only 10 per cent of those discovered in Sarawak and Sabah are of this design which is believed to be one of the earliest forms of surface decoration employed by prehistoric potters. This pattern also served a utilitarian function as it prevented slippage. Some Peninsular Malaysian vessels were incised with linear patterns, such as spirals, crisscrossing, curved lines and geometric shapes, while others were burnished with a smooth surface.

The majority of prehistoric earthenware objects found in Sarawak are either plain, polished, decorated with incised patterns or impressed with cord-bound paddles. In Sabah, nine types of vessel designs have been identified. The exteriors and rims of some vessels have been coloured with red slip, other wares have linear incisions or are impressed with carved or cord-bound paddles, and others have notched and scalloped lips and ridges.

Methods of production
It is still not certain what techniques and methods were used by prehistoric potters, but based on the limited technology available during the early Neolithic, it is most likely that earthenware was hand built with coils, which were then pinched and smoothed and dried in the sun.

As prehistoric cultures progressed, simple devices such as wooden sticks or paddles and anvil stones were introduced into pottery making. It is likely that a round stone was held inside the pot while it was paddled, thus producing a round-bottomed pot. This production method is still used by some ethnic groups of Sarawak and Sabah, such as the Iban, and it is probable that it was passed down through the

ages. Other techniques employed in prehistoric times included the use of segments. Some vessels could also have been turned on a primitive turntable made of either wood or clay. Pottery was fired at low temperatures in an open pit.

The absolute dates of Malaysian prehistoric pottery are still uncertain. However, some areas where these wares have been discovered have been positively dated by radiocarbon methods (see map). Figures from these indicate that the prehistoric earthenware period may have occurred at a much earlier date in Peninsular Malaysia than it did in Sabah and Sarawak.

The use of earthenware
Earthenware objects were both utilitarian and ceremonial. They served as cooking pots, as water vessels, and as eating and drinking utensils. Some Neolithic shards discovered at Bukit Tengkorak in Sabah were remnants of pottery stoves. This artefact type first evolved in China around 4500 BCE, and was used until recently by the Bajau Laut ('sea nomads') in the Sabah–Sulu region. However, while most prehistoric earthenware revolved around the need for food and drink, vessels were also utilized for religious ceremonies, or in rituals associated with prehistoric beliefs. For example, at Gua Cha, at the Niah Caves, and later at the protohistoric settlement site of Kuala Selinsing in Perak, earthenware was found together with human burials. This suggests that these communities had a belief in the afterlife.

From studying prehistoric pottery it is possible, in an indirect way, to ascertain how cultural development progressed from simple to more sophisticated technologies. These developments include the evolution of earthenware production, the changing techniques of combustion and design, and the functions which earthenware played in Malaysia's prehistoric societies.

Reconstructing a Neolithic vessel
Although much of the Neolithic earthenware excavated at Bukit Tengku Lembu, Perlis, comprised fragments, enough shards were found to enable the reconstruction of this goblet. It was found buried together with human remains and stone tools and is believed to date from the later Neolithic period.

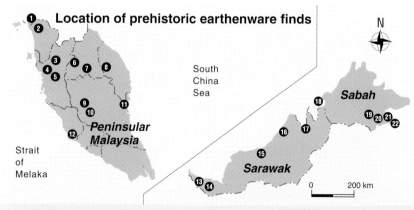

Location of prehistoric earthenware finds

1. Bukit Tengku Lembu
2. Kodiang
3. Gua Harimau *4929 ± 270 BP
   Gua Badak, Gua Kajang
   Gua Teluk Kelawar *6890 ± 80 BP
4. Gua Kerbau
5. Gol Bait
6. Gua Cha *3020 ± 270 BP
7. Gua Musang
8. Gua Taat *8920 ± 120 BP
9. Gua Kechil
10. Gunung Senyum
11. Gua Sagu *1240 ± 120 BP
12. Jenderam Hilir
13. Gua Bungoh
14. Gua Sireh *3990 ± 230 BP
15. Gua Sarang
16. Niah Caves * c. 3450 BP and c. 2950 BP
17. Lubang Angin
18. Pulau Burung
19. Tapadong Caves
20. Hagop Bilo (Baturong Caves)
21. Agop Atas (Madai Caves) *2650 ± 80 BP
22. Bukit Tengkorak 2870 ± 80 BP
    * radiocarbon dates   BP (before present)

Beads

Although beads are among the smallest of artefacts, they have played a prominent role in the cultural evolution of early Malaysian societies. Beads have been discovered at many of Malaysia's archaeological sites with some dating from as early as the Neolithic period. Long regarded as an essential part of human culture, beads have not only functioned as ornamental objects, but have also been used as currency, status symbols, gifts, marriage dowries and for religious and magical ceremonies.

In Sarawak, ancient bead necklaces are considered heirlooms and are still worn by the Kelabit, Kenyah, Kayan and Bidayuh peoples.

Location of bead finds

These rainbow-hued beads are part of the collection unearthed at Pengkalan Bujang, an archaeological site in Kedah's Bujang Valley, believed to have been an important entrepôt from the 10th to the 14th century CE. The opaque red beads, known as *mutisalah*, comprised 30 per cent of the more than 800 beads which were found at this site. This type of bead has been found in abundance at Southeast Asian megalithic, Dongsonian and protohistoric sites. It was manufactured on a large scale in South India, but there is no evidence for local production.

Origin and production

Not only are beads universal objects, found in most countries of the world, but they are also the most widely travelled of all prehistoric artefacts, as many were produced thousands of miles from their place of discovery. Since prehistoric times, they have been prominent items in both regional and international trade.

Bead-making is one of the world's oldest crafts. The first beads were made from seeds, shells, animals' teeth, claws and bones. Later, clay, stone, wax, resin, glass and metal were used. Stones used included agate, chalcedony, beryl, jasper, quartz, carnelian, amethyst, crystal, jade and granite. The oldest carnelian beads from the Royal Graves of Ur in Mesopotamia date to 2500 BCE. In India, carnelian beads were produced on a large scale from about 1500 BCE.

Stone beads, however, provide a limited source of information about cultural change, as they themselves have undergone little change over the last 2,000 years. Even if the beads were manufactured locally, many of the raw materials had to be imported, proof of early trade between Malaysia and countries such as Sri Lanka and India where these materials occur in large quantities.

Stones used for bead-making are usually those which are highly valued, including carnelian and agate, but favoured types vary from one ethnic group to another.

To produce stone beads, the selected stone is first cut into a suitable shape. This rough fragment is ground smooth and then polished. Finally, a hole is drilled through the centre of the bead.

It is still uncertain when humans first learned how to produce glass. However, studies have revealed that glass production had already begun in Georgia, north of Mesopotamia, about 3000 BCE. Beads from the Roman era were also widely distributed, and some beads found at Kota Tinggi, Johor, bear a remarkable resemblance to those produced during that time.

Various techniques are used in the manufacture of glass beads. Drawn beads are made from a drawn glass tube which is then cut into lengths; wound beads are produced by winding a glass filament around a wire or rod; mould-pressed beads are made by casting in a mould; composite beads are produced when a glass core is covered with another type of glass. Beads can also be made by the blown glass method. It is believed that the main centres for producing beads for the Southeast Asian markets were in India and Sri Lanka.

Evidence of local production

In Malaysia, most discoveries of ancient beads are the result of archaeological research. The oldest beads yet discovered in Peninsular Malaysia, which date to about 2,500 years ago, were found inside a granite cist grave in the Bernam Valley of south Perak. Beads dating from the Dongson cultural period (600 BCE–400 CE) have been found in Johor at Johor Lama and Makam Kota near Kota Tinggi, and at

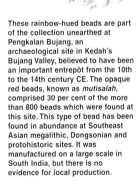

Early stone beads were pierced using a bow or pump drill, a method which required a lot of skill as the hole had to be drilled from both sides to avoid breakage.

Kampung Pencu near Muar; at Pantai Batu Buruk, Terengganu; and at Kampung Sungai Lang, Selangor. Large finds of beads have also been unearthed in Perak at Kuala Selinsing (200 BCE–10th century CE), the Bujang Valley of Kedah (5th–14th century CE), and at Takuapa and Patani in southern Thailand (8th–9th century CE). The types of beads discovered in Peninsular Malaysia are similar to those discovered in Sarawak and at other Southeast Asian sites.

Among the most popular beads found at Malaysian and Southeast Asian archaeological sites are those known as *mutisalah*. These are made from opaque, dark red glass, sometimes mistaken for carnelian, terracotta or coral. This type of bead has been discovered at South Indian megalithic sites, and at the ancient trade centre of Arikamedu, where there is evidence of large-scale manufacture.

In 1961, the archaeologist Alastair Lamb discovered small fragments of glass scrap which could have been used as raw materials for making beads in the Bujang Valley, Kedah. He also found similar materials at Kuala Selinsing, Perak, leading him to speculate that beads could have been made on site. Based on this evidence, and the finding of glass scrap at other Southeast Asian sites, academic opinion now leans towards a theory of local production, although the exact source of the materials and the location of the workshops is still unknown. It is assumed that the raw glass materials were originally brought on vessels from the Middle East, and were probably off-loaded at the west coast ports of the Malay Peninsula. These landfalls, such as Takuapa, Kedah and Kuala Selinsing, were the first ports of call in Southeast Asia, and have yielded the largest finds of beads. They also could have been made from discarded broken glass vessels, but this does not explain the presence of the raw glass materials found.

Other types of beads which have been discovered at Malaysian and other Southeast Asian sites are believed to have originated from many different regions, including the Indo-Pacific, the Mediterranean—site of the so-called 'Roman' beads— Africa and China.

The enduring popularity of beads

Archaeological sites the world over show that the popularity of beads is of great antiquity. Even today, the indigenous peoples of Southeast Asia, Africa and the Americas maintain great interest in beads, and regard them as more than mere decorative items. Among the various indigenous peoples of Malaysia, especially in Sabah and Sarawak, beads have been handed down from generation to generation. They are considered by both men and women as ornamental objects of great

significance and value, and are even believed to possess magical powers. Beadwork baby carriers used by the Kelabit, Kayan and Kenyah are believed to be the resting place of the child's soul for the first few months of his or her life. Because of the great demand for beads, the bead trade has played an important and widespread role in the region's economy. Such was the demand for beads by indigenous peoples during the 17th-century colonial expansion, that the Dutch East India Company established a bead factory in Amsterdam where 'trade beads' were manufactured on a large scale.

Beads play a significant role in researching the formation of early Malaysian cultures. They were extremely valued objects, not only during a person's lifetime, but even after death as beads have been found as part of the grave offerings in some early burials.

The function of beads covered all aspects of human life, such as birth, marriage, customs, religion and economics. In the archaeological context, beads are evidence that early societies possessed sophisticated social, cultural, economic and trading systems. The utilization of beads as a form of currency by early Malaysian societies also shows that they participated in a well-functioning economic system. In addition, the wearing of special, highly valued beads by particular people in the community clearly shows that there was a form of social hierachy in existence in Malaysia from prehistoric times.

0   1   2   3 cm

Thousands of beads have been unearthed at the archaeological site of Sungai Mas in the south of Kedah's Bujang Valley. These include blue-and-white 'eye' beads of possibly Mediterranean origin. The Sungai Mas collection resembles that from the protohistoric site of Kuala Selinsing which is believed to date from about 200 BCE to 900 CE.

Heirloom beads of Sarawak

How and when ancient beads arrived in Sarawak is still a mystery. Some of the most prized glass beads are strikingly similar to Eygptian and Mesopotamian beads produced more than two millenniums ago. However, to date, there is no evidence of trade between Sarawak and the Middle East during that time. The Kelabit people wear skullcaps (left) made of ancient beads, and in their system of bead values the oldest beads, especially those of blue glass (lower left), are the most valuable. The Kenyah call their most prized beads (lower right) *lukut sekala* and some resemble a type of bead found in Egypt which dates from 900 to 600 BCE. In Sarawak, large beads are known as *lukut*, as is the design of wrist tattoos. Both are believed to serve the same purposes of acting as a charm to ward off disease and prevent the soul from wandering.

Bronzeware

The most famous early bronzeware found in Malaysia is the decorated Dongson drums, named after the cultural centre of North Vietnam where they originated, and stylistically similar large bells, both believed to have been imported through trade contacts during the late Bronze Age from 600 BCE to 400 CE. Smaller bronzeware, believed to date from the early Bronze Age, include socketed celts which were also thought to be imports until the discovery of a mould for casting raised the possibility of Malaysian manufacture.

0   1   2 cm

Socketed celts
Described as adzes rather than axes, socketed celts came into use in Europe and China about 1300 BCE. This specimen, from a gold mine at Sungai Jenera, Kelantan, is believed to have been locally made. On analysis, it was found to be essentially copper with small amounts of tin and zinc.

A burial mound containing Dongson drums

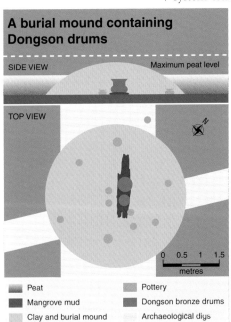

SIDE VIEW   Maximum peat level

TOP VIEW

0   0.5   1   1.5
metres

- ■ Peat
- ■ Mangrove mud
- ■ Clay and burial mound
- ■ Pottery
- ■ Dongson bronze drums
- ■ Archaeological digs

In 1964, a joint research team from the University of Malaya and the Department of Museums and Antiquities excavated the Dongson drum site at Kampung Sungai Lang, Selangor. The drums had been buried in an inverted position on a wooden plank which could have been the remains of a canoe. Pottery fragments and glass beads were found but no human remains or skeletal material.

Dongson drums

Based on archaeological discoveries in Thailand and Vietnam, the Bronze Age in Southeast Asia is believed to have started about the middle of the 2nd millennium BCE. Bronzeware discovered from the early period includes sharp implements like socketed celts, axes and spears, as well as personal ornaments such as bracelets. This bronzeware was made from a mixture of copper, tin and lead.

The overall picture of the Bronze Age in Malaysia is still vague. However, the discovery of bronze drums and bells in Peninsular Malaysia, as well as at archaeological sites on mainland Southeast Asia, Indonesia and southern China, has provided clear evidence that Dongson culture made an impact during the latter period of the Bronze Age when trade contacts enabled its influence to spread.

Dongson drums have been found in Peninsular Malaysia at Klang and Kampung Sungai Lang, Selangor; in the Tembeling Valley of Pahang; and at Kampung Batu Buruk and Besut, Terengganu. They are of the Heger 1 type, based on the classification system established by F. Heger in 1902.

Debate as to when the Bronze Age occurred in Peninsular Malaysia is ongoing. In the 1950s, W. Linehan was of the opinion that the archaeological data found did not indicate the existence of a true Bronze Age in Peninsular Malaysia, but was part of a combined Bronze–Iron Age. He believed that the bronzes originated from Funan, the powerful kingdom based in today's Cambodia, which had adopted the Dongson culture between the 1st and 3rd centuries CE. On the other hand, J. Loewenstein, working in the same decade, believed that the Bronze Age preceded the Iron Age in Peninsular Malaysia by a millennium. These conflicting theories came about partly because all the bronze artefacts which were studied were independent discoveries. They were unearthed before the advent of proper archaeological methods, and there was no contextual data to enable a more accurate chronology of each discovery.

Evidence of trade patterns

A clearer picture emerged in 1964 when more bronze drums were discovered at Kampung Sungai Lang, Selangor, and at Pantai Batu Buruk, Kuala Terengganu. When archaeological excavations were carried out at both sites, the discovery of remnants of iron implements provided evidence that both bronze drums and iron implements had been utilized at the same time. Various radiocarbon dates at Kampung Sungai Lang ranged from 580 BCE to 190 CE. Relative dating based on the iron tools narrows it from the end of the 1st millennium BCE to the early 1st millennium CE, the period which correlates with the diffusion of Dongson culture.

Prior to the discovery of the Terengganu drum, it was believed that this culture only made an impact on the west coast of the Malay Peninsula. This find confirms not only that Dongson culture had reached the east coast, but that trade relationships existed between both coasts during this time. Further evidence came to light in 1996 when another drum was found at Besut, Terengganu.

Dongson drums were luxury goods which were widely traded throughout Southeast Asia. Trade relations with other outside regions have also been proved through the discovery of imported items such as glass beads, which were discovered at drum sites on both coasts of Peninsular Malaysia.

This bronze bell, which measures 58 centimetres in height and 32 centimetres in diameter, was found by a villager in Kampung Pencu, near Muar, Johor, while levelling a mound for a house site.

Bells and other bronzeware

In comparison with the bronze drums, the distribution of bronze bells was more limited. Three were discovered in Klang, Selangor, and one in Muar, Johor. This type of bronze bell has only been found at one site outside Peninsular Malaysia, namely, the Battambang region of Cambodia.

It is believed that the bronze bells were not imported for commercial use, but as special objects to symbolize the power and status of their owners. The similarity of the design, shape and size of these bells prove that they originated from the same place.

Based on the thermoluminescence date of the bronze bell from Muar, it is believed that they were produced around 150 CE, which coincides with the expansion of the kingdom of Funan. The discovery of these bells provides clear evidence of the involvement of west coast Peninsular settlements in the trade and politics of Southeast Asia, especially with Funan.

In 1987, archaeological excavations carried out in Gua Harimau, near Lenggong, Perak, revealed a socketed bronze celt which was carbon dated to the earliest period of the Bronze Age—at least a millennium earlier than the date given for the Dongson drums. Prior to this discovery, the five socketed bronze celts discovered at Rasa, Selangor, at Tanjung Malim, Perak, at Keneboi, Negeri Sembilan, and at Sungai Jenera, Kelantan, were free finds which provided no contextual data. The Gua Harimau discovery was of great importance because a mould used for casting celts was also unearthed. Before this discovery, scholars believed that all the prehistoric bronze implements found in Peninsular Malaysia were imported because of the absence of easily worked copper ore deposits. The discovery of the mould gives rise to the question of whether some bronzeware was indeed produced in Peninsular Malaysia during the Bronze Age.

Bronze bowls, or remnants of these, have been discovered in the Tembeling Valley, Pahang, at Changkat Menteri, Perak, and at Chuping, Perlis. In Selangor, two bowls were found at Kampung Sungai Lang near where the Dongson drum was discovered, and three bowls were discovered in Jenderam Hilir. They are mainly undecorated although some bowls have crude linear patterns scratched on the outside. However, these decorations are not comparable to those of the Dongson drums. The bronze bowls are believed to have been produced considerably later than other early bronzeware, as they were discovered at sites

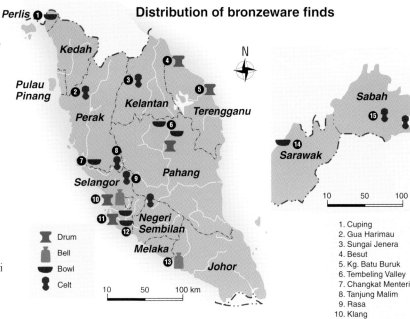

Distribution of bronzeware finds

Drum
Bell
Bowl
Celt

1. Cuping
2. Gua Harimau
3. Sungai Jenera
4. Besut
5. Kg. Batu Buruk
6. Tembeling Valley
7. Changkat Menteri
8. Tanjung Malim
9. Rasa
10. Klang
11. Kg. Sungai Lang
12. Jenderam Hilir
13. Muar
14. Niah Caves
15. Tapadong Caves
16. Agop Atas (Madai Caves)

where iron implements were also found. In the 1950s, both J. Loewenstein and G. De G. Sieveking dated these bronze bowls to the Iron Age. However, Leong Sau Heng (1989) dated the bronze bowls of Jenderam Hilir to the 14th century CE.

Finds from Sabah and Sarawak

Most of the bronze objects found in Sabah and Sarawak were independent finds, making dating difficult. These include two small hourglass-shaped drums, known as *moko*, which have only been found in Sabah and eastern Indonesia. They are believed to originate from Java or Bali and to have been taken to Pulau Alor, in the Lesser Sunda Islands of Indonesia, where they are considered important indicators of wealth.

In 1964, at Tapadong, Sabah, a socketed bronze celt and a cast for a bronze gouge were discovered, suggesting local bronzeware manufacture. Associated finds of polished stone tools, earthenware shards and an iron spearhead have led archaeologists to believe that the bronzeware dates from the 1st millennium CE. At Agop Atas, Sabah, some bronze remnants, earthenware shards, carnelian beads and an iron spear were discovered. These have been radiocarbon dated to about 500 CE .

Another important find in Sarawak, because of its archaeological context, is a bronze knife found at a burial site in the West Mouth of the Niah Caves. It was unearthed from the site of an extended burial where a copper implement was discovered in an urn for keeping human remains. As most of the burials are from the Neolithic period, this bronzeware is the oldest metal object yet found in Sarawak. Although absolute dates for the Iron Age in Sarawak are still unclear, it is possible that the early Bronze Age in Sarawak dates from the 1st century CE.

These remnants of a Dongson drum were discovered in 1944 at Klang, Selangor. Measuring 58.4 centimetres in diameter and 35.6 centimetres in height, the drum features characteristic Dongson designs, including herons in flight and a central sun or star with ten rays.

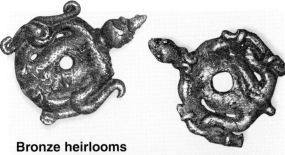

Bronze heirlooms
In the interior of Sarawak, some ancient bronze objects are kept as heirlooms by the Kayan community of Belaga. Among these is a figurine wearing a hornbill headdress, known as *Imun Ajo*, and turtle-shaped belt toggles. These are believed to be locally made and are related to the Kayan belief system. The form and decoration of these objects indicate that they are not of the early Iron Age.

Iron artefacts

Ever since the first ancient iron implements were unearthed in Peninsular Malaysia there has been much speculation as to their use, place of manufacture and production, and whether they were the products of a Malaysian Iron Age or were part of a joint Bronze–Iron Age. The majority of the implements are curious socketed, elbow-shaped tools, known to the Malays as tulang mawas, *literally 'ape's bones', which are the subject of many intriguing legends.*

The effect of centuries of exposure to Malaysia's hot, wet climate is evident in this collection of ancient iron implements from the National Museum.

The legendary *tulang mawas*

The origin of the term *tulang mawas*, literally 'ape's bones', which is the common Malay name for all the ancient, socketed iron implements, comes from the legend of a hairy, ape-like being with iron hands and forearms which roamed the interior forests of the Peninsula. Some scholars think that this legend could have been a reference to a different ethnic group of forest dwellers who had been observed using these unusual iron tools. It is still not certain how the tulang mawas were utilized, but there is speculation that the tools could have been swung from the elbow joint rather than the wrist, which could have inspired the legend of the 'iron forearm'.

Distribution and production

Apart from spearheads, all of the socketed iron implements found in Peninsular Malaysia bear no resemblance to those in use today. The implements, comprising axes, long-shafted axes, adzes, sickles, knives and spearheads, have often been discovered in hoards or in granite cist graves, and their similarity points to a common industrial tradition, believed to be evidence of an indigenous Iron Age.

The purpose of the tools is still uncertain, and even the way they were used continues to be debated. They are all disfigured by rust, and many have deteriorated since their discovery, but their basic shape can still be discerned. The socket probably supported a wooden handle although some scholars have suggested that it was used for a rattan cord which passed over the user's shoulder for carrying purposes. It has been suggested that the elbow-shaped tools could have been used as carpentry tools in ancient gold mines in Pahang. As iron implements have also been found near river beds, it has also been speculated that they were used as woodworking tools in the manufacture of boats.

The implements are of a very pure iron similar to present-day wrought iron. The abundant outcrops of iron ore found on the east coast are easily worked without advanced mining techniques as the ore is found close to the surface. The process of manufacture is difficult to determine. The sockets were probably cast, while the blades and shafts were probably hammered out. Smelting could have been carried out in the Tembeling region of Pahang, where tools have also been found, as quantities of iron slag, haematite and partly smelted ores have been found on the banks of the Tembeling River.

Iron finds in granite cist graves

The relationship between the cist graves—also known as slab graves—and the socketed iron implements found with them has been the subject of much debate since the first cist grave was discovered in 1895 at Changkat Menteri, south Perak. Since then, over a dozen more cist graves have been found in the same region, centred on the Bernam Valley and adjacent areas of southern Perak and Selangor. To date, there is no evidence of such graves anywhere else in Peninsular Malaysia.

The iron implements found in the graves include spearheads and socketed tools typical of other Iron Age sites in Peninsular Malaysia. Recent radiocarbon dates obtained from the cist graves range from the 1st to the 7th century CE.

It is believed that the graves were reserved for the élite as iron implements were reasonably rare and were probably only owned by people of high status. No human remains were found in the graves, although they were certainly funerary monuments. Associated finds of beads and shards show that the Bernam Valley was one of the most important early settlement centres in Peninsular Malaysia. However, detailed knowledge of the Iron Age communities is still lacking. Various origins have been posited for this Iron Age culture, including India, Indochina and Indonesia, or it could have been of local origin. Current academic opinion is that the settlement in the Bernam Valley was involved with trade via the transpeninsular route which led to the tin ore areas of Perak, the gold mining regions of Pahang, and the iron ore outcrops on the east coast.

Iron implements found in hoards

The discovery of different types of tools and weapons together in hoards indicates that the iron implements were of a single industrial tradition and formed a contemporary industrial assemblage.

Distribution of iron implements

Perlis

Kedah

Pulau Pinang

Perak

Kelantan

South China Sea

Terengganu

Strait of Melaka

Pahang

Selangor

Negeri Sembilan

Melaka

Johor

N

Iron Age cist grave

Socketed iron implements

0   50   100 km

Besides being found together in cist graves, iron implements have also been discovered in hoards elsewhere. At Sengat, near Ipoh, Perak, one hoard contained three long-shafted axes and a socketed sickle; another one from Tersang, Pahang, contained 10 long-shafted axes, while a hoard from Bukit Jati, Klang, Selangor, contained 21 socketed tools including knives and spearheads. Other hoards have been found in Selangor at Sungai Belata, Klang and Kampung Sungai Lang; in Perlis at Bukit Chuping; in Pahang in the Tembeling River valley, Raub and Kuantan; in Terengganu at Pantai Batu Buruk; and in Johor at Kampung Pencu, Muar. Isolated finds were discovered in Perak at Kuala Kangsar, Batang Padang and Tanjung Rambutan.

Of the five types of iron socketed implements, only the long-shafted axes, sickles, knives and spearheads were found in hoards. The normal axes and adzes have only been discovered in isolated finds. It has been suggested that the tools found in hoards represented a specialized tool kit, while the axes and adzes were used for timber felling and woodworking purposes.

Studies by G. de G. Sieveking revealed that the iron implements were manufactured using the same technology. He also believed that because the iron implements were found together they were of the same age. However, some scholars disagree with the latter, because the socketed spearheads also discovered with the tools are found throughout Southeast Asia and were in use during the early part of the Bronze Age and in later periods.

Collings and Sieveking believed that the Iron Age community responsible for the cist graves of the Bernam Valley existed at the same time as the protohistoric settlement at Kuala Selinsing. They based their theory on the similarity of beads found at both sites which were dated between the 1st and the 5th century CE. However, other scholars point out that similar glass and carnelian beads were found at many other Southeast Asian sites and were popular trade items throughout the region, and that their existence does not necessarily prove that the two settlements were connected. The comparison of other cultural data, such as the different burial modes used at both sites, does not support the theory of contemporaneous cultures.

Recent academic opinion favours the theory that the Bernam Valley cist grave culture was closely correlated to the Iron Age society which left hoards of iron implements together with Dongson bronze drums and bells at Klang and Muar. This theory is based on the similarity of the socketed iron implements found in both the Dongson and cist grave sites. The date of these Iron Age sites is based on the thermoluminescence date of the baked clay found on top of the bronze bell from Muar, which gave an absolute date of 150 CE.

Many iron implements have been found in the granite cist graves of southern Perak, which have been radiocarbon dated to between the 1st and 7th century CE. This artist's impression is of a reconstructed grave from Sungai Kruit, Perak.

Some scholars speculate that the elbow-shaped iron implements could have been used for shaping roof timbers in early Pahang mines, similar to those shown in this engraving from the *Illustrated London News*, 5 April 1890.

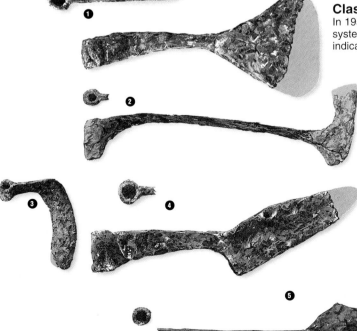

Classification of iron implements

In 1956, the archaeologist G. de G. Sieveking devised the following classification system for the socketed iron implements based on design differences which indicated differences of function:

(1) **Axes.** These tools are characterized by their heavy construction and strength. Only a small number have been found but all of them exhibit a single basic pattern with a heavy, downward-curving blade. Also included in this group are adzes, such as that pictured, found in the Tembeling River valley of Pahang.

(2) **Long-shafted axes.** These elongated tools are of light construction. The long outer margin was the working edge of the blade. Often found in hoards, they are unknown outside Peninsular Malaysia. The axe pictured is from Raub, Pahang.

(3) **Sickles.** These tools were probably fitted with a long, wooden handle and the cutting edge was on the convex part of the blade. The sickle shown here was found in a cist grave in the Bernam Valley of South Perak.

(4) **Knives.** These resemble the long-shafted axes but are of heavier make. They include both tanged and socketed varieties. It is unsure how they were used. The socketed knife pictured comes from a hoard unearthed at Klang, Selangor.

(5) **Socketed spearheads.** These form a separate class of weapons unrelated in form to the iron implements but found in association with them. The blades measure from 23 to 30 centimetres in length, while the socket and shank may be up to 15 centimetres long. The spearhead pictured is from a hoard found at Tembeling, Pahang.

Rock engravings

Rock engravings or carvings, also known as petroglyphs, refer to any man-made process whereby material is removed from a rock surface to produce a design or pattern. In Malaysia, most ancient rock engravings are found in Sarawak, particularly in the northeast, while a few are located in the adjoining region of Sabah. The only recorded rock engravings in Peninsular Malaysia are the carved megaliths at Pengkalan Kempas in Negeri Sembilan.

This Batu Narit, which means 'engraved stone' in the Kelabit and Lun Bawang dialects, is located at Punang Trusan near the Sarawak–Sabah border. The motifs consist mainly of spiral designs which cover about 2.5 square metres of the boulder's surface.

Engravings at Sungai Jaong

Dating perhaps from the 10th century CE, the most famous of the engraved boulders at Sungai Jaong, near Santubong, Sarawak, is a half life-size, spread-eagled human figure wearing a headdress (above top).

The motifs on the other boulders (above) consist mainly of smaller human figures either in bas-relief, produced by using a metal implement (chisel or axe), or in a pecked outline done by striking the rock with a sharp stone. The other common motif is a sausage-shaped object. It is likely that both types of engravings were produced by the same cultural tradition during the same period.

This rock engraving with a spiral motif is located near the longhouse at Long Banga in the upper Baram region. The engraving was said to have been made to commemorate the death of an illustrious leader.

Rock engravings in Sarawak

Of the five main rock engraving localities in Sarawak, Sungai Jaong is the only site located in the southwest. When excavations began there in the early 1950s, not only were shards of Chinese pottery from the Tang and Song dynasties, glass beads and iron slags discovered, but engraved sandstone boulders. The best known of these is the Batu Gambar (Picture Rock), which depicts a relief carving of a human, while other boulders also feature smaller humans in pecked designs chipped into the surface. Based on the recovered archaeological relics, and assuming that they are connected to the engravings, a date of around 900 CE has been suggested for the site.

In 1987, a rock engraving was recorded at Long Omok in northeast Sarawak. The pecked, wavy motif covers about 6 lineal metres of a river bank composed of pumice rock. An abandoned longhouse once stood at the now overgrown site. The local Punan regard the rock as sacred, believing it to be a Batu Kudi, a longhouse which became petrified due to some wrongdoing committed by the occupants.

Scattered groups of rock engravings and related megaliths found around Bario in the Kelabit Highlands were first recorded by Edward Banks in 1937 and by Tom Harrisson in 1958. The engravings were mostly made on sandstone boulders located along forest tracks and river banks. The motifs are mainly of human and animal figures in either pecked patterns or in bas-relief. One huge boulder, known as Batu Balang, has engravings of two animal figures, the larger one measuring about

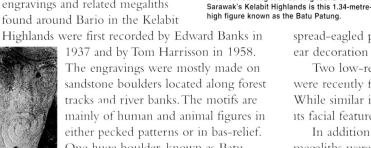

The most striking rock carving found in Sarawak's Kelabit Highlands is this 1.34-metre-high figure known as the Batu Patung.

6 metres tall. They are believed to depict two mythical *balang* (tigers) which were killed after terrorizing the local Kelabit. They are depicted with large eyes, pendant ears, long necks, barrel-shaped bodies and long, curved tails.

Another engraved boulder, known as Batu Narit, is located between Pa Ukat and Pa Lungan. It is said to portray the demise of a man-eating bird, somewhat resembling a hornbill. Human figures on the reverse of the boulder depict either the hunters or the victims. One engraving, from the late 1940s, was commissioned by the son of the chief of the southern Kelabit to commemorate the death of his father.

The most prominent bas-relief carving in the Kelabit Highlands is located high up on a cliff on the border between Sarawak and Kalimantan. Known locally as Batu Patung, the carving depicts an upright human figure in a spread-eagled posture, with prominent eyes, mouth, ear decoration and headdress.

Two low-relief engravings of human figures were recently found on a boulder near Pa Mada. While similar in style to the Batu Patung, they lack its facial features. One also wears a loincloth.

In addition to the rock engravings, other megaliths were constructed in the Kelabit Highlands for funerary purposes (see 'Megaliths'). Some of these megalithic remains are attributed to Tokid

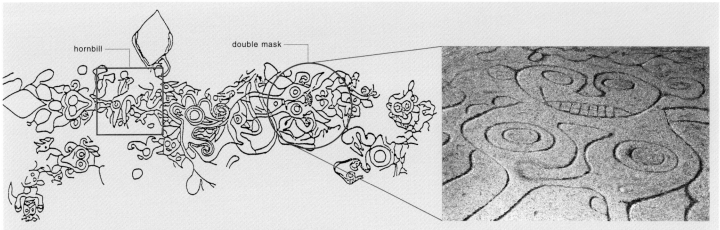

Prehistoric rock engravings at Lemuyun, Ulu Tomani
The tracing (left) illustrates in full the engravings which cover about 15 square metres of the surface of a boulder at Ulu Tomani in southwest Sabah. The overall design motif resembles Kenyah–Kayan harvest masks, while the coloured detail (right), pictures a double mask featuring two pairs of goggle-eyes and two noses sharing a single mouth, with prominently carved teeth and fangs (left, side view). Another figure (left, side view) resembles a bird, possibly a hornbill, as it has a beak, a horn and a slender neck.

Rini, a legendary Kelabit hero who is attributed with supernatural powers.

More engraved stones have been found near Long Semadoh and Ba Kelalan. One engraving is also known as Batu Narit by the Lun Bawang who are linguistically related to the Kelabit. Similar engravings have been found on menhirs. The local Lun Bawang believe that the engravings are *arit inawa*, 'romantic expressions' dedicated by Upai Semaring (their version of the Kelabit hero Tokid Rini) to his wife, Bau. Upai was said to have created the engravings by merely using his forefinger. Aligned depressions around the base of a boulder were explained as the imprints made by Bau's beaded waistlet. *Bau* in the Lun Bawang dialect also means 'beads'.

Rock engravings in Sabah

In Sabah, there are two recorded sites with rock engravings. The first, at Lemuyun in Ulu Tomani, was exposed in 1971 when the local Tagal community were clearing tree roots off a boulder. The dominant design consists of masks similar to Kenyah–Kayan harvest masks. The Tagal, who have occupied the area for about 45 years, have no tradition of megalithic activity. They believe the engravings were probably done by people who preceded them to the area, or by spirits. As the felled tree which exposed the carvings was well over a century old, it can be assumed that the engravings were at least of the same age.

Further south, near Pa Sia, a Lun Dayeh settlement, engravings of spiral motifs have been found on two boulders. The Lun Dayeh people are related to the Lun Bawang, leading Tom Harrisson (who researched in the mentioned areas of both states), to suppose that the engravings at Tomani possibly represented the northernmost extension of the Kelabit and Lun Bawang rock carving tradition. As the engravings at Pa Sia are similar to the Batu Narit at Punang Trusan and the Long Banga engravings in Sarawak, they were most probably done by the same people practising the same cultural tradition.

Rock engravings in Peninsular Malaysia

Although megaliths are found in Perak, Selangor, Negeri Sembilan and Melaka (see 'Megaliths'), the only engraved specimens are those found at Pengkalan Kempas near Linggi in Negeri Sembilan (see 'The Pengkalan Kempas inscriptions'). These megaliths are engraved with anthropomorphic, floral, and sun and moon motifs, while one is also carved with the Arabic inscription for Allah (God). Questions are still raised as to whether the engravings were done before the stones were erected, or after, and whether the Arabic word was carved at the same time as the other motifs or added later. It is generally believed that the megalithic activities in Peninsular Malaysia were done before the arrival of Islam.

It is clear that more research needs to be done on the dating, distribution, meaning and significance of the rock engravings in order to evaluate their role in Malaysian cultural development.

The photograph (above top) taken in 1920 shows the engraved stones *in situ* at Pengkalan Kempas before the site was restored by the archaeologist I. H. N. Evans. Cement casts of these three megaliths (above) are on display at the Negeri Sembilan State Museum in Seremban.

Location of rock engravings

• Rock engravings

Peninsular Malaysia

Strait of Melaka

Pengkalan Kempas

Melaka

South China Sea

N

Kota Kinabalu

Punang Trusan (Batu Narit)

Sabah

Lemuyun
Pa Sia
Long Semadoh
Ba Kelalan
Bario

Miri
Long Omok

Pa Lungan (Batu Narit and Ritung)
Pa Bengar (Batu Patung)
Pa Ramudu (Batu Balang)
Long Banga

Sungai Jaong (Batu Gambar)

Sarawak

Kuching

Kalimantan (INDONESIA)

0   200 km

Cave drawings

The prehistoric peoples of Malaysia, in common with their Orang Asli contemporaries, left records of their activities in the form of crude and simple drawings on the walls and ceilings of limestone caves. These cave drawings are sporadic and rare: there are only four sites in Peninsular Malaysia, four in Sarawak and one in Sabah. The meanings behind the drawings have remained largely mysterious due to a lack of in-depth research, while their future is also uncertain as they face natural as well as man-made agents of deterioration.

In these two views of the haematite cave drawings at Gua Tambun, Perak, a tapir is clearly visible (top, right-hand corner), while the animal in the lower left of the same panel is thought to be a pregnant female. In the lower panel, a human figure in a dancing posture holds a club in his right hand.

Cave art at Gua Kelawar

Charcoal drawings of human, animal and abstract motifs occur at 14 sites in the limestone cave of Gua Kelawar in Perak. The human figures are depicted in abstract forms and often in association with animals, including elephants and other large species, possibly pigs and monkeys. Both human and animal figures are usually filled in. There is a faded drawing (not shown) of a boat with three persons, one holding a pole and another steering a rudder. This drawing shows a distinct contrast in style and motifs to the modern objects with wheels pictured at Gua Badak, suggesting that its drawings probably predate those of Gua Badak, while they could also have been done by different groups of people. The Gua Kelawar drawings are of unknown age, and although they are believed to have been produced relatively recently, the tradition, as can be seen from other cave sites, is prehistoric.

Peninsular Malaysian cave art

In 1926, the first cave drawings to be reported in Malaysia were found on the walls of Gua Badak, a cave near Lenggong in Perak, by the archaeologist I. H. N. Evans. Attributed to the Negritos, an Orang Asli group who formerly inhabited the area, the charcoal drawings, depicting bicycles and motor cars, are obviously modern, but the practice could be ancient as attested by the second Perak discovery.

In May 1959, Lt. R. L. Rawlings chanced upon haematite cave paintings at Gua Tambun in the Kinta Valley of Perak. The motifs include human, animal and abstract designs. One human figure wears a headdress similar to that worn by the Orang Asli. The animal figures are quite large, with one in excess of 3 metres. Though the cave yielded some Neolithic artefacts and the motifs of the paintings resemble those found in New Guinea and Australia, it is unknown if there is a direct correlation between them in terms of age and cultural links.

In 1986, the staff of the Department of Museums and Antiquities found charcoal drawings at Gua Kelawar, a limestone cave near Sungai Siput in Perak. The drawings consist of human and animal figures, abstract designs and universal motifs such as the sun. Most of these drawings are deteriorating due to natural flaking of the cave surfaces, or have been defaced by modern-day graffiti. Gua Kelawar is said to be located within an area proposed for quarrying, while Gua Tambun has been excavated by guano (bats' excreta) diggers.

The existence of charcoal drawings at Gua Batu Luas in Taman Negara, Pahang, was reported by Abdul Latif Ariffin in 1985. They are believed to have been done by the ancestors of the local Orang Asli, and although they probably only date to about 1920, the tradition of cave drawing is much older. The motifs include what appear to be mountain panoramas, possibly the Gunung Tahan range with paths to the peak, 'maps' of rivers and camp sites, and designs used on Orang Asli blowpipes, combs and face decorations.

Cave drawings in Sarawak

The best known cave art in Sarawak is found in the Painted Cave, or Gua Kain Hitam, in the Niah Caves complex of Sarawak. The haematite paintings, first recorded by the art historian Barbara Harrisson in 1958, comprise about 100 individual drawings which stretch along 50 lineal metres of the interior wall. The motifs, comprising mainly human figures and boats, were possibly related to funerary rituals as several wooden 'boat coffins' were found nearby. It was believed that upon death the spirit of the deceased would journey to the underworld by boat. Scattered among the coffins were human bones, shells and pottery shards. One of the coffins was dated to around 2,000 years ago, which could also possibly be the age of the paintings if they were

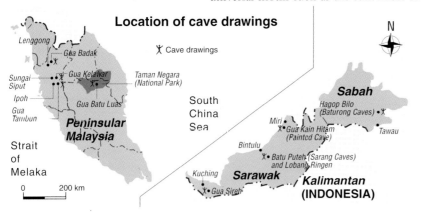

Location of cave drawings

Lenggong
Gua Badak
✗ Cave drawings
Sungai Siput
Gua Kelawar
Taman Negara (National Park)
Ipoh
Gua Batu Luas
Gua Tambun
Peninsular Malaysia
Strait of Melaka
0   200 km

N

South China Sea

Sabah
Hagop Bilo (Baturong Caves) ✗
Miri
✗ Gua Kain Hitam (Painted Cave)
Tawau
Bintulu
Batu Puteh (Sarang Caves) and Lobang Ringen
Kuching
Sarawak   **Kalimantan (INDONESIA)**
Gua Sireh

related and designed for the same purpose.

Charcoal drawings were found in two separate caves, namely Batu Puteh and Lobang Ringen, in the Sarang Caves in Bintulu Division by the archaeologist Tom Harrisson in 1966. The drawings at Batu Puteh were crudely executed and depict mostly human figures with geometric bodies. No animal figures could be deciphered. The drawings may portray some sort of procession.

The drawings at Lobang Ringen, covering about 6 lineal metres, depict human figures similar to those at Batu Puteh. The theme of the drawings could also resemble a procession. The present-day inhabitants, the Punan Tatau, could not account for the meaning of the drawings, nor had they noticed the drawings although they frequent the two caves to collect edible birds' nests.

Cave drawings also occur at Gua Sireh, a cave in the Serian District, where they cover 36 lineal metres of the interior walls. The main motifs are human figures with triangular or geometric bodies. A few figures wearing headdresses hold their hands outstretched as if in supplication. Some hold objects such as spears, shields and blowpipes, while others have parangs strapped to their waists and wear feathered items. A possible boat with a dancing figure on top and a musical instrument, perhaps the Bornean four-stringed *sape*, can be discerned. Other figurative designs include deer, turtles and monitor lizards. The non-figurative motifs consist of concentric circles and linear patterns. The general themes appear to portray daily activities, such as hunting and fishing, and occasional ones like fighting and dancing. Other themes may depict processions and ritualistic ceremonies as the main chamber yielded human burials. The present inhabitants of the area, the Bidayuh, could not explain the drawings, although some of them visit Gua Sireh on their way to collect birds' nests. The drawings are believed to be rather old, but the explorer Spencer St John, who visited Gua Sireh in 1862, did not report on them. Gua Sireh was first excavated in 1959 by the archaeologists Tom Harrisson and Wilhelm Solheim.

Designs used on Orang Asli blowpipes and combs are among the motifs found on the walls of Gua Batu Luas in Taman Negara.

Cave drawings in Sabah

The only confirmed and recorded charcoal drawings in Sabah were found in the rock shelter of Hagop Bilo in the Baturong Caves by the archaeologist Peter Bellwood and staff of the Sabah Museum who excavated the site in 1987. These unusual drawings, depicting events involving boats and humans, are probably less than a century old. However, Barbara Harrisson, who conducted research in the cave between 1966 and 1968, did not mention the drawings though she found wooden coffins and carved figures presumed to be remnants of Orang Sungai burial rituals.

Most Malaysian cave art sites were once remote. However, with development many of these sites are now accessible, which carries good and bad implications. Genuine visitors can now view the drawings, which are regarded as part of the national heritage, but less civic-minded visitors deface the originals by adding their own graffiti. Conservators are also faced with the problem of trying to arrest the natural deterioration of the drawings due to flaking of the limestone surfaces and the growth of algae.

The motifs used in Malaysian cave drawings are unique as those found in other Southeast Asian countries depict quite different motifs. The dating for most of the cave drawings is still uncertain. Obviously, much more research needs to be done so that these drawings can be understood and better appreciated, thus preserving them for future posterity.

Possibly 2,000 years old, the red haematite paintings at Gua Kain Hitam in the Niah Caves of Sarawak (above top) depict human figures with outspread arms who appear to dance on top of boats. Some hold spears and other objects, while some wear peculiar headdresses. The boats also resemble centipedes and scorpions—animals which abound in the caves and are feared for their lethal stings.

Stick figures with triangular or oval bellies are a main motif at Gua Sireh, Sarawak (above bottom). One unusual figure on the left features horns or ears, 'whiskers' and a tail or phallus between its legs. On account of its size and detailed features, it probably represents a deity or totemic symbol.

The charcoal drawings at Hagop Bilo

The only cave drawings found in Sabah depict four main compositions. The first has been identified as a native boat which used to ply the seas off eastern Kalimantan or Sulu in the mid-1840s. The second, a larger boat with no sail, has a crew armed with parangs. A symbolic head is pictured above the prow, while a bier with a corpse lies astern. The third composition consists of a large human figure drawn in association with a sambar deer (*rusa*) and other smaller human figures and geometric patterns. It is believed to depict the famous Idahan legend of Apoi and the Golden Deer. The fourth motif depicts a modern man, possibly an Orang Sungai, wearing a feather headdress, ear ornaments and possible body tattoos. His severed left hand could have been the result of the traditional Islamic punishment for theft. The two boats and the wounded man probably portray the social unrest and trying conditions during the mid-19th century when head-hunting and piracy raids were common.

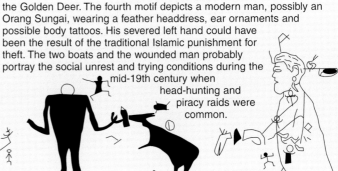

TOP LEFT: In this photo taken in 1955 near Temerloh, Pahang, an adult male of the Jahhut, one of the subgroups of the Senoi (Orang Asli), stands by a large fish trap made of split bamboo and lashed with rattan.

TOP CENTRE: Taken in the 1950s, this photo shows a Senoi male felling a tree using a metal tool. Neolithic stone axes may have been used in much the same manner by attaching the axe head to a handle using rattan twine.

ABOVE: On festive occasions Senoi musicians still use body decorations inspired by ancient tradition, including face markings and plaited leaf headbands with fringe-like streamers known as 'centipedes feet'. Their drums were originally made from hollowed-out tree trunks and monkey skins were used for the drumheads. Drums were considered the most important musical instrument and were usually owned by chiefs.

RIGHT: This colour plate entitled 'A Chief of the Forest People' which appears in *The Head-Hunters of Borneo* was drawn by the author Carl Bock who journeyed to Borneo in the 1870s. He relates that the subject of the drawing was 'the chief under whose guidance I visited the Forest People "at home"'. These people were the nomadic Punan–Penan (Bock's 'Orang Poonan') of Austronesian descent who have probably lived in Borneo since Neolithic times.

BELOW: These cave drawings of unknown date and origin found in Gua Sireh, Sarawak, are believed to depict cultural events. The large figure holds a shield, and, to his right, a figure dances on top of what could be a dugout. Below this motif a couple appear to embrace, while the larger figure at the end of the line of people may be wearing a deer headdress.

RIGHT: Grooved with crosshatching on one end, this unusual stone tool, one of several found at Neolithic sites in the Malay Peninsula, was used for beating bark to produce bark cloth. One of these objects is shown *in situ* as part of the grave goods of a Neolithic burial at Gua Cha, Kelantan. The position of the beater near the mid-section of the skeleton may have related to the bark cloth loincloth. Other grave goods, including the stone tool near the neck and the earthenware by the feet, probably also had cultural and religious significance.

ECONOMIC PATTERNS OF NEOLITHIC LIFE

The economic prehistory of the Malay Peninsula followed a slightly different course than that of Sabah and Sarawak. By about 10,000 years ago, during the Hoabinhian cultural period, the hunting and gathering lifestyle was established throughout the northern and central Peninsula, as well as a basic trade network along which travelled shells, stone resources, forest products and social information. There is no confirmed evidence that the population grew rice or practised systematic agriculture, but encouragement of plant resources most probably took place.

These charcoal cave drawings from Gua Sireh in Sarawak may depict a butchering scene.

During the Peninsular Neolithic (c. 4,500–2,500 years ago), there would have been some field agriculture of rice and foxtail millet. These crops are not proven by actual remains, but Peninsular Neolithic artefacts are closely paralleled in central and southern Thailand sites where rice cultivation is definitely attested about 4,000 years ago.

The origin of Malaysia's Neolithic people is often the subject of heated debates. Some academics believe that the Peninsular Neolithic populations (few commit themselves on Borneo) were indigenous to the Malay Peninsula and acquired agriculture and Neolithic artefacts by trade contact with people from Thailand. A contrary and popular theory, which uses linguistic evidence, is that the Peninsular Neolithic people were the ancestors of the present-day Orang Asli group, the Senoi, whose ancestors migrated down the Peninsula from southern Thailand about 4,500 years ago. No living archaeologists equate the Peninsular Neolithic with Austronesian migrations, although this was a popular view in the 1930s.

Hoabinhian pebble tool industries do not occur in Borneo, but the flake tool users of Sarawak and Sabah seem to have been hunters and gatherers. Rice remains from Sarawak's Gua Sireh have been dated to about 4,500 years ago. The knowledge of rice cultivation could have been introduced from Taiwan via the Philippines, or from the Malay Peninsula or southern Thailand. Present-day Austronesian-speaking groups were no doubt present during the Bornean Neolithic, but it is not known whether rice cultivation was connected with them or some other group, such as an Aslian population from the Peninsula. Neolithic pottery from Sarawak has more similarities with pottery from the Malay Peninsula than the Philippines. However, Neolithic pottery from Sabah (c. 3,500 years ago), relates to that of the Philippines and eastern Indonesia—areas which probably did not have a rice economy—and it is here that the Orang Laut (sea nomad) economy appeared based on fishing, shellfishing, trading, and tuber and fruit growing.

Overall, the economic patterns of Malaysian Neolithic life remain poorly known. Obviously, people continued hunting and gathering, just as before agriculture developed. In the rainforest environment, rice cultivation would have been restricted by climatic factors and poor soils away from the alluvial plains. Many other plant foods must have supported Neolithic life. Few remains of such plants exist in the archaeological record. However, the future for plant discovery looks set to change with the advent of new research methods.

Hunters and gatherers

Evidence suggests that prior to around 2500 BCE, when agricultural lifestyles first appeared in Malaysia, there was a universal economy based on hunting and gathering. After this date, the hunter-gatherer lifestyle began to erode, but it never entirely vanished. The Negritos, the Punan/Penan and the Orang Laut and Bajau Laut practised a nomadic lifestyle dependent on their immediate environment for their daily sustenance. Even today, small groups of these people still live in the traditional manner.

A group of hunter-gatherer Negritos from Ulu Kelantan are shown in this 1950s photo. The man in the foreground carries a woven fish trap.

Negrito bows and arrows

Formerly, the Negritos used bows and arrows to hunt, but around 90 years ago they switched to blowpipes which were introduced by the Senoi. A Negrito from Ulu Kelantan uses a bow and arrow in this 1950s photo (above). In the 1906 drawing by de Morgan (below), from Skeat and Blagden's *Pagan Races of the Malay Peninsula*, the 'Semang Implements' are described as follows: Semang bow (1), arrows (2, 3), arrowhead with two barbs (4), butt end of an arrow showing vanes and notch (5), arrows in their quiver (6), bamboo tubes used as poison receptacles (7, 8). The bow was made of hardwood, the string of twisted fibre, the shafts and quiver of bamboo, and the arrowheads were coated with *ipoh* poison.

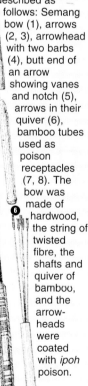

The Negritos of Peninsular Malaysia

Living in the mountainous regions north of Pahang, the hunter-gatherer Negritos are regarded as the earliest inhabitants of the Malay Peninsula. They are of Australo-Melanesian affinity, and probably descend from the people of the Hoabinhian cultural period whose burials date from 10,000 years ago. They speak an Austroasiatic language, as do their agriculturalist neighbours, the Orang Asli Senoi.

The Negritos number around 2,000 out of a total Orang Asli population of 92,000. They belong to various subgroups, namely, the Kensiu, Kintak, Lanoh, Jahai, Mendriq and Bateq. Those from Perak, Kedah and Pahang are also known as Semang (debt slaves) while those from Kelantan and Terengganu were called Pangan (forest people). The Negritos predated the arrival of the Senoi and Proto-Malay Orang Asli peoples, who probably arrived later, during the Neolithic period.

A Negrito camp usually comprises from 10 to 30 family members. They reside temporarily in wind screens or shelters, which are built by the women from bamboo, poles, rattan and palm leaf thatch. The shelter has a sleeping platform and a hearth for cooking, warmth and protection against wild animals and insects at night. The group stays in one place from several days to a few weeks and moves on after exhausting food resources in the vicinity. When a member dies, the deceased is washed and then buried in a flexed position together with his or her belongings far from the camp which is abandoned.

Different groups roam the forest within a vaguely defined but well understood territory. Certain trees, such as the durian and the poisonous Ipoh tree, are owned by a respective group and act as boundary markers. As the Negritos have no storage technology, they have to hunt and gather food daily. Early in the day, the women and children

Location of Orang Asli groups

Perlis
Kedah
KENSIU
KINTAK — JAHAI
Pulau Pinang
LANOH — MENDRIQ
TEMIAR — Kelantan — Terengganu
BATEK
Perak
SEMAI
Pahang
SEMAQ BERI
Strait of Melaka
Selangor
TEMUAN
JAHUT
CHE WONG
TEMOK
Negeri Sembilan
SEMELAI
MAH MERI
JAKUN
Melaka
ORANG KANAK
Johor
ORANG LAUT (Orang Kuala)
ORANG SELETAR

South China Sea

N

Semang-Negritos
Senoi
Proto-Malays
MAH MERI/TEMUAN Orang Asli groups
Group boundaries

0   50 km

set out with baskets and digging sticks to gather tubers, shoots, fruits, vegetables and shrubs, while the children search for snails, shellfish, insects and frogs. The men hunt squirrels, monkeys, rats, birds and wild pigs with bamboo blowpipes and poisoned darts. Traps are made to snare mouse deer, squirrels and birds, while fish and turtles are caught by barbed spears, traps and weirs.

Negritos possess and carry the bare necessities of life, such as clothes, baskets, and weapons. Originally, the women wore a short skirt and breech cloth made of bark cloth, belts, headbands and bracelets made of rock fungus and bamboo hair combs, while the men wore a loincloth of bark cloth. Their personal and household goods are carried on their backs in baskets woven from pandanus leaves.

The Punan/Penan of Sarawak

Present-day estimates put the number of Punan/Penan people in Sarawak at about 10,000. However, only about 400 individuals still lead a nomadic hunter-gatherer lifestyle and are called 'Penan' to differentiate them from the settled groups of Punan (see map). They differ from the Negritos as they are biologically and linguistically related to their Austronesian agriculturalist neighbours.

The Penan comprise various bands each consisting of around 10 family units making up to 40 closely related members. Three types of pole and leaf-thatch huts are built. The main camp, used from several weeks to months, is the base from which the group moves from one temporary camp to another within their designated area. It is also used for storing collected jungle produce and to shelter the old and sick while the able-bodied members go out to hunt and gather resources. The temporary hut is used for a few days when searching for food and jungle produce, while the travelling hut is built by hunters on their overnight trips. A camp is re-sited after the supply of food resources has been exhausted or when death occurs. The corpse is wrapped in a mat and left with his belongings in his hut. The camp is abandoned and the area avoided for some time as the Penan fear the soul's mischief.

The Penan have an intense affinity with their rainforest home. Their main source of carbohydrate is wild sago (*Eugeissona utilis*), which they protect through a preservation concept known as *molong*, whereby only a few mature trees are felled while the rest are marked and reserved for future use. This concept is also used to indicate claims over other resources, such as fruit trees, rattan groves or *ipoh* trees. The Penan also eat palm shoots, mushrooms and seasonal fruits like durian and wild rambutan. They often establish camp near fruiting trees so that they can feast leisurely on the fruits and lie in ambush for animals that come to feed.

Hunting is an important actitivity as it provides their protein. Blowpipes made of drilled hardwood (*nyagang*) and darts smeared with Ipoh poison are used to hunt small game like gibbons, monkeys, squirrels and birds, while spears and dogs are employed to hunt bigger animals such as bearded pigs and deer.

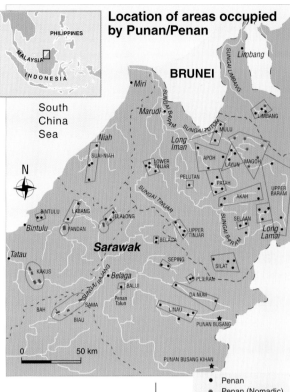

A Punan hunter-gatherer from Sarawak's Upper Baram region.

Traditionally, the Penan avoided large streams or rivers, and thus had no boat or fishing traditions. However, they have learned boat making and blacksmithing from their agriculturalist neighbours, the Kayan, and have become skilled at collecting and selling rainforest products. Their basketware is also highly prized and has been used as barter for salt, cloth, tobacco and cooking utensils. The Penan traditionally produced bark cloth to make short skirts for the women and loincloths for the men.

Seaborne hunters and gatherers

Another group of Austronesians who formerly practised a seaborne hunting and gathering lifestyle are the people collectively known as Orang Laut, or 'sea people'. Those from the coasts of eastern Sabah and the Sulu Archipelago are the Sama-Bajau speaking Bajau Laut, while those from the Strait of Melaka and the Riau–Lingga Archipelago speak Malay dialects. This latter group, who are now settled, comprise the Orang Kuala, or 'estuary people', and the Orang Seletar, or 'sea gypsies', both from Johor.

Present-day estimates of the Sama-Bajau speakers in Sabah are put at over 200,000. Since about 1930 most have settled down in 'water villages'—pile houses built over the coastal shallows—around Kampung Labuan Haji in the Semporna District. Only about 200 Bajau Laut still live permanently on boats.

The Bajau Laut of Semporna assert that their ancestors were sea nomads from Arabia. However, most agree that they originated from Sibutu Island in the Sulu Archipelago. This accords with linguistic evidence which places the Bajau Laut in this area since at least 800 CE, while archaeological excavations at Bukit Tengkorak in eastern Sabah have unearthed evidence for an economy based on maritime resources since 1000 BCE.

Originally, each Bajau Laut family lived aboard its own boat. They belonged to a mooring community of closely related families which had its permanent anchorage in a sheltered inshore area. Families came ashore only to collect firewood, food and water, to dry nets and to bury their dead.

Traditionally, a group came under the patronage and protection of the local ruler who had authority over their anchorage site. They collected fresh water and firewood and, in return, the patron received part of their catch. He would occasionally request trade commodities such as dried fish, trepang (sea cucumber) and mother-of-pearl, while the Bajau Laut received rice, cassava, fruits, betel nuts and leaves, cloth and other manufactured goods. They also traded with other groups, especially artisan communities, for forged iron items (knives, spears, fish hooks and harpoons), thatched roofing, sleeping mats, earthenware stoves, water jars and fishing boats. This patron–client tie declined with the establishment of Semporna as a trading centre in 1887 when the Bajau Laut began selling their commodities for cash.

Location of areas occupied by Punan/Penan

PHILIPPINES

MALAYSIA

INDONESIA

BRUNEI

Limbang

Miri

Marudi

SUNGAI LIMBANG

LIMBANG

South China Sea

Niah

SUNGAI BARAM

SUNGAI TUTOH

MULU

Long Iman

APOH

MAGOH

SUAI-NIAH

LOWER TINJAR

LAYUN

PELUTAN

PATAH

UPPER BARAM

AKAH

BINTULU

LABANG

JELALONG

UPPER TINJAR

SELAAN

Long Lamai

Bintulu

PANDAN

BELAGA

SUNGAI BARAM

Sarawak

SUNGAI TINJAR

Tatau

KAKUS

SEPING

SILAT

SUNGAI RAJANG

Belaga

BALUI

PLIERAN

Penan Talun

DA NUM

BAH

SAMA

LINAU

BIAU

PUNAN BUSANG

N

0   50 km

PUNAN BUSANG KIHAN

- Penan
- Penan (Nomadic)
- ★ Punan Busang
- Punan Bah
- BINTULU, APOH Punan/Penan subgroups
- ◇ Group boundaries

A few hundred Bajau Laut still practise a maritime hunting and gathering lifestyle around Semporna in southeastern Sabah. Families live permanently aboard traditional boats (below left) where children are taught to swim at an early age in order to dive for trade shells (below right).

Location of the Bajau Laut

N

Sabah

Lahad Datu

South China Sea

Sulu Sea

Lahad Datu (Darvel) Bay

Pulau Sibutu

Java Sea

Pulau Timbun Mata

Sulu Archipelago

Kampung Labuan Haji

Semporna

PHILIPPINES

Pulau Bumbun

Tawau

Bukit Tengkorak

Sulawesi Sea

0 10 20 30 40 km

Rice production

It is possible that rice was first cultivated in China at least 8,000 years ago, reaching Southeast Asia about four millenniums after this. Former beliefs that rice was introduced to Malaysia at a much later date have been revised following the highly important discovery in Sarawak of rice grains dating to around 4,500 years ago. As yet, the oldest rice found in Peninsular Malaysia is from 200 BCE.

Rice from Gua Cha
Carbonized rice grains (right), found at the rock shelter of Gua Cha in the interior of Kelantan by a 1979 archaeological team (top), has been radiocarbon dated to 930 years ago. Scholars speculate that the rice was either brought into the area by the local Orang Asli, or taken to the rock shelter by barter traders seeking forest products in return for imported goods. This latter theory is substantiated by associated finds of Chinese stoneware shards. Gua Cha is located on the bank of the Sungai Nenggiri, which eventually joins the Kelantan River, formerly a major trade route. Bamboo rafts, still used by the local Orang Asli (below), were utilized by the excavation team and were probably the means by which early barter traders found their way upstream from the coast.

The earliest evidence of rice
Sophisticated dating methods and detailed excavations undertaken by present-day archaeologists have resulted in finds which would have been overlooked a few decades ago. The cave of Gua Sireh, southeast of Kuching in western Sarawak, had undergone previous excavations, but in 1989, the archaeologists Peter Bellwood and Ipoi Datan discovered that some pottery shards from the site contained rice husk temper and even some whole carbonized grains. When these were radiocarbon dated they revealed an age of around 2500 BCE. This significant find is the oldest confirmed evidence of domesticated rice in the Malay Archipelago and is contemporary with proven rice cultivation sites in central Thailand.

This scanning electron microphotograph shows a rice spikelet base found in pottery at Gua Sireh in Sarawak. The discovery of the 4,500-year-old rice remnants proves that prior to the arrival of Austronesian-speaking people, perhaps during the 1st millennium BCE, some societies in Sarawak had been agriculturalists for over 3,000 years.

Location of early rice finds and reports

Dongson
THAILAND
Ban Kao
Ligor (Tan-ma-ling)
Bujang Valley
Kuala Selinsing
Patani (Langkasuka)
Gua Cha
Kuala Berang (Fo-la-an)
Tembeling
Peninsular Malaysia
Pulau Tioman (Tiyumah)
Mait (Johor?)
Gua Sireh
VIETNAM
South China Sea
Sabah
Sarawak
Kalimantan
Sumatra
0   400   800 km

The alluvial plain surrounding the limestone massif where Gua Sireh is located is presently used for paddy growing, and it is possible that the rice remains were cultivated there.

The oldest rice discovered during archaeological excavations in Peninsular Malaysia was found in 1979 by the archaeologist Adi Haji Taha at Gua Cha in the interior of Kelantan. This large rock shelter is one of Malaysia's richest archaeological sites of both the Mesolithic (Hoabinhian) and Neolithic periods. The carbonized rice, which has been carbon dated to the 11th century CE, is of unknown origin. There is no evidence to suggest that rice cultivation was ever carried out in the surrounding area, which is remote from any paddy-growing areas today.

The second find of rice in Peninsular Malaysia was made by the archaeologist Nik Hassan Shuhaimi during the 1988–90 excavations at Kuala Selinsing, a port site in Perak which existed from the 2nd century BCE till about the 10th century CE.

Rice (*Oryza sativa*), commonly grown by wet rice cultivation throughout Southeast Asia, is the same type as that found in the early Malaysian sites.

The rice is believed to date to over 2,200 years ago making it

the earliest physical evidence of rice so far found in Peninsular Malaysia. A wooden rice mortar, hollowed out of a tree trunk, was also recovered from one of the sites.

There are two theories on the origin of the rice from Kuala Selinsing. Either the settlement had contact with a paddy-growing society in the inland of the Peninsula, or the rice was imported by traders from Sumatra, South Asia or other Southeast Asian regions, as other artefacts found at the port show that Kuala Selinsing played a role in the trade network which linked India and China via the Strait of Melaka.

Tools and related evidence
Despite the belief that rice was a major form of sustenance during the Neolithic period, evidence of rice cultivation during this time is, so far, insignificant. The hypothesis that rice was brought in from areas outside the Malay Peninsula, possibly by foreign or local traders, has mainly arisen due to the small number of artefacts found which can be categorized as rice cultivation tools. This is further

complicated by varying interpretations of the function of these tools, since they could also have been used in ritual ceremonies, or in other types of farming. An unusually shaped stone tool, nicknamed the 'Tembeling knife' because most of its type were found around the Tembeling River region of Pahang, could have been used as a reaping knife.

The rice found at both Gua Cha and Kuala Selinsing has been identified as *Oryza sativa*, but it is not known as yet whether it was cultivated by wet or dry methods.

The traditional theory for the introduction of rice into the Malay Peninsula is that it was part of the Neolithic culture which was brought by migrating Austronesians from mainland Asia. On the other hand, there is also strong archaeological evidence that the change to Neolithic culture at Gua Cha and other areas was the result of long-established links through overland trade between the inhabitants of the Malay Peninsula and central and southern Thailand. This theory is based on the similarities between earthenware and stone tools found in these regions. Tripod pots from Peninsular sites show affinities with pottery from central Thailand, while similar archaeological assemblages occur at various points southwards into the north of the Malay Peninsula. Several Thai sites provide evidence of rice cultivation 4,500 years ago.

Remains from the Bronze Age, including Dongson drums and bells from North Vietnam, which have been found at various Peninsular Malaysian sites (see 'Bronzeware'), suggest that these communities, if not actively involved in rice cultivation, probably had contacts with people who came from a sophisticated rice-producing society.

Evidence from protohistoric times

Evidence of rice production and trade during the protohistoric period is equally as sparse as from prehistory. However, documentary sources provide clues that early Malay Peninsular settlements and kingdoms were engaged in these activities. Chinese reports of the Song Dynasty (960–1279 CE) mention Tan-ma-ling, thought to have been located at either Ligor (southern Thailand) or at Tembeling in Pahang, as well as Langkasuka, at present-day Patani in southern Thailand, as places where foreign merchants traded in rice. Fo-lo-an, believed to be

Avenues of menhirs, originally from Negeri Sembilan, could have been linked to beliefs and rituals associated with rice cultivation.

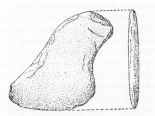

The 'Tembeling knife'
Various terms, such as 'luxate axes' and 'bent fan axes', have been used to describe what is now commonly known as the 'Tembeling knife', a Neolithic stone tool found in the greatest quantity in the Tembeling River valley in the interior of Pahang. Interpretations vary as to its use, but some scholars speculate that it could have been used for reaping paddy. As Tembeling was located along a land route linking the east and west coasts of the Peninsula, it is likely that rice grown in this valley could have reached both Gua Cha and Kuala Selinsing where early rice remains have been found. The grey stone 'knife' (left) was found at the Tui Gold Mine in Pahang under 5 metres of alluvial deposits. The black hornstone specimen (above right) was found near Kuala Lipis, Pahang, while the two specimens (above, and above left) were unearthed in the Tembeling region.

Kuala Berang in Terengganu, is mentioned as a place where 'foreigners barter rice for indigenous products'.

The Arab geographer Idrisi (12th century) writes that 'one finds in Tiyumah (Pulau Tioman), sandalwood and rice', while at Mait (Johor) he lists rice as an indigenous product.

The early kingdom sites in the Sungai Muda, Sungai Mas and Pengkalan Bujang area of South Kedah are today surrounded by an important paddy-growing district. This region may have been influential in the early development of rice cultivation. A miniature silver ploughshare and a silver yoke found in a foundation deposit under a temple may be religious symbols related to rice cultivation, although they are not proof of actual rice production.

Other finds related to rice cultivation include mortar stones used for making rice flour. These stones have been found in Sabah and Sarawak alongside megaliths which are usually located in paddy fields (see 'Megaliths'). On the west coast of Sabah, the Kadazan used menhirs to bestow fertility and guard their fields against evil spirits.

In Peninsular Malaysia, most of the early rituals associated with rice cultivation have now vanished, but surviving traditions in Sabah and Sarawak may be of great antiquity. Further research into these cultural beliefs will no doubt shed more light on early rice production.

Relics from the Bujang Valley
Irrigated paddy fields (above) surround the archaeological sites of the Bujang Valley in South Kedah where an early kingdom thrived from the 4th to the 14th century CE. It is believed that rice was cultivated there from the earliest period. However, the only tangible evidence yet unearthed which connects the valley with early rice production is a silver yoke (3 mm high (above, top)) and a silver ploughshare (44 mm high (above, right)). They were part of the contents of a bronze casket (below) unearthed from the foundations of a 10th–11th century Hindu temple at Site 16A on the Bujang River.

Barter trade networks

Prehistoric barter trade in Malaysia may have evolved about 10,000 years ago when coastal and inland inhabitants began exchanging goods. Later, during the Neolithic period, the frequency of barter trade increased and long-distance overland exchanges between the Malay Peninsula and Thailand began. The early belief that Neolithic cultural changes were due to seaborne migrations is now obsolete. Some scholars now favour the theory that these changes came about through trade, and that maritime trade networks began about 500 BCE during the Metal Age.

At Kota Gelanggi, near Jerantut in Pahang, archaeologists research into prehistoric exchange networks dating back to the Mesolithic.

Evolution of barter trade

8000 BCE
MESOLITHIC

7000 BCE

Freshwater shells found inside a cave at Gunung Senyum, Pahang, may have been used as trade exchanges during the Mesolithic period on the Malay Peninsula.

6000 BCE

5000 BCE

Bifacial pebble tools from Peninsular Malaysia, typical of Hoabinhian culture during the Mesolithic, could have been traded with coastal communities in exchange for marine products.

4000 BCE

NEOLITHIC
3000 BCE

2000 BCE

Polished stone tools are a hallmark of the Neolithic period when barter trade networks expanded. During this period, long-distance overland trade between Malaysia and Thailand began.

1000 BCE

METAL AGE

CE 1

Finds of Dongson drums and other bronzeware during the Metal Age are proof of early maritime trade networks.

Overland trade patterns

Exchanges of marine and inland forest products possibly took place between the coastal and inland inhabitants of Malaysia from Mesolithic (Hoabinhian) times. But trade movements were very slow and the volume of trade was insignificant. A seashell found at Gua Sagu near Sungai Lembing in Pahang, tentatively dated to 12,000 years ago, may be evidence of these early trade exchanges. But most seashells found in inland caves, including a shell spoon made from a mussel from Gua Cha in Kelantan, date from the Neolithic. These shells probably passed through several hands before reaching their inland destination where they were exchanged for forest products such as rattans, resins, bark and probably stones for making stone tools.

When the Neolithic began, perhaps as early as 3000 BCE, the rhythm of exchanges increased. Evidence of this is revealed by abundant finds of earthenware and polished stone axes, adzes and rings at inland Malaysian sites. Recent studies of these goods have shed new light on trade networks during this period. As a result, some scholars now believe that technological advancements and the new material culture of Neolithic sites could have been due to overland trade between Peninsular Malaysians and people from central and southern Thailand, and not necessarily to seaborne or overland migrations. There is also no direct evidence to indicate that long-distance maritime trade took place in the region during this period.

The emergence of Neolithic culture in the Malay Peninsula has been linked with the more advanced societies in

This Neolithic bowl, of a style similar to Thai earthenware of the same period, was discovered at a cave site at Gunung Senyum in Pahang's interior.

Thailand on the basis of similarities in material culture. On the whole, Malaysian Neolithic pottery is similar in both vessel shapes and surface decoration to that from Thai Neolithic sites. Tripod pots found at Ban Kao in central Thailand and at numerous Peninsular sites, including Jenderam Hilir in Selangor, are virtually identical. More evidence of overland trade comes from unusual T-sectioned stone rings found at Gua Cha, which have been discovered at both Neolithic and Bronze Age sites throughout mainland Southeast Asia. All these similarities lead to the theory that the Peninsular artefacts probably derived from central Thailand and reached their destinations in the Malay Peninsula through various contact points where products were exchanged. As the artefacts in Thailand were found in close association with bronze objects, and as tin was used in the production of bronze, it is possible that this mineral was sourced from the Peninsula, particularly as many of the T-sectioned stone rings were recovered from areas which are known for the presence of rich alluvial tin or gold.

Neolithic origin theories

A few scholars in the past have used stone artefact technology as the basis for their theory that migrating Austronesians originating from southern China were the cause of the sudden cultural progression from Mesolithic to Neolithic in the Malay Peninsula. Other characteristics attributed to the Austronesians which arrived around the same time throughout Southeast Asia, were the cultivation of rice and millet, the use of the perforated stone knife for reaping rice, the brewing of beer from rice and millet, the raising of pigs or buffaloes for sacrificial purposes, the custom of head–hunting, plus megalithic monuments, houses built on piles, bark cloth and outrigger canoes.

Earthenware similarities at sites in the Malay Peninsula and Thailand have been used to support the theory that the change from Mesolithic to the much more sophisticated Neolithic material culture occurred suddenly, and was due to an invasion of people from the north who introduced agriculture, stock breeding and the new techniques of stone polishing, pottery manufacture and weaving into the existing Mesolithic food-gathering economy. It was posited that the arrival of the more technically advanced Austronesians suddenly intruded on the Mesolithic culture of the Malay Peninsula.

The intrusive nature of this change was mainly based on the belief that some earthenware assemblages, and the quadrangular adze culture, derived from seaborne migrations from southern China. However, detailed studies of the stone adzes of Southeast Asia have not provided convincing proof of this. Peninsular Neolithic sites, besides having the same pottery types, appear to have their own special characteristics. The archaeologist Leong Sau Heng has shown that two types of stone artefacts—beaked adzes and stone bark cloth beaters—do not occur at Ban Kao. Moreover, many of the Neolithic stone tools from Peninsular Malaysia, including the beaked adze, have not yet been recorded outside the Peninsula. Because of the presence of so many variants, and the fact that the Neolithic artefact assemblages are a mixture of stone tools, earthenware and, very infrequently, iron goods, it is theorized that these could not have originated from one source as the Austronesian immigration theory suggests. As stone bracelets occur in both Peninsular and Thai sites, and as many of the bark cloth beaters were found in Peninsular alluvial tin fields, it is probable that the later Neolithic inhabitants of the Malay Peninsula had established contacts, probably of a commercial nature, with the Metal Age societies of Thailand.

This iron implement from Raub, Pahang, could have arrived at its inland destination by barter trade.

The beginning of maritime trade

Evidence for the rise of maritime trade networks by the latter half of the 1st millennium BCE is mainly based on the discovery of bronze drums and bells of the Dongson type in Peninsular Malaysia (see 'Bronzeware'), which are believed to have strong links with several Bronze Age sites in present-day North Vietnam. The Malaysian drums were identified as Dongson drums on the basis of their common decorative motifs, which comprise concentric bands of a ladder pattern, circles, and flying birds around a central star motif. The function of the drums is still not certain. It has been proposed that they were used as commemorative objects to mark the death of important men of a tribe. The burial of the drums in an inverted position may suggest that they were connected with certain festivals as the inverted position may help to preserve the strength of their magic. The finding of these artefacts indicates that the people of the Peninsula were in contact with the Metal Age society in Vietnam using the maritime trade route via the South China Sea. The absence of copper ore in the Peninsula, at least in early worked deposits,

may have been responsible for the importation of the drums. However, the iron implements which have been discovered at many inland localities (see 'Iron artefacts') are believed to have been locally manufactured. The settled people of the west coast lowlands probably produced these iron implements which were used in barter trade with collector-traders from the inland.

By 500 BCE, maritime trade links were established not only between Peninsular Malaysia and mainland Southeast Asia, but also with Sri Lanka, India and perhaps the Mediterranean world. This assumption is based on the discovery of stone and glass beads at late prehistoric Peninsular sites. Beads found with the bronzeware, and in Metal Age cist graves, indicate far-flung trade networks. As some beads originated from India, Sri Lanka, Burma and perhaps the Mediterranean and Africa, they may not necessarily have been imported by the same people who brought the Dongson bronzeware from Vietnam. Both the bronzeware and the beads reached the Peninsula via maritime trade from about 2,500 years ago.

It is theorized that the cultural change from the Neolithic to the Metal Age, like the earlier change from the Mesolithic to the Neolithic, was mainly due to trade. During the Metal Age, the Peninsular peoples traded with India, Sri Lanka and Burma in the west, and Vietnam, Cambodia and probably China and island Southeast Asia in the east via maritime trade. Meanwhile, the inland regional trade patterns which began during the Neolithic period between the inhabitants of the Malay Peninsula and central and southern Thailand, and in Sabah and Sarawak between the various peoples of Borneo, were still very active.

Dongson bronzeware

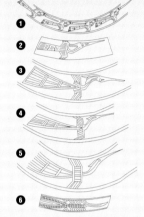

Distribution of Dongson bronzeware

Originating from the Dongson culture of present-day North Vietnam, bronze drums and bells were widely traded throughout Southeast Asia during the Metal Age. Several have been found at Malaysian sites. A relief from Angkor Wat (top) shows two men carrying, and a third striking, a temple bell which resembles the bells found at Klang, Selangor, and at Muar, Johor. A common motif on the drums are concentric bands of flying birds. The above diagram shows variations on this theme from drums at the following locations: (1) (Origin unknown) Vienna Museum, Austria ; (2) North Vietnam; (3) Battambang, Cambodia; (4) Klang, Malaysia; (5) Dongson, North Vietnam; (6) (Origin unknown) Victoria & Albert Museum, London.

Some of the beads found at the archaeological site of Sungai Mas in the Bujang Valley of Kedah could have originated from South Asia. These stone and glass beads may have been used as barter for rainforest products.

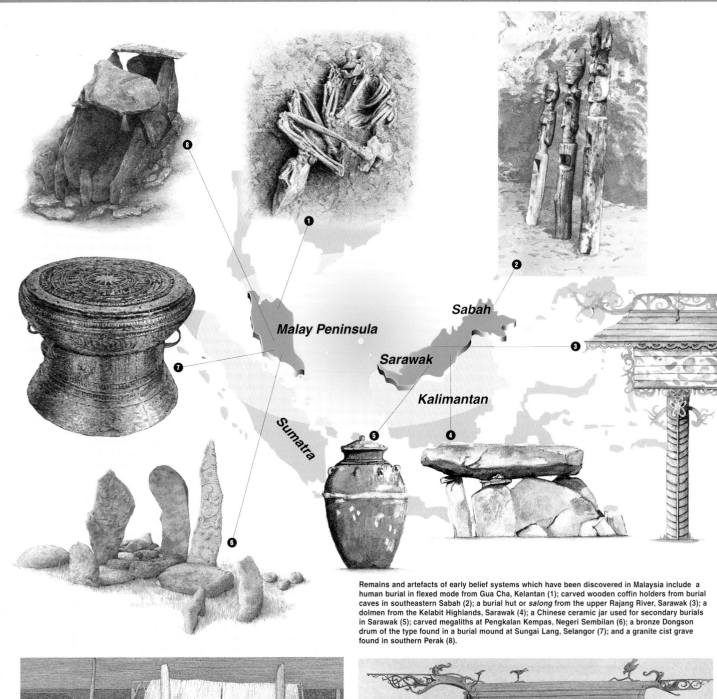

Remains and artefacts of early belief systems which have been discovered in Malaysia include a human burial in flexed mode from Gua Cha, Kelantan (1); carved wooden coffin holders from burial caves in southeastern Sabah (2); a burial hut or *salong* from the upper Rajang River, Sarawak (3); a dolmen from the Kelabit Highlands, Sarawak (4); a Chinese ceramic jar used for secondary burials in Sarawak (5); carved megaliths at Pengkalan Kempas, Negeri Sembilan (6); a bronze Dongson drum of the type found in a burial mound at Sungai Lang, Selangor (7); and a granite cist grave found in southern Perak (8).

The Norwegian naturalist and explorer, Carl Alfred Bock (1849–1932), journeyed through Borneo in the late 1870s. His sensationalized travels, ethnographic accounts and illustrations appeared in his book *The Head-Hunters of Borneo* (1881). A carved wooden coffin (above) holds the remains of a Dyak chief. A wooden animal figure hangs from the front of the coffin to ward off evil spirits. Bock reported that although 'the body had been dead 15 days there was not the slightest smell in the room, the coffin being hermetically closed with a sort of putty made of gutta-percha'.

The 'Mausoleum of Rajah Sinen's family', one of Carl Bock's illustrations, is an elaborate *salong*, a type of wooden burial hut built on hardwood poles which still survives in remote parts of Sarawak. Remains of the deceased family members would be stored in the hut in burial jars or log coffins. Many of these animist practices had their origins in prehistoric times. Hornbill and *naga* (serpent/snake) motifs adorn the walls of the *salong*. These animals were especially significant in the cosmology of the Iban and Orang Ulu peoples.

BELIEF SYSTEMS IN PREHISTORIC TIMES

Archaeology has shown that during the late Pleistocene in Europe, West Asia and Australia, the emergence of spiritual consciousness was already evident. Cave drawings and rock engravings from this period were not merely aesthetic endeavours, but manifestations of religious beliefs. Red ochre, or haematite powder, found with human burials from the late Pleistocene time onwards, suggests that burial rites were already being practised, and grave offerings are evidence of a belief in an afterlife. In Malaysia, the climatic conditions are not conducive for the preservation of such early remains. Nonetheless, numerous burials from the later prehistoric and protohistoric periods have been found, including the 10,000-year-old skeleton of Perak Man. The multiplicity of ways in which the dead were disposed of, including flexed and extended modes, jar, canoe, boat, mound and slab grave burials, as well as the associated funeral rites, testify to the diversity of Malaysian societies since prehistoric times.

The Iban of Sarawak decorated their baby carriers with beaded animist designs to scare away evil spirits.

The earliest Malaysian belief systems derive from communal memories of encounters with natural forces and struggles with sickness and death. These memories included tales handed down by oral traditions of the extraordinary feats of forefathers. Eventually, people began to conceive the idea that there were powers operating at a realm well above theirs. Animism, the belief that inanimate objects and natural phenomena have a soul or spirit living in them, was a common religious belief. Droughts, floods, forest fires and sickness were thought to have been caused by spirits. Sacrifices and rites were conducted to propitiate them, taboos were instituted to avoid offending them again, and amulets were used for protection against evil spirits and wild beasts. Ritual healings conducted by shamans were commonly practised to cure the sick.

Benevolent spirits were worshipped for protection and favours, particularly ancestral spirits of men of prowess and founders of settlements. Cults centred around such benevolent spirits designated special places for worship and the performance of ceremonial rites. Large, undressed stones in Negeri Sembilan, Sabah and Sarawak may have been used to mark these sacred places.

Ethnographic records show that celebrations for important spirits were marked by animal, and sometimes human, sacrifices. Food and intoxicating drinks were offered to the spirits along with incantations, dances, music and feasting. In some cases, special ceremonial objects were part of the rites, such as the famed Dongson drums, used as cult objects throughout Southeast Asia during the Metal Age. Six of these have been found in Malaysia, and it is believed that they could have been utilized in the burial rituals of important persons.

Animals' teeth and prized beads have been used for powerful amulets among the Orang Ulu of Sarawak since prehistoric times.

Many animist beliefs still practised by some Orang Asli and ethnic groups in Sabah and Sarawak may have originated in the prehistoric period.

A southern Perak cist grave re-erected at the Perak Museum, Taiping (above top). A burial pole from the Rajang River re-erected at the Sarawak Museum (above middle). Megaliths from Negeri Sembilan re-erected at the Petronas Megalith Park, Kuala Lumpur (above).

Flexed and extended burials

In the absence of written records, burials are an important source of information on the culture and belief systems of early societies. Burial methods and funerary rites vary according to the beliefs of particular communities or ethnic groups. In Malaysian prehistoric sites, the most common modes of interment are flexed and extended burials. More elaborate burials were usually reserved for the élite, and sometimes completely different burial modes were employed.

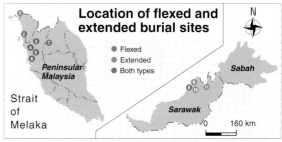

Location of flexed and extended burial sites

- ● Flexed
- ● Extended
- ● Both types

Peninsular Malaysia
Strait of Melaka
Sabah
Sarawak
0   160 km

1. Bukit Tengku Lembu
2. Guar Kepah
3. Gua Gunung Runtuh
4. Gua Kerbau
5. Gua Baik
6. Gunung Cheroh
7. Gua Cha
8. Niah Caves
9. Gua Magala
10. Lubang Jeragan
11. Lubang Angin

Formerly believed to be about 38,000 years old, Malaysia's oldest skull was excavated from the West Mouth of the Niah Great Cave by Tom Harrisson (pictured below, top right-hand corner) from the Sarawak Museum, who headed the archaeological digs at Niah Caves during the 1950s and 1960s. This date is currently under revision as current research suggests that the skull may be of a later period.

Flexed burials

Nearly all the earliest prehistoric burials found in Malaysia come from cave rather than open-air sites. Most of these do not date before the terminal Pleistocene (about 10,000 years ago) as Malaysia's hot and wet climate is not conducive to the preservation of earlier skeletal remains. The oldest burials, most of which are in the flexed mode with a few fragmentary and seated burials, are from the Niah Great Cave in Sarawak. These have been radiocarbon dated to the terminal Pleistocene. In Peninsular Malaysia, early human burials have also been found in rock shelters and limestone caves. The majority of these are flexed burials. Except for the burial from Gua Gunung Runtuh, most of these burials are from the latter part of the early Holocene. One fragmentary burial has also been recorded from an open shell midden site at Guar Kepah in Seberang Perai.

These were deliberate burials, as opposed to accidental burials, as the bodies were laid to rest in a foetal position, with the knees bent and drawn up just below the chin. This arrangement of the limbs had to be executed before the onset of rigor mortis. In general, flexed burial is a fairly common mode of burial in many parts of the world. It has even been recorded in some Neanderthal burials in Europe and West Asia.

In Malaysia, flexed burials are associated with the Hoabinhian phase (beginning about 10000 BCE) as they are usually found with Hoabinhian-type stone tools. Most flexed burials have been excavated from earlier levels than the Neolithic burials, which mostly comprise extended, supine burials. Flexed burials have been found in Perak cave sites at Gua Cheroh, Gua Baik (or Gol Baik) and Gua Kerbau, but the most famous is the 'Perak Man' from Gua Gunung Runtuh, which dates to 10,000 years ago.

At least nine flexed burials have been excavated from the Hoabinhian occupation levels of Gua Cha rock shelter, but they contained very few grave goods. Three were single primary burials, but four other individuals were found interred together. Only the main parts of their skeletons were found and the bones of all these individuals were no longer separable. Multiple burials are rare in Malaysian archaeology, but it is not possible to confirm whether this was a secondary burial, or even some form of cannabilism. Two more flexed burials were excavated in 1979 from this rock shelter. One of these used a stone slab as a pillow to support the skull. The body was first covered with a thin soil layer, then with a layer of white tufa chunks (soft, porous rock) dusted with haematite powder. The other skeleton had no stone pillow, but two stone slabs covered its midsection.

Haematite, also known as red ochre, is a natural mineral pigment which can be mixed with liquids or animal fat to produce a red tint resembling blood. The ritual use of haematite in burials was widespread during the earliest period of Malaysian prehistory. The 1979 Gua Cha excavations clearly demonstrated its use in mortuary rites associated with Hoabinhian flexed burials. Pieces of haematite, as well as grinding slabs stained with haematite, have been found at several Hoabinhian sites in Peninsular Malaysia. However, as these came from non-burial contexts, this mineral could have been used for body painting or even for cave painting. The use of

---

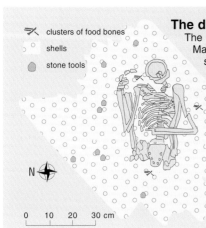

- ⚒ clusters of food bones
- 〰 shells
- ▣ stone tools

N

0 10 20 30 cm

The discovery of the 'Perak Man'

The 10,000-year-old flexed burial excavated by the archaeologist Zuraina Majid in Gua Gunung Runtuh revealed a remarkably well-preserved skeleton. Nicknamed the 'Perak Man', the deceased was a 40- to 45-year-old male. Careful excavations produced a clear picture of the burial rites. Apparently, much effort was expended to ensure that the deceased was accorded a proper burial. Of the mortuary goods placed in the grave, only those fashioned from stone have survived, along with food offerings of meat and riverine shellfish. The 'Perak Man' was very well provided for in his afterlife as meat offerings from five types of animals were found. Freshwater shells were scattered over the floor and completely covered the burial. The great array of food offerings was perhaps the best that his hunter-gatherer community could give. This burial is the richest of the flexed burials so far discovered in Malaysia.

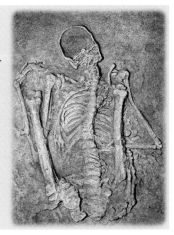

Neolithic earthenware, such as this jar with impressed paddle decorations, formed part of the grave offerings of extended burials in the Niah Caves.

haematite in fragmentary burial has also been reported from the Hoabinhian site at Guar Kepah where quantities of powdered haematite were strewn over the face. Some early flexed burials from the Niah Caves were also treated with haematite.

Extended burials

From about the mid-Holocene, extended burials replaced flexed burials as the most common burial mode. For example, most of the extended burials excavated from Gua Cha were from higher levels than the flexed burials, and were found in shallow graves. These burials have been ascribed to the Neolithic period. According to radiocarbon dating, the Neolithic began at Gua Cha about 3,000 years ago. In an extended burial, the deceased is laid to rest in a supine position with the arms by the sides of the body. Extended burials from Niah Caves, however, displayed a variety of arm positions which may be indicative of the sex of the deceased.

Another important Neolithic site, which was probably used for burial purposes, is the rock shelter site at Bukit Tengku Lembu in Perlis. The mode of burial practised was probably primary extended burials like those found in the upper levels of Gua Cha. However, the site was badly disturbed by guano extraction activities before the museum authorities were alerted to it. Finds retrieved from the site included fragments of human bones, some polished stone adzes, a stone bracelet, a bone axe and a large collection of cord-marked earthenware, including several intact vessels which were probably grave furniture.

In Sarawak, extended burials have been excavated from Niah Caves, at Gua Magala and Lubang Jeragan nearby, and at Lubang Angin in the Gunung Mulu National Park. Most of the burials are Neolithic, but a few may be from the Metal Age. Some radiocarbon dates for the extended burials from the Niah Caves date to the 4th millennium BCE, although the more acceptable dates are between 1750 and 500 BCE. The Neolithic burials at Gua Magala and Lubang Jeragan

have been dated to c. 1500–1000 BCE, while those at Lubang Angin have been dated to 1000 BCE.

Burial activity, including flexed burials, might have taken place since the terminal Pleistocene at the famed West Mouth of the Niah Caves. Long after this, during Neolithic times, the site was again used as a major burial cave for extended burials and also cremations. As many as 66 extended burials have been found in the inner portion known as the 'cemetery sector'. These burials differ from those of Peninsular Malaysia. For example, at Gua Cha, most were found placed in burial containers such as log coffins or cigar-shaped casings made of bamboo strips. Some bodies were wrapped in pandanus mats before being placed in the containers. Wooden stakes were used as grave markers. Traces of haematite were found on many burials. Some of the skeletons also showed signs of having been partially burnt, which could have been part of the last rites of lustration, in this case purification by fire, conducted *in situ* at the graves. The burials were accompanied by relatively few funerary goods, comprising earthenware and bone, stone and even wooden objects. Most of these grave goods were treated with haematite.

The extended burials at Lubang Angin did not have coffins or any sort of containers. However, traces of bark cloth suggested that some of the deceased were wrapped in this material before their interment. Compared to the extended burials at Niah, the Lubang Angin burials were poorer in terms of funerary furniture, although the local earthenware shards are similar to those found at Niah comprising three-colour ware and double-spouted vessels.

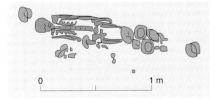

At Gua Cha, extended burials were accompanied by a variety of grave goods, including cord-marked earthenware vessels, mussel shell spoons, polished stone adzes and a stone bark cloth beater. Some of the deceased also wore ornaments, such as stone and shell beads and polished stone bracelets.

Cist graves and boat and mound burials

Archaeological records indicate that prehistoric Malaysian burial customs not only varied according to region, but sometimes even within a community. Some of the more uncommon types of ancient burials found in Malaysia include secondary burials in boat-shaped coffins and primary burials in dugout canoes, clay mounds and cist graves.

These boat-shaped coffins (above) in Gua Kain Hitam, Sarawak, were probably related to the 'ships of the dead' depicted in the accompanying cave paintings (above top). Believed to be at least 1,000 years old, the coffins were not left directly on the cave floor but were reverentially placed on stands or trestles with the heads of the coffins pointing towards the interior of the cave.

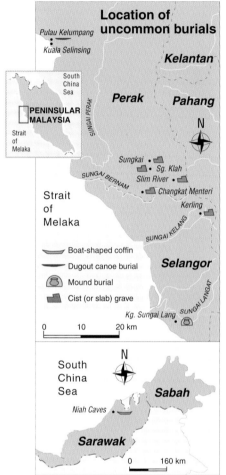

Location of uncommon burials

Pulau Kelumpang
Kuala Selinsing

Kelantan

South China Sea

PENINSULAR MALAYSIA

Strait of Melaka

Perak   Pahang

N

Sungkai
Sg. Klah
Slim River
Changkat Menteri

Kerling

SUNGAI PERAK
SUNGAI BERNAM
SUNGAI KELANG

Strait of Melaka

Boat-shaped coffin
Dugout canoe burial
Mound burial
Cist (or slab) grave

Selangor

SUNGAI LANGAT

Kg. Sungai Lang

0   10   20 km

South China Sea

N

Sabah

Niah Caves

Sarawak

0   160 km

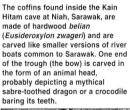

The coffins found inside the Kain Hitam cave at Niah, Sarawak, are made of hardwood *belian* (*Eusideroxylon zwageri*) and are carved like smaller versions of river boats common to Sarawak. One end of the trough (the bow) is carved in the form of an animal head, probably depicting a mythical sabre-toothed dragon or a crocodile baring its teeth.

Boat-shaped coffins

The most impressive of the unusual types of burials are those in wooden, boat-shaped coffins found in Gua Kain Hitam (also known as the Painted Cave) at Niah in Sarawak. They are secondary burials as the bones have been exhumed and reburied. This remarkable burial cave also contains Borneo's only prehistoric haematite paintings. Stretching over 60 metres in length and comprising more than 100 drawings, the paintings are undoubtedly related to the boat-shaped coffin burials. Several boats portrayed in the cave paintings have been interpreted as 'ships of the dead', carrying the souls of the deceased to the afterworld.

The finds at Gua Kain Hitam document one of the most sophisticated funerary practices ever recorded in Malaysia. No other burial caves have been found with such a spectacular manifestation of funerary art. Obviously, this was an élite burial cave. According to local tradition, its topographical setting— where the mountain and the river merge—is spiritually ideal for a burial cave. Also, the cave mouth floor is well trodden and polished, perhaps from large-scale human dancing conducted during the ceremonies.

The possibility that these boat coffins held the remains of high-status individuals is further corroborated by their valuable grave goods. These comprise imported Chinese stoneware, imported glass beads, fragments of bronzeware, carved bones and local earthenware, including double-spouted vessels. Based on the associated finds of imported Chinese stoneware of the Tang and Sung dynasties, burial activity at the cave probably took place some 1,000 years ago. Radiocarbon dates from one boat-shaped coffin revealed a date of c. 780 CE.

Dated to around 200 BCE, this occupant of Kuala Selinsing, Perak, was buried in a dugout canoe accompanied by his steering paddle (right).

Burials in dugout canoes

The use of a dugout canoe as a burial receptacle for a single primary burial is known from only one Malaysian site, namely, the mangrove forested island of Pulau Kelumpang in Kuala Selinsing, Perak. At this site, three canoe burials have been found. The hull fragment of one of the canoes measured 5.64 metres, and was probably longer as both ends of the vessel were broken. The burials were accompanied by funerary goods such as glass beads and pottery, some of which were decorated with impressed patterns made with *cardium* shells. One burial also contained a wooden steering paddle and a hair ornament made from the spine of a stingray.

The location of these burials and the material culture reflected by the associated finds suggest that these burial practices were performed by a sea-oriented community. Discovered in 1932, the burials were found in a shell layer about 1.5–1.8 metres below the present surface. These burials have been ascribed to the first phase of occupation at Kuala Selinsing which has been carbon dated to about 200 BCE.

Further excavations unearthed other burials (see 'Flexed and extended burials'), but no other canoe burials. However, both types of burials were found at similar depths, indicating that more than one type of burial method was in practice at the same time. This indicates that canoe burials were reserved for only a few important individuals.

Burials in clay mounds

In 1964, when land at Kampung Sungai Lang, Selangor, was being cleared, a large mound 'protruding like an island from the surrounding peat soil' was discovered. A greater surprise was in store for the smallholder when his persistence in levelling the mound led to the discovery of two large bronze Dongson drums buried in the mound (see 'Bronzeware'). This form of burial in a clay mound has only been discovered at this single Malaysian site. The 4.6-metre-diameter mound was originally constructed on the surface, but the growth of later swamp forests resulted in the formation of a thick peat layer which buried it.

The mound was constructed over a sacred site, possibly a boat burial, as the bronze drums were found on a wooden plank made of *cengal*, a hardwood still used for the construction of boats and dugouts. The plank is probably the remains of a dugout canoe. Other boat burials with bronze drums have been found in Southeast Asia, including at Viet Khe in North Vietnam and in the Ongbah Caves in Thailand.

Concentrations of earthenware shards, red glass beads and a fragment of an iron implement were also unearthed, suggesting that ceremonial rites were conducted before the clay mound was erected. Traces of two other clay mounds were also found nearby, together with rock crystal beads, earthenware and two bronze bowls. Valuable goods, such as bronze drums and bowls, were often interred at burials of high-status individuals. Bronze drums were important status symbols during the late Metal Age and they have been found in rich burial sites in Southeast Asia and Yunnan. Their occurrence at Kampung Sungai Lang is strongly suggestive of a similar meaning for the site. No human remains have been found in the Kampung Sungai Lang burial mounds, but in this equatorial climate human skeletal remains are unlikely to be preserved in open-site burials.

Radiocarbon dates from the plank ranged from 580 BCE to 190 CE. This wide date range can be narrowed down by relative dating of the socketed iron tools also found in the burial which appear from about the end of the 1st millennium BCE to early in the 1st millennium CE.

Cist graves

Dating from the Iron Age, cist graves are burials in slender, rectangular-shaped stone cists, which only occur in southern Perak and northern Selangor, particularly in the Bernam Valley (at Changkat Menteri) and adjacent areas near rivers (see map). The graves are constructed of large granite slabs, hence they are also known as 'slab graves', or even as megalithic tombs.

In the construction of the cist graves, the slabs were always arranged so that they sloped inwards with the original smooth surface of the granite boulder on the outside, thereby giving a 'finished' appearance. The graves were always provided with a heavy, top-covering stone, the side stones often overlapped, and the floors were also lined with granite. It is evident that the cist graves were reserved for important members of the community.

Radiocarbon dating of some recently excavated cist graves have yielded dates from the 1st to the 7th century CE. However, the actual settlements of these Metal Age communities have yet to be located. Based on some loose finds collected from Changkat Menteri and its vicinity, these settlements probably lasted to at least the 8th century CE. It is believed that the settlements were strategically located to handle or, more likely, to control trade via the Bernam River, a transpeninsular route which led into the far interior of the Malay Peninsula during the 1st millennium CE. The display of wealth found in some of the cist graves is a good indicator of the successful economy of these Metal Age settlements.

Transporting the stones for the cist graves

A great deal of effort was involved in the construction of the Bernam Valley cist graves. As the granite needed for the graves was not available in the area, it had to be quarried from sources much further upstream in the foothills of the Banjaran Titiwangsa (Main Range). Large slabs, nearly 2 metres in length and varying in thickness from 3 to 6 centimetres, had to be carefully split from huge boulders to prevent breakage. The slabs were extremely heavy, requiring at least four or five men just to lift them, let alone carry them for some distance. Considerable manpower was required to transport the granite slabs downstream (probably by rafts), and also to haul them to the grave sites, many of which were located on high ground some distance from the river bank. It is believed that elephants might have been employed for this purpose. The slabs would have probably been tied onto the elephants' backs with rope made of rainforest fibres.

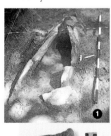

Tombs for the élite of the Iron Age

It is most unlikely that the Peninsular Malaysian cist graves were for common folk. They were most likely constructed as tombs for the élite as the graves were all richly furnished by Iron Age standards, indicating the high status of their occupants. Apart from earthenware pots, which were probably containers for food offerings, most of the graves were furnished with highly valued imported items. These included personal ornaments, such as beads made of glass and semiprecious stones such as carnelians and rock crystals. Glass fragments found in some graves might have come from glass bangles or even glass vessels. Many of the burials were accompanied by iron artefacts, such as spearheads and sickle-shaped tools (see 'Iron artefacts'). Since not very many of these ancient iron artefacts have been found, it is surmised that they were rare items. They were probably available only to high-status individuals who also had access to other exotic goods and were important enough to have these valuables buried with them. The grave at the K2 site at Changkat Menteri, Perak, shown (1) after it was fully excavated. Grave goods were found, including socketed iron implements (2), a whetstone (3) and imported beads (4). Beads from the K1 grave also at Changkat Menteri (5) and another grave (K3) at the Ulu Bernam Estate before the grave was opened (6).

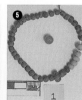

Jar and log coffin burials

Beginning in the late prehistoric period, a great variety of burial modes were practised in Malaysia. In Sabah and Sarawak, secondary burials using jars as containers—hence the term 'jar burials'—were common. In Sarawak, where this custom continued until the early 20th century, elaborately carved wooden burial poles and burial huts were constructed to house the burial jars of important people, while in Sabah, primary and extended burials housed in decorated log coffins continued until the early historic period.

Constructed from an unusual, double tree trunk, anthropomorphic carvings adorn the *klirieng* of a Kajang chief from Sarawak's Belaga District. The burial pole now stands in the grounds of the Sarawak Museum.

The burial jar containing the remains of a chief is placed in a hollowed-out chamber of the *klirieng* (burial pole).

As the carvings and the erection of the *klirieng* (above) involved a great deal of labour and time, only upper-class families could afford them.

Secondary jar burials

Among the earliest of the Southeast Asian secondary jar burials are those from the Niah Great Cave in Sarawak, one of which has been radiocarbon dated to the late 2nd millennium BCE. In these burials, locally made earthenware vessels were used to rebury cremated and burnt remains. In the latter method, more bones survive because of the use of lower heat.

Besides jars, other types of containers used for secondary burials include basket caskets and rectangular, wooden-lidded boxes cut from hollowed-out tree trunks. In a few cases, the burial jars and wooden boxes contained the remains of more than one individual. Most of the cremations and their grave goods were treated with haematite. In contrast, burnt burials were rarely found with haematite, but dammar residues suggest that these were used to assist in the burning process.

The most distinctive type of artefact found with the Niah secondary burials is the double-spouted earthenware vessel. These were probably used specifically for ritual or funerary purposes in Sarawak during prehistoric times.

Jar burials dating from the Metal Age and later periods have been found in burial caves and rock shelters in Sabah and Sarawak. Unlike the early Niah burials, these secondary burials did not always involve the use of fire, but the removal of the flesh was done before the remains were finally deposited in the burial caves. In eastern Sabah, jar burials using locally made earthenware jars were popular during the Metal Age (beginning c. 500 BCE). The caves where jar burials were found (see map) were traditional burial grounds possibly owned by the ancestors of the Orang Sungai and the Idahan who still live in the area.

Burial goods from these caves included tools and personal ornaments, such as finely polished stone adzes, earthenware shards, a bronze (or copper?) axe head, a mould for a metal object, glass beads and iron knives. In many of these caves, jar burials lasted until about 1000 CE when they were replaced by log coffin burials.

In Sarawak, jar burials continued well into the historic period when Chinese stoneware jars replaced locally made earthenware jars—a practice only discontinued a few decades ago.

Burial poles and huts

Some ethnic groups of Sarawak did not use caves for their burial jars but elaborate structures such as burial poles, known locally as *klirieng*, which were constructed to house the burial jars of high-ranking individuals, especially chiefs. Klirieng have been reported from the upper Rajang–Belaga areas among the Kajang peoples, the near coastal areas of Oya (among the Berawan) and in the region of the Mukah and Tatau rivers near Bintulu.

The burial poles are usually made from *belian* (ironwood). These majestic structures are carved from top to bottom with elaborate motifs which are often anthropomorphic. Some burial poles are over 30 metres in height and have a girth of about 4 metres. When chiefs were buried, slaves were said to have been sacrificed and their bodies placed in the lower niches of the klirieng. The use of klirieng must have been in existence for several hundred years. The oldest extant klirieng is believed to be about 200 years old, and even older ones would have already deteriorated.

Another type of wooden structure built to house the burial jars of the upper class is the *salong*. This elaborately decorated (sometimes with painted designs), single-chambered burial hut is also made of belian and is constructed like a pile dwelling, resting on one to nine tall posts. This burial custom has

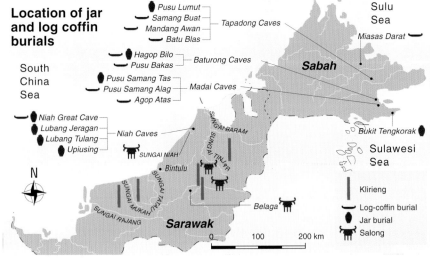

Location of jar and log coffin burials

- Pusu Lumut
- Samang Buat
- Mandang Awan — Tapadong Caves
- Batu Blas
- Hagop Bilo
- Pusu Bakas — Baturong Caves
- Pusu Samang Tas
- Pusu Samang Alag — Madai Caves
- Agop Atas
- Niah Great Cave
- Lubang Jeragan — Niah Caves
- Lubang Tulang
- Upiusing

South China Sea

SUNGAI BARAM
SUNGAI TINJAR
SUNGAI NIAH
Bintulu
SUNGAI TATAU
SUNGAI MUKAH
SUNGAI RAJANG
Belaga
Sarawak

Sabah

Miasas Darat

Bukit Tengkorak

Sulu Sea

Sulawesi Sea

N

0   100   200 km

Legend:
- Klirieng
- Log-coffin burial
- Jar burial
- Salong

been associated with the Kayan people of the upper Rajang River, and is one of the practices of the Punan in the Niah River area. Salong also occur in the Belaga districts, and the Tatau and Tinjar districts of the Fourth Division. In these high-status mausoleums, remains from secondary burials were either placed in the chamber in jars, together with the burial jars of other important people, or interred in wooden coffins.

Log coffin burials

Log coffin burials are found in burial caves and rock shelters in Sarawak and eastern Sabah. These burial caves were usually communally owned by a particular ethnic group. In Sabah, for instance, some burial caves were found packed with log coffins and some were even piled on top of one another.

The earliest log coffins, believed to date from the Stone Age, are from the Niah Great Cave. They were found in a poor state of preservation because they were made from medium- or low-density timber. In contrast, log coffins from later periods were made from extremely hard and heavy hardwoods, an innovation which was only possible with the advent of iron cutting tools.

Hardwood log coffins for primary burials have been found in a number of burial caves in eastern Sabah. Unlike the early log coffins of Niah, those of Sabah were not buried but were placed on the cave floors, on rock ledges, or on wooden trestles. Large log coffins which were ossuaries for the bone remains of a family or clan have also been found in at least three eastern Sabah burial caves.

Klirieng were sometimes topped with a large stone slab to protect the niche containing the burial jar

Log coffins were constructed from large tree trunks split lengthwise. The lower half served as the receptacle for the body, while the upper half served as the lid. The coffin was sealed with dammar gum, and sometimes bound with rattan. All the coffins had end extensions or flanges which acted as handles—perhaps for easier handling during their arduous journeys to the caves, many of which are situated high up in cliff faces, or are only accessed through narrow tunnels within the limestone massifs. Some of the log coffin extensions are just short, projecting handles, while some have either upward- or downward-curving flanges which may represent the open jaws of a crocodile. Although the majority of the log coffins are plain, some have incised motifs as well as carved decorations. For example, some end flanges are carved in the shape of the head of a buffalo or a barking deer. Coffin lids are sometimes decorated with fluted or faceted patterns, simple incised geometric motifs or, more rarely, zoomorphic motifs of crocodiles or flying lizards carved in relief. Decorated hardwood coffins were probably reserved for important or wealthy people such as chiefs.

Sometimes the coffins are plain, but their stands or trestles are carved. For example, at Hagop Bilo, trestles are carved in the form of human figures. As only two large coffins were found at this rock shelter, it was apparently an exclusive burial place for high-ranking individuals, unlike the communal burial caves where log coffins are piled on top of each other. Similarly, those found in extremely inaccessible caves, such as Mandang Awan, are probably coffins of important people. The use of log coffins in eastern Sabah is undoubtedly an ancient burial custom long practised in the region by the ancestors of some present-day ethnic communities. Radiocarbon dates indicate that this custom could date to about 1,000 years ago. Research in the Baturong–Madai caves region has shown that log coffin burials ended around the 16th century, after the adoption of Islam. In more remote parts of eastern Sabah, these burials continued until fairly recent times. However, as suitable hardwoods became scarce, only the very rich could afford to have this type of coffin.

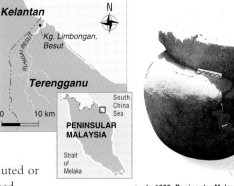

In 1985, Peninsular Malaysia's only jar burials were found at Kampung Limbongan, Terengganu. They probably date from the 1st millennium CE, or much later. Associated finds from the sites included gold beads (above right).

The advent of iron cutting tools in the Metal Age meant that coffins could then be built from large hardwood trees. Log coffins occur most frequently in East Sabah where these elaborate receptacles for the dead feature incised motifs and carvings. These log coffins with buffalo-head flanges are displayed at the Sabah State Museum but were originally found piled on top of each other in Miasas Darat, a cave near the Lokan River, a tributary of the Kinabatangan.

The *salong*
Carl Alfred Bock (1849–32), the Norwegian naturalist and explorer, was also an artist of merit. This illustration from his book *The Head-hunters of Borneo* depicts a *salong*, or upper-class burial hut, which he describes:
'The tombs of the Rajahs were most substantially built and elaborately decorated structures of ironwood . . . walls were carved, and rudely painted with representations of birds or quadrupeds.'

Megaliths

Although megaliths are not a widespread phenomenon in Malaysia, a fairly wide range of types are known, including stone cist graves, menhirs, petroglyphs, dolmens, stone jars, stone seats and stone tables. None of these predate the Metal Age, from 200 BCE to 1000 CE, while some were still in ritual use up till historic and even recent times. The most common form of Malaysian megaliths are menhirs, which are found in Melaka, Negeri Sembilan, Sabah and Sarawak.

Stone avenues
Stones aligned in avenues are found around Alor Gajah in Melaka, and Kuala Pilah and Jelebu in Negeri Sembilan. These formations comprise pairs of menhirs, consisting of a large menhir and a smaller one, arranged in a row. Each pair is erected facing each other with their tapered end bending forwards as if nodding or bowing.

This megalithic alignment was excavated from a Negeri Sembilan site and reconstructed at the Petronas Megalith Park in Kuala Lumpur.

Megalithic culture
Megaliths are rough cut stones or natural boulders which have been erected or arranged in formations by human endeavour. They occur in many parts of the world, and were constructed for a variety of purposes. However, it is still unclear whether Malaysian megalithic traditions are connected with those of other geographic regions.

Judging from their widespread distribution and the effort needed for their construction, it is apparent that Malaysian megaliths were important cultural items of the various communities who built them. Their occurrence in so many forms is a reflection of the rich belief systems and rituals which characterized early Malaysian societies.

The fact that stone was selected as the construction medium, rather than timber which was easily available in the Malaysian rainforest environment, reinforces the idea that megaliths were important structures erected as permanent monuments. Stones were carefully chosen and were sometimes laboriously transported from distant sources. According to ethnographic reports from historic times, megalithic construction was a coordinated, communal effort involving much labour, which often culminated in a feast.

Stone cist graves, which mainly occur in the Bernam Valley of Peninsular Malaysia, are the oldest of Malaysia's megaliths (see 'Cist graves and boat and mound burials') and are believed to date to the Metal Age. A few slab graves have also been reported in the Kelabit Highlands of Sarawak, and although these have not been systematically excavated, ethnographic reports sugggest that they probably date from historic, rather than prehistoric, times as they are associated with the folklore of the local Kayan communities.

Menhirs
Menhirs are found in Melaka, Negeri Sembilan, Sarawak's Kelabit Highlands, and on the coastal plain of Sabah from Papar to Tuaran. The majority are located in paddy-growing areas, giving rise to the belief that they were associated with the movements of early farming communities. In Sabah and Sarawak, some menhirs may be of fairly recent origin since the tradition of erecting them was practised until only a few decades ago.

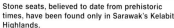

Stone seats, believed to date from prehistoric times, have been found only in Sarawak's Kelabit Highlands.

Menhirs are essentially upright-standing stones, usually tallish in shape, slightly bent or curved in their upper part and tapering at the top. Malaysian menhirs comprise either roughly cut stones or large slabs flaked from boulders. The menhirs of Peninsular Malaysia are composed of granite, while those in Sabah and Sarawak are usually of sandstone. Menhirs are the most simple form of megaliths to construct which perhaps accounts for their relatively widespread occurrence. However, there is still little evidence to connect menhirs found in one region with those of another.

Most of the menhirs found in Malaysia are plain. With the exception of the three carved menhirs at Pengkalan Kempas in Negeri Sembilan (see 'The Pengkalan Kempas inscriptions'), there has been no attempt to give the menhirs a smooth finish, let alone carve or engrave them.

The most interesting aspect of Malaysian menhirs is the variety of ways in which they are arranged. In Sabah, they commonly occur as single stones, whereas in Sarawak and Peninsular Malaysia they are found in pairs, with one larger than the

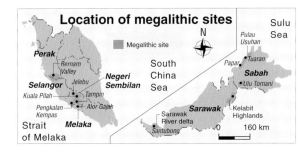

other, or in clusters, usually with one large menhir surrounded by smaller ones.

Alignments of menhirs, known as stone avenues, are very common in northern Melaka and Negeri Sembilan, although they have not been reported in Sabah, and are rare in Sarawak. These alignments are usually erected on top of long earth mounds which were deliberately constructed. These mounds are unknown in Sabah and Sarawak, and although they are just under a metre in height, their construction must have involved a great deal of effort and manpower. Some local inhabitants still consider these sites *keramat* ('sacred'), and refer to the menhirs as *batu hidup* ('living stones') because of the belief that they grow in height. However, this phenomenon is due to erosion of the mounds. Another associated belief is that the menhirs mark the graves of forefathers or the leaders of the pioneer group who founded the first settlements. But excavations at many sites have unearthed no skeletal remains.

The meanings of menhirs

It has been suggested that the reasons for the erection and the arrangement of the various menhirs probably differed from region to region. Ethnographic observations among the Kelabit in Sarawak have shown that menhirs were constructed at the end of an *irau*, a festival connected with the burial rites of the rich or the aristocracy. After the distribution of the deceased's property, some kind of monument was constructed to commemorate the dead, such as a menhir, a dolmen, a stone vat, or even a ditch cut in the ground. This memorial served as a status symbol for the host family.

In Sabah, menhirs also served a variety of functions. The Kadazan constructed them for a number of reasons, including the distribution of property by the heirless, status feasting, tests of bravery, funerary rites and memorializing. Local beliefs in northwest Sabah also associate menhirs with 'oath stones' and boundary stones. In Pulau Usukan and other offshore islands of northwest Sabah, small, rough cut, upright-standing stones were also used as grave markers by the Bajau, a Muslim ethnic group who were originally sea nomads.

This menhir, photographed with field workers in 1978, is located in a paddy field on the road to Papar, Sabah.

The reasons why menhirs were constructed in Peninsular Malaysia are still unknown. Recent excavations at a few sites have demonstrated that they were not burial grounds, while finds of Chinese ceramic shards indicate that they were not of prehistory, but of early history. Nonetheless, some local communities, including those of Minangkabau origin at Kampung Ipoh, Tampin, in Negeri Sembilan, still view them as keramat, and agricultural rites are held at important menhir sites at the beginning of the planting season to ensure a good harvest.

Petroglyphs, dolmens and other megaliths

At Ulu Tomani in Sabah, at Santubong and in the Kelabit Highlands of Sarawak, petroglyphs (pecked or incised designs and figures) have been found on boulders and rocks (see 'Prehistoric art'). They are apparently of ancient manufacture, but no one knows when or why they were made.

Sarawak has the greatest variety of megaliths in Malaysia, although megalithic activity seems to have been focused on two areas: the Sarawak River delta area and the Kelabit Highlands. The latter area was a major area for these activites, as not only menhirs, cist graves and petroglyphs occur, but also other types of megaliths which have never been recorded in other parts of Malaysia. These include dolmens— two upright stones surmounted by a horizontally placed stone—stone tables, stone seats, stone urns and other minor types of megaliths such as stone walls, stone dams and grottoes cut in clifflets. Many of these megaliths were constructed during the irau festivals as memorials. None of them predate the advent of iron in the Borneo region, slightly more than a millennium ago, and many may date much later. The earliest types probably comprise the large menhirs, as well as the dolmens. As only a few dolmens and other large megalithic structures have been found in Malaysia, they are viewed not merely as stone monuments, but as a lasting testimony of the early communities who erected them.

Dolmens of the Kelabit Highlands

The most exhaustive survey of Kelabit megaliths was done by Tom Harrisson (shown above standing barefoot on a collapsed dolmen) from 1949 to the 1970s. During this time, he participated in large-scale megalithic rituals with the Kelabit who attributed the building of the dolmens to unknown ancestral folk figures. Great skill and manpower were required in their construction as the horizontal stone had to be properly placed on top of the two uprights. Their erection no doubt involved much community effort and celebration.

Large menhirs known as *ibu*, literally 'mother', are often placed in the centre of the stone alignments. This specimen from Negeri Sembilan measures 2.44 metres in height and weighs 240 kilograms.

ABOVE TOP: This 19th-century engraving by William Daniell entitled 'Malaye Proas' depicts characteristic Malay praus of a type which were used throughout protohistory, especially by the nomadic sea people, the Orang Laut. Cages of singing birds, a Malay passion even today, are suspended from the boom of the boat on the right, which has a thatched cabin.

ABOVE: The Malay Peninsula is shown as 'Malaca' in this early Portuguese map entitled 'Indiae Orientalis'. Other recognizable Malaysian place names include Quedoa (Kedah), Pera (Perak), Mubar (Muar), Paam (Pahang), Calatan (Kelantan).

FAR RIGHT: This 'View of Pekan, the Capital of Pahang—the Sultan's Old Town which has been in Great Part Removed', appeared in the illustrated magazine, The Graphic, in the late 19th century. Settlements have existed near Pekan on the bank of the Pahang River since protohistoric times, as the most popular route from the west coast of the Peninsula to the east was via the route known as the Penarikan, meaning 'portage'. This route followed the Muar River upstream, then joined the Pahang River after a short portage between the two rivers.

THE PROTOHISTORIC PERIOD

In Malaysia, protohistory refers to the period from about the end of the first century CE to the beginning of the 15th century when the historic period began with the emergence of Melaka. To reconstruct the protohistoric period, scholars utilize archaeological findings and textual sources of Greek, Egyptian, Indian, Chinese and Arab–Persian origin. Among the earliest of these to include reference to Malaysia were Greek texts dating from the 1st century CE.

Beads made from fish bones found at the protohistoric port of Kuala Selinsing, Perak.

Indian sources consist of Hindu and Buddhist literature, and Tamil writings. Obscure references to Suvarnabhumi ('Land of Gold') and Suvarnadvipa ('Golden Island') are believed to refer to Malaysia, while Kataha is thought to have been Kedah. More information on Kedah comes from early Indian sources, such as the Nalanda inscription, dated 850 CE, and the Cola inscription of 1025.

The largest volume of knowledge on Malaysia's protohistoric period derives from China. Important sources include narratives by Buddhist monks, such as Faxian (5th century CE) and Yiqing (late 7th century). Political and trade relations were recorded by chroniclers such as Zhou Chufei (12th century) and Zhao Rukua (13th century). These documents record the names of various states, their locations, natural resources, culture, administrative structures and social hierarchy. However, because some place names in Chinese dialects have been difficult to decipher, the exact locations of some early kingdoms are still unknown. These include Chi tu, in the interior of Kelantan; Langkasuka, near Patani (Southeast Thailand); and Pan-pan, on the Peninsular east coast.

Reports on Southeast Asia by Arab–Persian travellers emerged in the 9th century when the expansion of Islam accelerated trade between West Asia, India and China. These sources also posed difficulties in locating places such as Kalah, probably Kedah, and Zabaj and Tiyumah, now known to be Srivijaya and Pulau Tioman, respectively. By comparing Arab and Chinese texts, and relating them to archaeological finds, scholars have slowly deciphered these locations.

Archaeologists have also successfully located important protohistoric sites, including remnants of early Hindu–Buddhist kingdoms in the Bujang Valley (Kedah), Beruas (Perak) and Santubong (Sarawak). At the port sites of Kuala Selinsing (Perak) and the Bernam Valley (Perak/Selangor), it is evident that animism was being practised. Even today, the Orang Asli and some ethnic groups of Sabah and Sarawak still retain animist beliefs. On the east coast of the Peninsula, finds of engraved stones and gold coins are evidence that Islam had begun to be established in Kelantan, Terengganu and Pahang before the founding of Melaka in the early 15th century.

The glaze on this jarlet has deteriorated due to half a millennium spent under water. It was recovered from a 15th century Thai ship, called the 'Nanyang' shipwreck, which went down with a cargo of ceramics from Sawankhalok, Thailand, off the coast of Pahang.

From prehistory to protohistory

Although the development of writing marks a quantum leap forward in the ability of a literate culture to gather and store new knowledge, historians now believe that the relationship between writing and other aspects of civilization is not so simple. The impact of writing may not have been as immediate nor as far-reaching as older theories assumed. Similarly, the pre-literate period may have been characterized by a more complex civilization than earlier theories gave Malaysia credit for.

The Sungai Mas Stone, now in the Bujang Valley Archaeological Museum, Kedah, features an inscribed stupa and Sanskrit scripts of the following Buddhist formula: 'From ignorance acts accumulate, of birth, acts are the cause; from knowledge no acts accumulate, through absence of acts they are not reborn.'

Colonel James Low of the East India Company, who discovered the Cerok To'kun boulder in 1845, left his signature there as have many graffiti artists since.

This anonymous Sanskrit inscription, one of seven different scripts inscribed on a boulder at Cerok To'kun, in the grounds of St Anne's Church near Bukit Mertajam, translates as *prathame vayasi*, 'in the time of youth'.

The earliest written evidence

The oldest surviving written sources in Malaysia are stone inscriptions found in the northwest of the Peninsula. They are among the most ancient extant evidence of writing in Southeast Asia, and based on the style of writing, historians conclude that the stones were carved around 400 CE. The scripts are similar to those used in South India at that time, but with deliberate deviations, which suggests that the writers were working in a literary system which had already undergone local development.

The inscriptions are written in Sanskrit, a learned language used as a lingua franca in ancient India, but the script and the type of stone confirm that the inscriptions were carved locally.

The first antiquities in the Kedah area were discovered in the 1840s by James Low, an officer in the East India Company. At Bukit Meriam he found a stone inscribed with two Buddhist texts. Inscriptions of this text have also been found in Borneo, Brunei and Java, but nowhere in India. Unfortunately, this stone has since disappeared.

South of the Muda River, in the region now known as Seberang Perai, Low found another inscription bearing a depiction of a stupa, the same karma text, and another text of particular historical relevance which mentions 'the great sea captain Buddhagupta, a resident of Raktamrttika'.

'Buddhagupta' is a common Sanskrit name, but 'Raktamrttika' is unknown in India. He may have come from the Malay Peninsula as the name means 'Red Earth' (Tanah Merah), a common Malay place name.

Another inscribed stone, 46 centimetres high, was discovered in 1979 at Kampung Sungai Mas by local residents. Believed to date from the 5th or 6th century CE, it depicts a square building supporting a stupa, surmounted by a multi-tiered ceremonial parasol, only part of which remains. The inscription contains the karma text, with a brief addition in an unknown script. The carving is less shapely than the Buddhagupta Stone, indicating that a different hand was responsible for creating it.

An indigenous style develops

These various inscriptions show that the area between Gunung Jerai and the Muda River was already part of an extensive sphere of communication and trade by 400 CE. The writing style and original texts came from India, but even these earliest texts show that local Buddhists emphasized ideas and writing styles which differed from those of India.

Other ancient writings in the same area include several inscriptions on a boulder at Cerok To'kun near Bukit Mertajam, Seberang Perai, and an inscribed stone from Bukit Coras, north of Merbok, Kedah. The Bukit Coras inscription, also in Sanskrit, has a common Buddhist expression of faith found widely in both early Southeast Asia and India. The Cerok To'kun boulder is intriguing because it bears seven different texts in slightly different alphabets, suggesting that they were carved by different people at different times, around the 5th century CE. Texts

Location of inscriptions

Perlis

Pulau Langkawi

Strait of Melaka

Kedah

Bukit Coras Stone

Gunung Jerai ▲ 1217 metres

SUNGAI MUDA

Bukit Meriam Stone

SUNGAI MERBOK

Sungai Mas Stone

Buddhagupta Stone

Bukit Mertajam

Cerok To'kun Boulder

Pulau Pinang

Seberang Perai

Perak

South China Sea

PENINSULAR MALAYSIA

Strait of Melaka

0   20 km

In 1979, while this irrigation channel was being dug at Sungai Mas in South Kedah, an inscribed stone (see above) bearing Buddhist scripts dating from the 5th or 6th century was unearthed.

include the karma verses, and a reference to a king, Ramaunibha. He may be the first Malaysian ruler whose name is recorded in history.

It is likely that writing became established in the Malay Peninsula before 400 CE. However, the precise date of this technological innovation cannot be established as common writing materials used in ancient times were perishable, lasting no more than one or two centuries.

The cultural impact of writing

More important than the exact date of this new technique is its impact on Malay culture. Formerly, scholars assumed that the introduction of writing signified an important discontinuity in social development. It was thought that writing, together with new religious beliefs, ideas of government, commercial systems, and settlement patterns, were all transformed as the result of a sudden expansion of Indian culture, which was eagerly if passively absorbed by uncivilized natives.

It is now realized that the true picture was much more complicated. Archaeological discoveries in various parts of Southeast Asia have cast doubt on the assumption that Indian culture underwent a period of sudden expansion, causing a revolution in Southeast Asian culture. Instead, the picture which now emerges is one of gradually intensifying communication over a period of several centuries, beginning before the 1st century CE. Southeast Asia was not trapped in a static backwater before it was set in motion by a new current from the West. In the Malay Peninsula, prehistoric burial methods suggest that concerns of religion and social status were already established in late prehistoric times. Bronze and iron were being worked and rice was being grown.

The importance of maritime trade

The reason for Kedah's early prominence is not difficult to discover. Sailing due west from Kedah, the route just misses the northern tip of Sumatra, crosses the Bay of Bengal, and eventually strikes the southern tip of India or Sri Lanka. Ancient sailors, who did not possess clocks, could not calculate longitude. However, they could determine their latitude by observations of the stars. By simply following the line of latitude west from Kedah, they could be sure of reaching southern India.

Seaborne trade was a significant feature of early historic life in what is now modern Malaysia. It is likely that this was also the case in late prehistory, and that links were forged between Kedah and other ports in the Peninsula, and trading partners around the Strait of Melaka and the South China Sea. It is also likely that much of the traffic between Southeast Asia and India was transported by Southeast Asian ships and shippers. Graeco-Roman traders who had established trading quarters in South India

Early historic sailing routes

in the 1st century CE describe huge non-Indian ships coming from the east with rich cargoes, probably from the Strait of Melaka region. The Malays were not passive recipients, but were probably active participants in a two-way exchange of commercial and cultural commodities. Indian cultural traits may have provided a kind of catalyst, enabling certain evolutionary processes in Malay society to proceed more rapidly than would have been the case in the absence of an external stimulus, but the transition to the historic period seems to have been a continuation of processes already in motion, rather than a sudden break with the past. Indian literature and art merely provided new metaphors and new motifs in which to express Malay cultural concepts.

The impact of trade on early Malaysian culture

Maritime routes across the Bay of Bengal from India to the Malay Peninsula played an important role in the importation of Indian culture. In the early historic period, around 2,000 years ago, Southeast Asian ships dominated the sea lanes. It is probable that Indian merchants first came to Malaysia in Southeast Asian vessels. The place names on the map were the major trade centres of the early historic era.

The Buddhagupta Stone

Discovered in the 1840s in South Kedah, this inscribed stone is known as the Buddhagupta Stone because it tells of a sea captain of that name. Originally part of a column, the stone is thought to date from about 400 CE. Inscribed in the centre is a stupa with a spherical base surmounted by a tiered pagoda-style roof. In Sanskrit script beside the stupa is a common Buddhist mantra about karma and rebirth. On the right-hand side of the slab is mentioned 'the great sea captain Buddhagupta, a resident of Raktamrttika', while the left-hand side translates as 'He and his fellow travellers by all means . . . be successful in their voyage'.

'Raktamrttika', meaning 'Red Earth', may have referred to the Peninsular east coast kingdom of the same name, which the Chinese knew as Chi tu.

65

Protohistoric settlement patterns

Although the protohistoric period in Malaysia begins around 400 CE, sources of original Malaysian data before about 1000 CE are so scanty that historians depend to a large extent on foreign documents to compile a detailed picture of the situation in the Malay Peninsula during this span of time, known as the protohistoric period.

A terracotta Seated Buddha image found at Pengkalan Bujang, South Kedah, is dated c. 1000–1100 CE.

Found inside a limestone cave in 1994, Buddhist votive tablets made of clay indicate the existence of a protohistoric settlement at Bukit Cawas in Kelantan's interior.

Earliest confirmed sites

To rely on archaeology for protohistoric population and settlement patterns may be misleading as many areas of Malaysia remain practically unexplored by archaeologists. Only certain types of structures leave remains which can be easily found and interpreted. For example, religious structures of masonry survive whereas palaces of wood, no matter how grand, do not leave lasting traces.

The oldest protohistoric settlement is on Pulau Kelumpang, in the Kuala Selinsing area of Perak. The date of the site is still a mystery, but shards of Chinese porcelain unearthed here, dating from the Song Dynasty (960–1279 CE), suggest that the site may have continued in use until that time. A stone found here is inscribed 'Sri Visnuvarman', a name used by South Indian rulers in the middle of the first millennium CE, leading scholars to conclude that the site was founded around 200 CE. It does not seem to have been particularly wealthy or important; no religious structures have been found, but some gold artefacts were discovered.

Other important data come from the 5th–9th century site of Sungai Mas in South Kedah. However, evidence of religious activity in this region is much older, as inscriptions found in the vicinity date from around the 5th century CE.

It is possible that some sites characterized by late Metal Age artefacts (500 BCE–1 CE) derive from the early protohistoric period. If these sites are included, a more complex image of settlement distribution is obtained. Late prehistoric to early protohistoric (1–600 CE) sites in the Malay Peninsula form three main clusters. Two of these are on the west coast, namely the Bernam Valley area of southern Perak and northern Selangor, and the Klang Valley of Selangor, where iron and bronze tools, weapons, bowls and ceremonial objects, stone-lined chambers and wooden boats, possibly buried during burial rituals, have been found. Another settlement centre lies in the interior, along the Tembeling River Valley of Pahang.

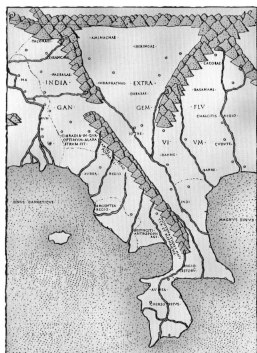

On a 16th-century map of Southeast Asia taken from the 13th-century *Geographike Huphegesis*, the Malay Peninsula is marked as 'Aurea Chersonesus' and an imaginary transpeninsular river system is shown.

Clues from early European maps

One of the most important sources for the study of protohistoric Malaysian settlement patterns is the *Geographike Huphegesis* or 'Guide to Geography'. This 13th-century map of the lands bordering the Indian Ocean and the South China Sea was based on data collected by an Alexandrian Greek named Claudius Ptolemaeus who lived around 100 CE. It is difficult to assign a firm date to any particular name or location on the map, which shows a feature called the 'Golden Khersonese' or peninsula, vaguely corresponding to the Malay Peninsula. On it are several toponyms: the first is 'Takola, an emporion'. 'Emporion' refers to a place where foreign trade was regularly conducted and taxed. Takola lay in the Thai or Burmese portion of the peninsula. Near the southern tip is another emporion called Sabara. A third coastal town called Kole is also mentioned.

A manuscript accompanying the map mentions a river system in the peninsula, flowing from a central range of mountains. Another section of the manuscript mentions four towns, namely, Kalonka, Konkonagara, Tharra and Palanda 'in the Golden Khersonese'; presumably these were located inland.

Transpeninsular routes

The geographer/historian Paul Wheatley surmised that the above manuscript describes a transpeninsular portage system similar to that reflected in 16th-century European reports. The Tembeling Valley probably lay on or near this route.

Tasik Chini, a series of lakes in Pahang near the Penarikan transpeninsular route, is also associated with legends of early settlement. Some chance finds of ancient Chinese porcelain have been reported from that area, but they date from the 13th century or slightly later. Nevertheless, their presence suggests

Early transpeninsular routeways and protohistoric settlements

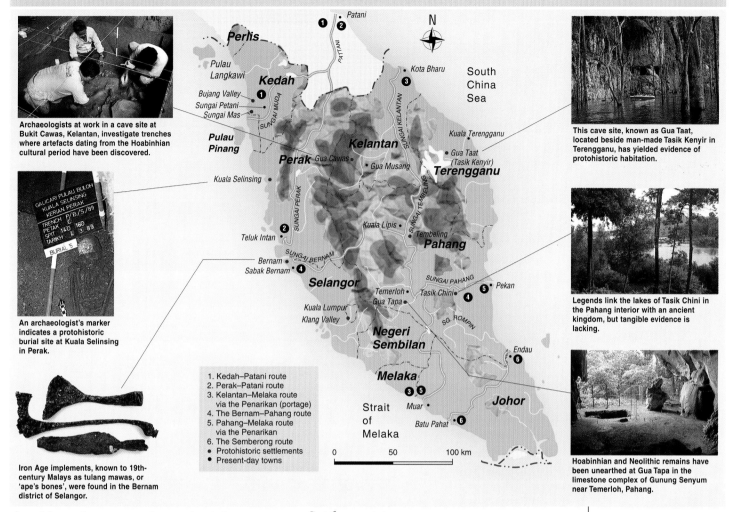

Archaeologists at work in a cave site at Bukit Cawas, Kelantan, investigate trenches where artefacts dating from the Hoabinhian cultural period have been discovered.

An archaeologist's marker indicates a protohistoric burial site at Kuala Selinsing in Perak.

Iron Age implements, known to 19th-century Malays as tulang mawas, or 'ape's bones', were found in the Bernam district of Selangor.

1. Kedah–Patani route
2. Perak–Patani route
3. Kelantan–Melaka route via the Penarikan (portage)
4. The Bernam–Pahang route
5. Pahang–Melaka route via the Penarikan
6. The Semberong route
● Protohistoric settlements
● Present-day towns

0   50   100 km

This cave site, known as Gua Taat, located beside man-made Tasik Kenyir in Terengganu, has yielded evidence of protohistoric habitation.

Legends link the lakes of Tasik Chini in the Pahang interior with an ancient kingdom, but tangible evidence is lacking.

Hoabinhian and Neolithic remains have been unearthed at Gua Tapa in the limestone complex of Gunung Senyum near Temerloh, Pahang.

that older settlements may have existed there.

The pattern of site distribution also suggests that the most important sites were located along transport routes. In the case of Tembeling, there may have been another incentive for the population to cluster here as sources of gold lie nearby. The name 'Golden Khersonese' suggests that traces of pre-colonial gold mines found in this area may date from such an early period.

The distribution of agricultural land does not seem to have fostered dense populations in protohistoric Malaysia. Pioneer sites of wet rice cultivation were located in upstream areas rather than along broad river valleys or near river mouths. Even in Kedah, Malaysia's major rice-growing area, there is no evidence for extensive wet rice growing until the Melaka Sultanate.

The donation of revenue from taxation of villages and craftsmen to temples, common in other parts of ancient Southeast Asia, does not seem to have existed in either Malaysia or Sumatra. In the Peninsula, too, most centres of traditional settlement were in the lowlands. However, the reverse situation occurred in Sumatra where early centres of dense population were mainly in the highlands.

Settlement types

The assumption that sites such as those in South Kedah, or the emporion of Sabara mentioned by Ptolemaeus were early cities is incorrect as there is no evidence for such a physical structure as a city anywhere in Malaysia during protohistory.

Warfare over land often resulted in the formation of early fortified cities. In protohistoric Southeast Asia, however, sites were not strongly fortified. Manpower was scarce and more precious than land. Rather than lose lives by defending a location, rulers preferred to retreat and establish a new settlement elsewhere.

The probable settlement pattern of protohistoric Malaysia consisted of a few downstream areas, such as the Merbok estuary in Kedah, inhabited by a sizeable but dispersed population. Other concentrations probably existed along streams near the foothills of the Banjaran Titiwangsa, the main mountain chain of the Peninsula, while a third important settlement area probably occupied significant points along the transpeninsular route, from Muar on the west coast to the Pahang and Lebir valleys on the east.

This ancient ceramic *kendi* was found in the Bujang Valley of South Kedah.

Pottery shards unearthed at Sungai Mas in the Bujang Valley of South Kedah are used by archaeologists to date this trading settlement, believed to be the earliest population centre of the ancient kingdom of Kedah.

Chi tu: An inland kingdom

By the 5th century CE, several kingdoms and entrepôts appeared on the Malay Peninsula and other parts of Southeast Asia. The majority of these were situated on the coast, although there were some inland kingdoms, the most prominent being Chi tu, or the 'Red Earth Land'. Its location is still not confirmed, but academic opinion favours the interior of the Peninsular Malaysian state of Kelantan.

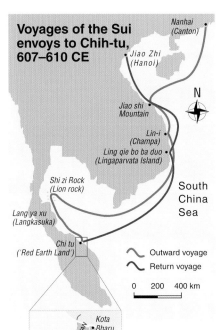

Voyages of the Sui envoys to Chih-tu, 607–610 CE

Nanhai (Canton)

Jiao Zhi (Hanoi)

N

Jiao shi Mountain

Lin-i (Champa)

Ling qie bo ba duo (Lingaparvata Island)

Shi zi Rock (Lion rock)

South China Sea

Lang ya xu (Langkasuka)

Chi tu ('Red Earth Land')

Outward voyage
Return voyage

0   200   400 km

Kota Bharu

SUNGAI KELANTAN

Gua Cha

Kelantan
Ulu Kelantan

The information obtained from the 7th–century embassy to Chi tu considerably expanded Chinese knowledge of the mysterious South Seas, the location of many desirable exotic commodities. Bearing gifts for the king of Chi tu, the Sui envoys set sail from Canton, stopped over in Champa (present-day Vietnam), and then sailed south. Debate continues on the route described from there to the kingdom of Chi tu, but most scholars believe that the sailing directions refer to the islands named on the map (above). The envoys sailed past the kingdom of Langkasuka to the borders of Chi tu where they were met by the king's representative at the head of a fleet of 30 ships. From there they proceeded upriver to the capital, believed to be in the Ulu Kelantan region.

Documentary evidence

A detailed description of Chi tu appears in the Chinese *Chi tu guo ji*, a documentary account of a visit to the kingdom by Sui envoys from 607 CE to 610 CE. Chi tu was described as being part of the empire of Funan (based in present-day Vietnam), and was located in the South Seas, 100 days journey by sea from China. The account mentions that the name of the kingdom derived from the colour of its soil which is 'mostly red'.

Based on the Chinese description, the location of Chi tu has been much debated by scholars. The most favoured position is the northern part of the Malay Peninsula, around the upper regions of the Kelantan River. Apart from general considerations, including geography, climate and soil colour, one of the main reasons for locating the kingdom there is that the capital of Chi tu, called either Seng zhi, or Shi zi, was described as being reached after a one-month journey upriver. The Kelantan River is the obvious choice as it is a major waterway, navigable by fair-sized boats for about 160 kilometres upstream, as well as being the means of access to the goldfields of Kelantan and Pahang. This region, known as Ulu Kelantan, has been inhabited for at least 8,000 years, as evidenced by prehistoric burials found at the cave site of Gua Cha. Recent excavations in the same region have revealed a large cache of Mahayana Buddhist votive tablets perhaps dating from Srivijayan times (9th–11th century CE). However, to date, no tangible evidence of the inland capital of Chi tu has been found.

Description of the kingdom

Chi tu established a political relationship with China in about 607 CE when the Sui Emperor Yang di decided to open up communications with 'far distant lands'. He sent an embassy to Chi tu under the leadership of Chang zhu, the Custodian of Military Property, assisted by Wang Zhong

Zheng, Controller of Natural Resources. China had been unified under the Sui in 589 CE and this wealthy new dynasty craved exotic luxuries, many of which were imported from the South Seas. The ambassadors bore 5,000 different sorts of gifts for the king of Chi tu, and on their arrival they were presented with 'local products as tribute'.

Many of the sociopolitical and cultural aspects of the kingdom are described in the Chinese account of this visit. According to this source, the kingdom was ruled by a family known as Chu dan. The king, Li fo duo se, ascended the throne when his father abdicated in order to preach Buddhism to the world. At the time of the envoys' visit, the king had ruled for 16 years and had three wives who were the daughters of neighbouring kings. His residence was in the upriver capital of Seng zhi, which is described as having 'triple gates more than a hundred paces apart' painted with images of bodhisattvas and hung with flowers and bells. They were guarded by women dressed as giants. Those who were stationed on the outside of the gates held weapons, while those on the inside held white cloths and 'gathered flowers into white nets'.

The *Chi tu guo ji* lists various officials in the king's administrative body, including one for governing political affairs and one for administering criminal law. Chi tu also controlled several other city-kingdoms which were administered by appointees of the king.

Cultural practices and beliefs

The envoys' account states that it was customary for both men and women of Chi tu to pierce their

Only accessible by boat, the cave sites of Kelantan's interior, such as Gua Cawan, are proof of early riverine settlements which could have preceded Chi tu.

ears, anoint their bodies with scented oils, and wear rose- and plain-coloured cloth. The women wore their hair in chignons at the nape of their neck. People had to obtain permission from the king to wear a special gold locket, and even wealthy families had to acquire royal dispensation for this privilege.

Wedding ceremonies were conducted on auspicious days. The bride's family celebrated for five days before the wedding ceremony. On the seventh day, the nuptial rites were completed and the couple were considered united. After the marriage, the couple moved to a separate house. However, the youngest son was obligated to live with his father.

On the death of a parent or brother, mourners shaved their heads and wore plain clothes. The body was cremated in a chalet roofed with bamboo and built over a river so that the ashes could fall into the water. The cremation was accompanied by the burning of incense and the blowing of conch shells and drumming. Both the upper-class nobles and the commoners were cremated in this fashion, but the king's ashes were preserved in a golden jar and deposited in a temple. Their religious beliefs were reported as being Buddhist, but 'greater respect is paid to the Brahmans', which suggests that Hinduism had a strong influence, as does the practice of cremation.

The staple food of the kingdom was rice, and accounts of the feast presented to the Sui envoys mention yellow, white, purple and red cakes, 'together with beef, mutton, fish, turtle, pork and tortoise-meats of more than a hundred sorts'.

The king's son Na ya jia accompanied the envoys back to China to offer local products, including a gold 'hibiscus' crown and camphor, as tribute for the Emperor, who in turn bestowed him with gifts and an official rank.

The *Chi tu guo ji*

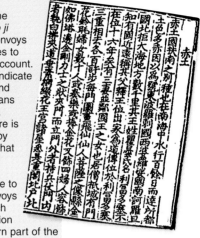

The most important documentary evidence of the kingdom of Chi tu is contained in the *Chi tu guo ji* (right), the account written by the Sui Dynasty envoys after a visit to the kingdom in 607–610 CE. Clues to the whereabouts of Chi tu are revealed in this account. Constant high temperatures and heavy rainfall indicate an equatorial location, as do the crops of rice and sugar cane. The translation of Chi tu, which means 'Red Earth Land', or Tanah Merah in Malay, is a popular Peninsular place name even today. There is a town and district in the Kelantan River valley by that name, which gives credence to the theory that the kingdom was situated in inland Kelantan. However, Tanah Merah also occurs in Negeri Sembilan and Kedah. Perhaps the best evidence to support the Kelantan theory is that after the envoys left Chi tu it only took ten days of sailing to reach Champa (South Vietnam). This is a clear indication that the kingdom was located in the northeastern part of the Malay Peninsula.

The royal court of Chi tu

This artist's impression of a court scene at Chi tu is inspired by the following passage from the 7th-century *Chi tu guo ji*: *The king sits on a three-tiered couch, facing north and dressed in rose-coloured cloth, with a chaplet of gold flowers, and necklaces of varied jewels. Four damsels attend on this right hand and on his left . . . . To the rear of the king's couch there is a wooden shrine inlaid with gold, silver and five perfumed woods, and behind the shrine is suspended a golden light. Beside the couch two metal mirrors are set up, before which are placed metal pitchers, each with a golden incense burner before it. In front of all these is a recumbent golden ox, above which hangs a jewelled canopy, with precious fans on either side. Several hundred brahmans sit in rows facing each other on the eastern and western sides.*

Kuala Selinsing: A mangrove settlement

Kuala Selinsing, a mangrove-forested estuary on the coast of Perak, is the location of several archaeological sites believed to have been the settlement of a late prehistoric seafaring community. Using evidence from human burials and artefacts, including pottery, beads, shells and glassware, the mangrove settlements are believed to date from the 3rd century BCE till about the 11th century CE.

Geologists taking soil samples from boreholes near Pulau Kelumpang 2 for radiocarbon dating and pollen analysis. The peat and clay layers revealed shards, shells and charcoal fragments.

Pile dwellings

The settlements were built over the mud flats on the fringe of the mangrove forest. Houses were pile dwellings made of wood and thatch. The basic design of these houses has remained unaltered for centuries, as shown by the similarities between this 19th-century etching (above) and present-day fishermen's dwellings at nearby Kuala Gula (above top).

Location of the settlement

Hidden deep within the wetlands of the Matang Forest Reserve, 12 kilometres northwest of Kuala Sepetang, the archaeological sites are known to the local woodcutters and fishermen as Pulau Buluh (Bamboo Island) or Pulau Kulit Kerang (Shell Island). However, they are not separate islands but, rather, high mounds on Pulau Kelumpang, an island in Kuala Selinsing.

In 1932, I. H. N. Evans made the first archaeological excavations comprising two mounds (Kelumpang 1 and 7), located about 600–700 metres from the Selinsing River mouth. Later, aerial photographs indicated further sites. This was confirmed by a field survey in 1988, led by Nik Hassan Shuhaimi, which revealed five more mounds (Kelumpang 2–6), about 1 kilometre away from the original site.

The mounds vary in size—the longest is about 280 metres—and consist of earth and shell remains, the result of accumulated household refuse cast out from the original pile dwellings. During and after the settlement's occupation, the mangrove forest has crept seawards with the advance of the land due to the constant deposit of riverine detrius.

Artefacts indicate trade contacts

All the mounds are scattered with molluscs, and amongst these occur bones, shards, stone artefacts, metal objects and beads. The most numerous artefacts are beads, which are mostly made from semiprecious gemstones, including beryl, sodalite, moldavite, plasma, jasper, aventurine, quartz cat's-eye and analicima. The beads were cut, ground and polished, although much of the lapidary work was rather crude. Many of these gemstones, apart from jasper, do not occur in the Malay Peninsula. Beryl, plasma, aventurine and sodalite have been mined for centuries in India, and Iran and Iraq are well known for producing sodalite and aventurine. The Chinese used plasma and aventurine as jade substitutes. Beads of agate, carnelian and rock crystal were also found but were not as common. Glass beads, and beads fashioned from fishbones and shells, as well as shell bracelets and spoons were also present.

Metal finds included tin rings and ear pendants, some of which were found in association with burials. A few badly corroded bronze objects have also been found, together with iron slag.

Other finds include objects of horn, bone and ivory, including what could be an unfinished knife handle made from a deer horn. Bone points, which

Changing shorelines of Kuala Selinsing

These maps show how the settlement sites on Pulau Kelumpang have become further inland as a result of estuarine sedimentation, which was probably the reason for their abandonment in the 11th century.

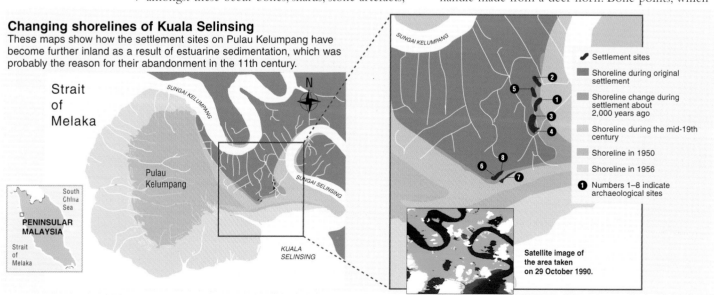

Strait of Melaka

South China Sea

PENINSULAR MALAYSIA

Strait of Melaka

Pulau Kelumpang

SUNGAI KELUMPANG

SUNGAI SELINSING

KUALA SELINSING

N

- Settlement sites
- Shoreline during original settlement
- Shoreline change during settlement about 2,000 years ago
- Shoreline during the mid-19th century
- Shoreline in 1950
- Shoreline in 1956
- Numbers 1–8 indicate archaeological sites

Satellite image of the area taken on 29 October 1990.

could have been hairpins, have been found in association with burials, particulary near the skulls.

Rocks of various shapes and sizes are classified as artefacts because they were specially brought to the settlement—some from as far away as the Bujang Valley in Kedah. The most common of these are slabs with numerous deep and parallel grooves, which could have been used for finishing shell bracelets. Large numbers of sharpening stones also occur, as well as pestle-like specimens. It is quite common to find unshaped stones with burials, laid either beside the bodies or over their middle parts.

Local earthenware and imported ceramics

Several types of earthenware shards have been found in all the mounds. Altogether four whole pots were recovered—three of these from burials. Prominent incised decorations include chevrons, wave and scroll patterns, as well as many linear, geometric and punctate designs. Impressed shards are common, with surface patterns including cord, net, mat and basket marking, and carved designs.

Imported glazed wares are rare and have been dated no later than the 10th century CE. This assumption is based specifically on the dark green glazed shards found in Kelumpang 6, which might have come from Iran or Iraq. Similar shards have been found at Sungai Mas in the Bujang Valley, and at Takuapa in southern Thailand. Other grey glazed shards may be Yueh stoneware.

Lifestyle of the mangrove settlers

Altogether 25 identifiable species of shells were obtained during the 1988–89 excavations. The commonest is the bivalve *Anadara granosa*. These food molluscs were mostly obtained from the mud flats around the site, whereas the thick-shelled gastropods used for ornaments were probably imported from rocky shore environments.

Perhaps the most interesting finds came from the lowest waterlogged levels, which contained materials discarded from the pile dwellings into the tidal shallows beneath. Coconut shells, bottle gourds, split bamboo and charred kindling left from cooking fires were found. Betel nuts were also unearthed and, by association, the teeth of two adults buried at the sites were stained by betel chewing. Excavators also brought up sections of adzed and sewn planks, stumps of house posts and fragments of what may have been a dugout canoe. Another interesting find was a perfectly preserved mat, presumably made from bamboo, together with pieces of pandanus matting.

Preserved in peat deposits sandwiched between

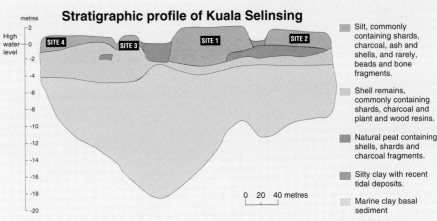

Stratigraphic profile of Kuala Selinsing

Silt, commonly containing shards, charcoal, ash and shells, and rarely, beads and bone fragments.

Shell remains, commonly containing shards, charcoal and plant and wood resins.

Natural peat containing shells, shards and charcoal fragments.

Silty clay with recent tidal deposits.

Marine clay basal sediment

This cross section of archaeological sites Kelumpang 1–4 shows how the settlement mounds were built up over time. The mounds contain high levels of human-induced deposits, while the lower levels are natural deposits. Sites 3 and 4 contain large quantities of cockle shells (still abundant in the area), which indicates that they were a major food source for the prehistoric inhabitants of Kuala Selinsing. Their availability may have been one of the reasons for the choice of location.

layers of waterlogged mud were animal bones and rice husks. If botanical analysis confirms preliminary observations, then this may be the earliest physical evidence of rice so far found on the Malay Peninsula. An exciting related find was a wooden rice mortar made from a hollow tree trunk.

Excavations also unearthed 11 burials, some of which contained grave goods comprising beads, pottery, stone ornaments and food. Graves appear to have been shallow.

Preliminary observations indicate that the people of Kuala Selinsing may not have been Hindus, as had been suggested by Evans. He based his theory on the Pallava seal and a gold ring found at Kuala Selinsing which bore designs of Visnu or Garuda. However, these are insufficient evidence to suggest that the people followed Hinduism. Other evidence, especially the burial practices, points to indigenous belief systems such as ancestor worship. Even though the settlement was in contact with the Indianized population of South Kedah, the people of Kuala Selinsing were still ideologically in a non-Indianized state.

Radiocarbon dates suggest that the settlement was in use between 200 BCE and 1000 CE. It is apparent that the settlement did not come to a violent end, as the dead were properly buried, even during the latest phase. The people were evidently seafarers, judging by the presence of bones from deep sea fish found at the sites, and they had contacts with an inland rice-growing people, as evidenced by the rice husks. A final observation is that the first settlers of Kuala Selinsing were a metal-using people who were presumably in contact with the community who built the cist graves in South Perak and Selangor.

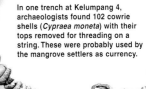

In one trench at Kelumpang 4, archaeologists found 102 cowrie shells (*Cypraea moneta*) with their tops removed for threading on a string. These were probably used by the mangrove settlers as currency.

This pot was reconstructed from shards found in a burial site. It is uncertain whether the wares were hand- or wheel-made. The clays used are quite coarse, with colours ranging from buff to orange and various shades of brown.

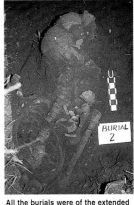

All the burials were of the extended type with the body in a supine position. The excavator (below) points out a skull in a waterlogged grave where the skeletons were better preserved than in the drier top layers.

Pulau Tioman: A port settlement

Mountainous Pulau Tioman, the largest island off the east coast of Peninsular Malaysia, was known to ancient mariners plying the trade routes of the South China Sea at least a millennium ago. The island features on early Arab and Chinese maps, and ceramics discovered there, which date from the 10th-century Song Dynasty, are evidence that the island was a port of call for ships engaged in the lucrative maritime trade between South China, Southeast Asia, India, the Middle East, and ultimately Europe.

Among the ceramics found on Pulau Tioman are these spouted water vessels, known as *kendi*, which are made of burnished earthenware. They were produced locally in Southeast Asia. A similar vessel found in Sarawak has been dated to the 10th century CE.

Nenek si-Muka, one of two horn-like granite peaks in the south of Pulau Tioman, can be seen far out to sea and has served as a navigational beacon for South China Sea mariners for over a thousand years.

Location of the ceramic finds

Tranquil bays protected from the wrath of the northeast monsoon, plentiful freshwater streams, and a wealth of rainforest and sea products contributed to Pulau Tioman's attraction as a landfall port for ancient mariners.

The discovery of ancient ceramics

Pulau Tioman's current status as a popular tourist getaway is due to its geographical splendours. The mountainous interior is still covered in virgin rainforest, much as it was when the early mariners stopped over, and the distinctive granite peaks, over 1000 metres in height, are a prominent landmark for sailors even today. According to oral tradition, the name Tioman derives from *burung tiong*, the hill mynah, a large black bird with a distinctive whistle, which is still abundant on the island.

The two most important archaeological sites are at Kampung Juara, located beside a protected bay on the east coast of the island, and at Kampung Nipah beside Teluk Nipah, a bay on the west coast, which is screened from the monsoon by the horseshoe-shaped mountain range behind.

Early ceramics were first discovered in 1962, when a University of Malaya expedition came across the remains of over 40 ceramic vessels in Gua Serau, a cave near Teluk Nipah. Further excavations from 1970 to 1973 revealed more ceramic shards at Teluk Nipah, believed to be the earliest settlement site on Pulau Tioman. In 1975, shards were revealed during land clearing near the resort hotel south of Kampung Tekek, and another discovery came a year later when ceramics were discovered at Juara, on the opposite coast, when villagers were levelling ground for a football field. As they were only shards, the finds did not cause any excitement among the local inhabitants. However, in 1979, when further work was being done on the field, complete ceramics—some in perfect condition—were discovered. Many were kept by the villagers, some were given to tourists, and others were sold to antique dealers before the curator of the Sultan Abu Bakar Museum at Pekan, Pahang, was informed of the discoveries in 1980. The villagers were then educated on the importance of safeguarding the site and its heritage. Three years later, when the National Museum

Department and Sultan Abu Bakar Museum carried out excavation work, nine ceramic vessels were unearthed and a further 104 ceramic vessels were purchased from the villagers. Also during 1983, excavations were carried out by the same team at Teluk Nipah.

Analysing the discoveries

Ceramics were important trade items as they served as commodities of exchange for the natural forest and sea products of Southeast Asia. They were also used as gifts for Southeast Asian rulers, who regarded them as status symbols.

According to ceramicists, more than half of the discoveries from Gua Serau and Teluk Nipah were produced in Guangdong Province, South China, during the Northern Song Dynasty (960–1126 CE). Other finds from both those sites, and from Kampung Juara, were produced during the 12th–14th century Song and Yuan dynasties in Jiangsu, Zhejiang and Fujian provinces, South China. Other foreign ceramics discovered include 15th–17th century Thai and Vietnamese wares, 17th-century blue-and-white Kraak wares from Jiangxi, Swatow ceramics from Fujian, late 19th-century Chinese and Thai kitchenware, as well as some European pieces. Earthenware, including cooking pots and *kendi* (water vessels) produced locally in Southeast Asia, were also discovered. These earthenware vessels are difficult to date. However, during excavation they were found together with the foreign wares in all soil layers, leading archaeologists to date them between the 11th and 19th centuries.

Small stoneware storage jars found on Pulau Tioman have been identified as being produced in South China during the 12th-century Song Dynasty.

Used for storing water and food, paddle-decorated vessels like this cream-coloured earthenware from Pulau Tioman have been found at other Southeast Asian ports.

Evidence of early port settlements

The ceramics discovered at Pulau Tioman are important indicators of the history of the island and the development of Malaysia's early trade patterns. The oldest ceramics were found at Teluk Nipah, affirming local belief that this was the island's earliest settlement site. The presence of these trade traces strengthens the view of historians and archaeologists that the island served as one of the links in the chain of landfall ports which flourished along the East–West maritime trade route.

Arab sources mention a place called Betumah, and also Tiyumah, which have both been identified as Pulau Tioman. The *Akbar as Sin wa'l Hind* [Tales of China and India], written prior to 1000 CE, mentions that '. . . the ships sail to a place called Betumah where fresh water can be found for anyone who desires it'. In the 9th century, Ibn Khurdadhbih also mentioned the island, saying: 'After leaving Mait [the southern tip of Peninsular Malaysia or the southern archipelago], one would discover to his left, the island of Tiyumah which produced aloes wood of the type called Hindi, as well as camphor. From that place one would arrive at Qmar [Cambodia].' Another Arab, Idrisi, writes that 'one could get sandalwood and rice at Tiyumah'. He also mentions an island called Sumah (thought to be a reference to Tioman) where there 'were edible birds, coconuts and superior camphor. There is plenty of wind and rain, and it is surrounded by many small inhabited islands, some peopled by Panhang [Pahang] people.'

More evidence comes from Chinese sources. The island

appears on the Wubeizhi Chart, which was printed in 1630, although it is believed to derive from the sailing directions of Admiral Zhenghe's (Cheng Ho) expeditions to Southeast Asia, India and the Middle East between 1403 and 1433. On this map, Pulau Tioman is named Zhumashan, 'the Mountain of Rami', which takes its name from the rope-making fibre *rami*, obtained from a native plant which was used for rigging on sailing ships.

From these various sources, it is clear that by the 11th century Pulau Tioman was a strategic and well-known landfall port which played a major role in the development of international trade in the Asian region in general, and Malaysia in particular, before the emergence of Melaka in the early 15th century. Due to its prominence in Arab writings, indications are that Pulau Tioman was the most important stopover port in the South China Sea for early Arab mariners. It was easily found while sailing to Cambodia and Champa (Vietnam), and henceforth to China. Ships, sheltered in the protected coves during the monsoon season, replenished their supplies of fresh water and food, and stocked up on rainforest products such as rope-making fibre, timber, aloes wood and camphor.

Ceramics similar to those found on Pulau Tioman have also been discovered at other ports in the trading link, including Kedah, Srivijaya, Malayu (Jambi), Kota Cina, Beruas, Santubong, and Po ni (Brunei). Song Dynasty ceramics were exported from Canton and have also been traced to Egypt, Sri Lanka, the Maldives, the Persian Gulf, South Thailand, Indonesia and the Philippines.

Qingbai ceramics

During the Southern Song and Yuan dynasties (960–1368 CE), when trade with the South Seas (Nanhai) was at its peak, ceramics were a major barter item. White wares, known as qingbai, were produced at various kilns in Fujian Province, South China, and were exported from Quanzhou, which was the most important port during the Song–Yuan period. Qingbai wares found on Pulau Tioman include a vase with a lotus-designed base, various covered boxes with moulded bases, and a bowl and vase incised with chrysanthemum designs.

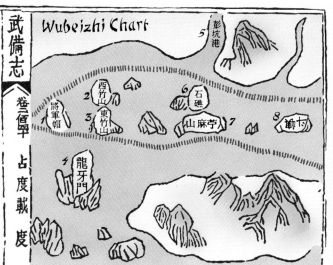

The east coast in the Wubeizhi Chart

This section of the 17th-century Wubeizhi Chart shows the east coast of the Malay Peninsula. The present-day geographical features which have been identified are as follows:

1. Pulau Tinggi (Tall Island in Malay) or 'General's Hat Island'(*Chiang chun mao*).
2. One of the twin peaks of Pulau Aur or 'West Bamboo Mountain' (*Hsi Chu Shan*) which appears as two islands from a distance.
3. One of the twin peaks of Pulau Aur or 'East Bamboo Mountain' (*Tung chu shan*).
4. Singapore Strait or 'Dragon Tooth Strait' (*Lung ya men*).
5. Pahang River estuary (*P'eng k'eng chiang*).
6. Pulau Seribuat (*Shih shiao*).
7. Pulau Tioman (*Ch'u ma shan*).
8. Pulau Tenggol or 'Peck Island' (*Tou hsu*).

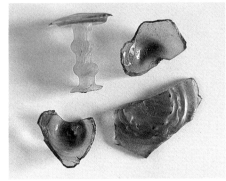

Glass remnants, believed to originate in the Middle East, have been unearthed at the archaeological site of Pengkalan Bujang in the Bujang Valley of South Kedah. Trade remnants such as these are proof that the kingdom of Kedah participated in an international trade network.

BELOW: This artist's impression, after a 13th-century print in the Bibliothèque Nationale de France, depicts an Arab merchant ship, possibly of the same type which plied the maritime trade route to the Malay Peninsula.

In this extract after a map of the Indian Archipelago by Willem Lodewycksz, c. 1596, the Malay Peninsula is shown as the Chersonese Aurea (the early Greek name), while the Muar River is mistakenly depicted as running from one side of the Peninsula to the other. This error was due to early reports of the transpeninsular route which involved a portage between the Muar and the Pahang rivers.

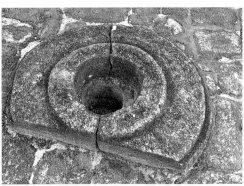

This stone temple platform and a pillar mount atop a drain for ceremonial liquid are part of the surviving ruins of a Hindu temple known as Candi Bukit Batu Pahat (The Temple on the Hill of Cut Stone) beside the Merbok River in the Bujang Valley of South Kedah.

WIDER CONTACTS IN PROTOHISTORIC TIMES

By the 3rd century BCE, Indian storytellers were aware of the existence of the Malay Peninsula as their tales include a place called Malayadvipa, literally 'Malay Island (or Peninsula)'. By the 1st century CE, Graeco-Roman traders in India told of large ships bringing spices from Southeast Asia, probably from the vicinity of the Strait of Melaka, while a Greek sailing guide to the Indian Ocean mentions the Aurea Chersonesus, or 'Golden Peninsula', believed to be the Malay Peninsula.

Thai ceramics from the 15th century were recovered from a shipwreck off the coast of Pahang.

Chinese envoys were exploring the transpeninsular route to India by 250 CE, and once the maritime link between the Indian Ocean and the South China Sea had been formed, it was inevitable that the Malay Peninsula would assume a position of importance in the Asian economy.

For much of the first millennium CE, Asian maritime trade was largely in the hands of shippers from the Strait of Melaka. In the 5th and 6th centuries, a number of trading kingdoms appeared in Malaysia. At this time, traders from India visited, but did not form resident colonies. Southeast Asian sources from the first millennium CE compare foreign merchants to migratory birds who came and left at specific times of year. This seasonal nature of trade was due to the predictable monsoons. As the Malay Peninsula is situated at the approximate limit of one monsoonal voyage from both India and China, this region became a transshipment point for cargoes from one end of Asia to the other. Local rulers took advantage of this trade to acquire exotic status symbols such as textiles, ceramics and bronzeware.

The most significant protohistoric Malaysian kingdom was located in the Bujang Valley of South Kedah. A stone stele found there inscribed with prayers for safety by a Buddhist sea captain known as Buddhagupta was apparently erected before he set out on the hazardous voyage to India around 500 CE. He was from the 'Red Earth Land', probably in Kelantan, which suggests that Malaysian shippers congregated at Kedah before setting off across the Indian Ocean.

Kedah was also a stopover for Chinese Buddhist pilgrims en route to India. The most famous pilgrim, Yiqing, provided information regarding Kedah's political situation. On his first visit in 671 CE, Kedah was independent, but on his return voyage in 685 CE it had become part of the Sumatran kingdom of Srivijaya. However, its suzerainty seems to have been mainly ceremonial as contemporary Indian sources depict Kedah as an important political entity in its own right.

This stone, inscribed with an unknown motif, was found in South Kedah.

Other protohistoric Malaysian sites which were in contact with international trading networks are few. These include the west coast sites of Kuala Selinsing, Perak, and Jenderam Hilir, Selangor. However, recent research on the Peninsular east coast suggests that this region may yield much more evidence of trading activities in the future.

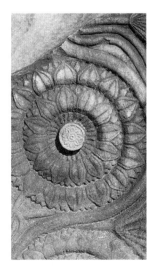

TOP: The early port site of Santubong in southwestern Sarawak has revealed a variety of artefacts, including this Buddha image believed to date from the 7th century CE.

CENTRE: An 11th-century stone lintel from India is on display at the Bujang Valley Archaeological Museum located at Merbok, South Kedah.

ABOVE: This stoneware water vessel, recovered from a 15th-century shipwreck, is on display at the Pahang State Museum in Pekan, Pahang.

Expansion of trade

The pursuit of trade has been a commonplace activity in Southeast Asia for several thousand years. At the beginning of recorded history, Southeast Asians were already engaged in long-distance barter trade. The people of the Malay Peninsula were strategically situated to participate in this trade, due to both the demand for local products and to the Peninsula's location on regional trade routes. At the beginning of the first millennium CE, the volume of trade between Southeast Asia and the two flanking regions of India and China began to expand, bringing many benefits to the people of Malaysia.

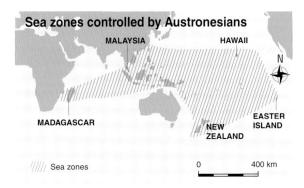

Sea zones controlled by Austronesians

///// Sea zones   0   400 km

A three-part economy based on exchange networks

Malaysia's early domestic economy was the result of three interlinking specialized communities. The first of these were the population groups of the hinterlands. These people were primarily involved with, and adept at, gathering forest produce, particularly tree resins, such as dammar, which gave off a fragrant smoke when burnt.

Nomadic boat dwellers comprised the second community. They inhabited the swamps and small offshore islands and spent most of their lives on the water. In addition to making use of crustaceans, fish and other marine food sources, they were efficient gatherers of such materials as tortoiseshell and pearls.

The third group inhabited the banks of streams from the estuaries to the point upstream where travel by dugout canoe and raft became impractical. The peoples in this group were ideally suited to become the foci of networks of exchange which in their original state were probably limited to one river system and the nearby offshore islands.

The advantages of mutual interdependence among several groups exploiting different environments are obvious. By linking their economies, individual groups obtained some measure of security which enabled them to survive when fluctuations in the ecosystem caused temporary food shortages. It was also more efficient for some groups to become specialists in the manufacture of commonly needed craft items, such as pottery. In addition, the establishment of a meeting place where exchange could take place under certain rules, with safety ensured by an authority, was obviously in the interests of all parties.

Early international trade

The region now known as Malaysia first appears in written history as the result of trading contacts with India and China. However, there were sophisticated commercial societies in Malaysia long before this. The Austronesian-speaking people, of whom the Malays form one branch, possibly began making long-distance sea voyages between 3,000 and 4,000 years ago. It is quite probable that one of the principal factors which encouraged them to undertake these difficult and dangerous journeys was the prestige they accrued when they returned from distant lands bearing rare and interesting objects. By the time written documents first mention Malays, branches of Austronesian speakers controlled the sea routes over an expanse of ocean stretching more than halfway around the earth, from Madagascar to Hawaii.

Domestic and regional trade patterns

Written documents do not exist from the earliest phase of this expansion. Therefore, a description of Malay trading patterns before the expansion of trade 2,000 years ago depends partly on archaeological discoveries and partly on analogy with later societies. These sources yield indications that the Malaysian population in late prehistoric times comprised three types of specialized communities which had adapted to different environmental opportunities. These were the interior forest dwellers, the nomadic boat dwellers, and the estuarine and riverside villagers.

The seacoasts and hinterlands of the Malay Peninsula were linked from early times as evidenced by the discovery of oceanic cowrie shells in prehistoric strata of caves in the Pahang interior. This suggests that some intermediary site linking the peoples of the coasts and hinterlands was already in existence.

Centres of authority probably began to form in the late prehistoric period (500 BCE–200 CE). Archaeological discoveries, such as bronze Dongson drums found on both coasts of the Peninsula, indicate that certain individuals took advantage of their geographical position, and other less tangible resources, to amass the wherewithal to obtain especially rare and elaborately made artefacts. During this period, regional exchange networks also began to form. The discovery of bronze drums and other artefacts indicates Peninsular centres were in communication with other parts of the region, including areas as far north as Vietnam (the origin of the Dongson style), and probably with islands in the Indonesian Archipelago as well.

The lure of gold

In the mid-3rd century CE, the Chinese were already aware that the Malay Peninsula formed an important intermediate point on the sea route to India, which indicates that the Peninsula had already been in regular contact with India for some time.

Indian sources do not describe Southeast Asia in enough detail to differentiate between the Malay Peninsula and other parts of the region. However, one of the major commodities of interest to the Indians was gold, which was available in the mountains of Pahang. This geological situation may have given rise to the ancient Greek term 'Golden Khersonese', which most probably referred to the Malay Peninsula.

During the first millennium CE, trade between Malaysia and both China and India gradually expanded. However, trade with India was more important and influential.

Two thousand years ago, Indian sources referred to places called Suvarnabhumi ('Land of Gold') and Suvarnadvipa ('Golden Peninsula (or Island)')—the literal equivalent of the Greek 'Golden Khersonese'— where merchants travelled to seek riches. However, geographical precision was not an objective of these early Indian stories.

Both Indian and Chinese sources reveal increasing interest in Southeast Asia in the first few centuries CE. Sometimes they refer specifically to places which were probably in the Malay Peninsula. This growing interest could have been related to the unrest in central Asia, which made overland communication between the two areas unsafe. At the same time, rising populations and increasing political sophistication in Sumatra and the Malay Peninsula probably made maritime travel through the Strait of Melaka less prone to attacks by pirates. In 250 CE, the main communication route between

the Indian Ocean and the South China Sea still necessitated the use of portages across the Malay Peninsula, the most important of which probably lay near the Isthmus of Kra.

The rise of regional maritime travel

By the beginning of the 5th century CE, the record of a voyage made by the Chinese Buddhist pilgrim Faxian shows that the Strait of Melaka was used as a link between India and China. The security of this passage would have made seaborne commerce between the Indian Ocean and the South China Sea more efficient by lowering transport costs, which, in turn, would have stimulated the volume of trade. Malaysian shippers, together with Sumatrans and Javanese, would have been the main beneficiaries of this increase. However, there is no evidence that any sailors other than Southeast Asians participated in the transport of cargoes before about 1000 CE.

Detailed knowledge of Malaysia's early long-distance trade is imprecise. However, data on the internal trade of Malaysian ports with other Southeast Asian regions is even more vague. The discoveries of bronze items of presumed local manufacture in such places as Kuala Selinsing, Perak, and the similarity in pottery designs over an area encompassing the Malay Peninsula, eastern Sumatra and western Borneo, suggest that the lively intercourse between Malaysia and her neighbours, which began in prehistoric times, did not cease but continued to flourish. For example, metallurgical analysis of gold used in ritual deposits placed beneath a 10th–11th century CE temple in South Kedah came from western Borneo.

Although much remains to be learned, available data makes it clear that around 2000 years ago a number of circumstances conspired to increase the volume of international trade entering Malaysia's ports. The wealth and new information which arrived with the trade commodities provided resources which local leaders utilized to increase the complexity and sophistication of their societies.

Regional trade patterns can be deduced from artefacts found at archaeological sites. Some reliquaries discovered at 11th-century temple sites in the Bujang Valley of Kedah contained gold objects, which are believed to have originated from Borneo.

The oldest pictorial example of the type of boat used by early shippers of the Malay Archipelago is carved on a frieze at Borobudur, the world's largest Buddhist monument built in Java during the 8th and 9th centuries CE. Similar sailing vessels could have been those described by the Greeks as dominating the Indian Ocean seaborne trade in the 1st century CE.

Map: Gold-mining areas of Pahang

SUNGAI JELAI · Kuala Lipis · Tembeling · SUNGAI TEMBELING

SUNGAI KUANTAN · Kuantan

SUNGAI LEPAR · SUNGAI PAHANG

Pahang

Temerloh · SUNGAI PAHANG · Pekan

Gold mining-area

0 — 50 km

N

Inset: PENINSULAR MALAYSIA · South China Sea · Strait of Melaka

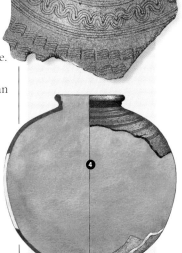

Trade patterns proved through pottery designs

Shards discovered on both Peninsular Malaysian coasts show design similarities— evidence that these settlements were linked by trade. Shards (1) and (2) were found at Kuala Selinsing, Perak, while shards (3) and (4) were part of the pottery cargo of the ancient boat found at Kuala Pontian, Pahang.

Trade routes and trade centres

The locations of many early Malaysian trade centres have yet to be identified. No doubt, many sites still exist and will eventually be discovered, although some may already have been destroyed by recent development without being recognized or recorded. It is probable that the expansion of trade during the first centuries CE, and the routes used to reach the main overseas markets in India and China, had some effect on the patterns of settlement which formed at this time.

The identification of ceramics by archaeological researchers provides viable evidence of early trade routes and centres. This student is sorting shards from the early kingdom site of Sungai Mas in the Bujang Valley of South Kedah.

The importance of transpeninsular routes

Trade was not a subject which merited much discussion in traditional Asian literature, which is overwhelmingly dedicated to religion. Trade centres can be detected by archaeological means. But, if trade routes are not specifically described in written sources, their locations can only be inferred.

Kedah, Malaysia's most important early trading kingdom situated in the Bujang Valley, was uniquely favoured by its location to become a trading centre in ancient times. Its location at the entrance to the Strait of Melaka, on the same latitude as southern India, meant that ships could sail due east or due west between these two points on opposite sides of the Bay of Bengal without danger of becoming lost. Previously, most voyaging in the Indian Ocean and the Mediterranean had depended on keeping land in sight at all times, although the Austronesians who colonized the Pacific had evolved navigational techniques which allowed them to cross great distances of open sea. Additional factors favouring the development of a trade centre at Kedah included the presence of rivers, in particular the Muda, which gave access by transpeninsular routes to the east coast. In the earliest period of long-distance maritime trade, the transpeninsular routes were necessary, as the route through the Strait of Melaka does not seem to have been in general use.

Other portage routes made use of the Peninsular river system, including that known as the Penarikan which linked the Muar and Pahang rivers. However, these portage routes were not very efficient. Accounts of the time taken to make the one-way journey vary from six days to three weeks. Only certain lightweight and non-breakable commodities could be transported this way. The existence of this route does not appear to have fostered the growth of any significant centres of trade or population.

West coast trade centres

Early west coast trade centres are few in number as they were overshadowed by Kedah. This entrepôt was so well known in India that even after it was subjugated by the empire of Srivijaya in the late 7th century CE, Indian sources continued to depict Kedah and not Palembang, South Sumatra, as the fulcrum of the kingdom.

The evolution of Kedah is linked closely with its position on a trade route. However, there were other contributing factors in its development. Shell midden sites in the region testify to a relatively dense population in late prehistoric times. Shell middens are also found in Sumatra, directly across the Strait of Melaka from Kedah, but no firm

The southern portage

This artist's adaption of the 16th-century map of Melaka District by the Portuguese cosmographer Emanuel Godinho de Eredia, shows the route linking the Muar River to the Pahang River via their tributaries, the Jempol and Serting rivers, and the portage marked as the Penarikan. Eredia's map is the oldest extant map of Melaka District and many of his place names are still in use today. In the upper right-hand corner, *caminho pera Pam*, is 'the route to Pahang', while *Por Panarican passao de Malaca a Pam en 6 dias de caminho* translates as 'By the "Penarikan" they travel from Melaka to Pahang in 6 days' journeying.' The word 'Penarikan' derives from the Malay *penarikan* meaning 'drawing or pulling', that is, dragging boats from one river to another. This transpeninsular route existed in the early 19th century, and was described by early British travellers.

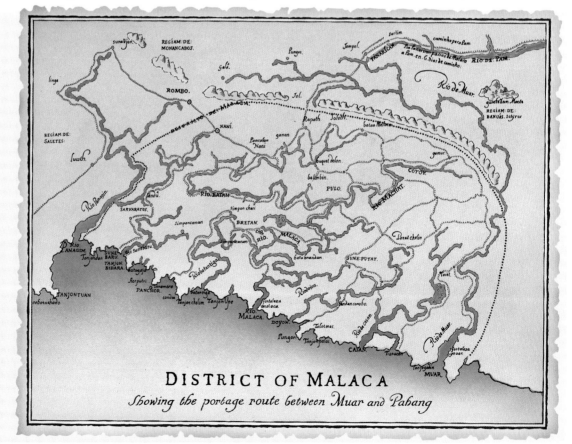

DISTRICT OF MALACA
Showing the portage route between Muar and Pahang

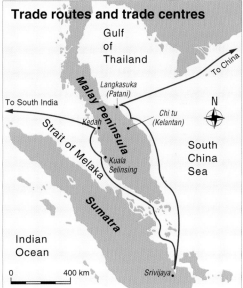

Trade routes and trade centres

Many of the locations of early Peninsular Malaysian trading centres are still being debated. However, abundant archaeological evidence has proved that the early entrepôt of Kedah was situated in the region of the Muda River estuary (1) dominated by Gunung Jerai, a prominent mariner's landmark. Kuala Selinsing, a lesser west coast port, was once by the river bank but its remains are now surrounded by dense mangrove forests (2). Narathiwat, a fishing village south of Patani in southern Thailand (3), was probably once part of the east coast kingdom of Langkasuka, while the Kelantan River (4) is believed to have been the route used to reach Chi tu, the 'Red Earth Land', probably located in the interior of Kelantan.

evidence of early trading ports in that area has yet been found. Thus, the development of early Kedah was the result of the interaction between trade in local resources and the opportunities provided by maritime commerce.

Archaeological research has yielded evidence of a trading port at Kuala Selinsing, Perak, believed to have existed between the 2nd century BCE and the 10th century CE. Finds include a stone seal, possibly from the 6th century CE, inscribed with Sri Visnuvarman, a name used by several Pallava rulers of South India; green-glazed Chinese porcelain of the Northern Song Dynasty (960–1126 CE); and a piece of 8th–9th century gold jewellery.

Kuala Selinsing does not seem to have been large or important as no references to it can be detected in ancient records. However, it possessed wealth as gold objects have been found there. Some of the inhabitants may have been goldsmiths, since the discoveries included small lumps of melted gold and scraps typical of those found around a goldsmith's workbench. Gold is not found in the vicinity, so this material had to be imported. Kuala Selinsing was probably representative of a second tier of sites, smaller than the major entrepôts such as Kedah. It is probably significant that the Kuala Selinsing area, like the Bujang Valley, is also characterized by the presence of shell middens.

East coast trade centres

On the east coast of the Peninsula, the kingdom of Langkasuka was a prominent port of call for Chinese Buddhist pilgrims voyaging westward. The route from China toward the Strait of Melaka more frequently led straight from South Vietnam to southeast Sumatra, then up to Kedah, but some ships took the less direct route to the northeast of the Malay Peninsula.

Langkasuka's precise location is unknown, but most scholars are in agreement that it was somewhere in the vicinity of Patani in present-day southern Thailand. In about 607 CE, a Chinese

embassy mentioned passing 'the mountains of the country of Langkasuka' just before reaching their goal of Chi tu. This latter kingdom, probably in inland Kelantan, had a highly organized court, espoused Buddhism, and possessed considerable wealth (see 'Chi tu: An inland kingdom').

Langkasuka became an important stopover for Buddhists from China on their way to India, which indicates that it was an important commercial centre. Just as Kedah is best known from Indian sources, Langkasuka is frequently mentioned in Chinese texts, such as the *Liang-shu*, which states that Langkasuka sent missions to China in 515 CE, and also in 523, 531 and 568, indicating a busy record of diplomatic activity. It also records that Langkasuka was founded as early as the 2nd century CE.

Langkasuka's importance was partly due to its location on a direct sailing route across the Gulf of Thailand. Like Kedah, it perhaps became significant because of its latitude, in this case almost due west of the southern tip of Indochina in present-day South Vietnam. Sailors rounding this cape could set a course due west and be confident of arriving at their destination. Another factor favouring the development of Langkasuka was its local forest produce, especially camphor of the highest quality, which was extremely prized in the Chinese market.

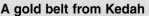

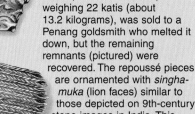

A gold belt from Kedah

These four pieces were all that remained of a gold belt pulled up by a boy while fishing in a tributary of the Sungai Merbok, Kedah, in 1914. The belt, weighing 22 katis (about 13.2 kilograms), was sold to a Penang goldsmith who melted it down, but the remaining remnants (pictured) were recovered. The repoussé pieces are ornamented with *singha-muka* (lion faces) similar to those depicted on 9th-century stone images in India. This pattern indicates that the belt was either crafted in India and imported to Kedah, or that a local Kedah goldsmith was familiar through trade contacts with this design.

Indian traders

Malaysia came into contact with India in late prehistoric times, but evidence remains vague. Indian literature provides proof that Indian traders visited early Malaysia, although it is still not sure whether they, or the more active seafaring Southeast Asian traders, were responsible for bringing Indian cultural ideas to Malaysia. This communication had important effects on early societies, particularly in Kedah which, as archaeological and historical evidence suggests, was always the main focus of Indian commercial interests in Malaysia.

Remnants of Hindu deities found at Site 4 in the Bujang Valley of Kedah include the head of a granite Nandi, the sacred bull (above top), and a terracotta Ganesa, the elephant-faced god (above). On the basis of associated finds, the sculptures have been dated from the 11th to the 13th century CE.

The evolution of South Asian culture and religion

In both South and Southeast Asia, trade and commerce were important activities in ancient times. The Indus Valley civilization, centred in present-day northwest India and Pakistan, carried on regular commercial dealings with the Sumerian city-states of the Tigris-Euphrates valley around 4,000 years ago. However, the highly evolved Indus Valley civilization left no records other than a few brief inscriptions which have not yet been deciphered. During the next thousand years, South Asia provides no evidence of playing an important part in Asian long-distance commerce.

During the late centuries BCE, South Asia witnessed the evolution of two world religions, Hinduism and Buddhism, into forms similar to those which still exist. Simultaneously, large kingdoms began to evolve. The first of these was established by the conqueror Asoka in the 3rd century BCE. Horrified by the slaughter which he

Built of laterite blocks, this Hindu temple at Site 50 in the Bujang Valley has been dated from the 12th to the 13th century CE.

had caused, he converted to Buddhism and played an important role in its spread. At the same time, the Sanskrit language and caste system were also being introduced to South India. The Aryans, originally invaders from central Asia speaking a language related to modern European tongues, were becoming assimilated with the local population. Their gods from the holy books, or Vedas, with names like Indra and Rudra, were becoming subordinate to other deities, especially Siva, who exemplified values and attributes similar to those known in India since at least the time of the Indus Valley civilization.

The appearance of Indian culture in Malaysia

The appearance of Indic inscriptions and religions in Malaysia and other parts of Southeast Asia a few centuries after these traits first appeared in South Asia led early scholars to conclude that the same process—imperialistic expansion through military conquest—was responsible in both regions. However, history and archaeology provide no support for this thesis, sometimes termed the *ksatria* theory after the warrior-king caste of Hinduism, and it has now been discarded.

Another theory on the adoption of South Asian cultural elements in Southeast Asia suggested that the *brahmana* caste was responsible. Early Southeast Asian texts mention Brahmans at various royal courts, and Southeast Asians were educated in ritual and other matters which belonged to the special sphere of the brahmana caste. The main objection to this theory is that Brahmans were considered to have lost their caste if they travelled across the sea. It is generally believed that most Brahmans mentioned in early Southeast Asia are more likely to have been Southeast Asians rather than Indians.

The third group considered as possible agents of the introduction of Indic traits are the *vaisya*, the caste of artisans and traders. The main obstacle to the acceptance of this theory is that the traders were unlikely to have been sufficiently cognisant of the sacred lore of the Brahmans to have been able to introduce it to Southeast Asia.

In current opinion, it is now considered most likely that the major group responsible for the introduction of South Asian cultural traits to Southeast Asia were the Southeast Asian merchants themselves. Trade between South and Southeast Asia was a two-way affair, and Southeast Asians were active and expert seafarers.

However, if the merchants of South Asia were not the main party responsible for cultural evolution in Southeast Asia, they were certainly present in

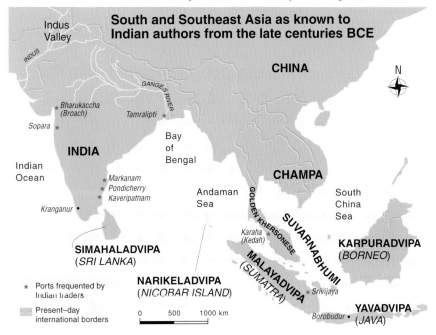

South and Southeast Asia as known to Indian authors from the late centuries BCE

Indus Valley

INDUS

Bharukaccha (Broach)

Sopara

GANGES RIVER

Tamralipti

CHINA

N

INDIA

Bay of Bengal

Indian Ocean

Markanam

Pondicherry

Kaveripatnam

Kranganur

Andaman Sea

GOLDEN KHERSONESE

Karaha (Kedah)

CHAMPA

South China Sea

SUVARNABHUMI

KARPURADVIPA (BORNEO)

SIMAHALADVIPA (SRI LANKA)

MALAYADVIPA (SUMATRA)

Srivijaya

NARIKELADVIPA (NICOBAR ISLAND)

★ Ports frequented by Indian traders

Present-day international borders

0   500   1000 km

Borobudur •

YAVADVIPA (JAVA)

Indian-influenced architecture and artefact finds in Kedah

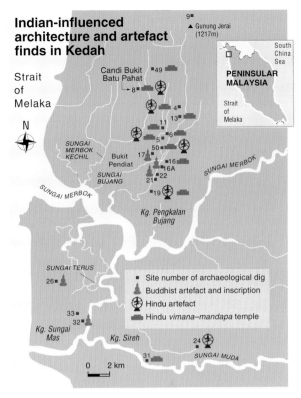

Strait of Melaka

PENINSULAR MALAYSIA
Strait of Melaka
South China Sea

- ■ Site number of archaeological dig
- 🔔 Buddhist artefact and inscription
- ⊕ Hindu artefact
- ▦ Hindu *vimana–mandapa* temple

0 2 km

early Malaysia. Unfortunately, archaeological evidence can only confirm that trade between Malaysia and India took place in the early part of the first millennium CE, but it does not indicate whether the traders were Indians or Malaysians. In the absence of firm information, such basic matters as the identities of the active parties, their motivations and the specific geographical locations involved still cannot be confirmed.

The best evidence that Indian traders visited early Malaysia comes from Indian literature, in Sanskrit verse or Tamil court poetry. Southeast Asia appears in such genres as collections of fairy tales and Buddhist texts. In general, these tales portray Southeast Asia as a land of promise where ambitious traders might make their fortunes.

Kedah as the focus of Indian commerce

Specific names of places in Southeast Asia rarely appear in this early literature, and in many cases they seem to be nicknames or literary devices rather than real place names. One of the names which has a closer relationship to geography than most is Kataha, believed to refer to the South Kedah region known as the Bujang Valley.

Documentary and archaeological evidence points to Kedah as the pivot of Indian commercial interests in Malaysia. Although it is difficult to prove, it is likely that many Indian merchants did visit Kedah during protohistoric times, and that some of them resided there for a period of time. Judging from later sources, for instance, accounts of trading communities in Melaka, Indian merchants resident in Kedah would have settled in their own kampong or ward within the trading settlement. The head of the foreign settlement negotiated with the local authority regarding such matters as trade

regulations and legal matters.

In South Asia, early sources mention numerous ports (see map) as points of departure for the Golden Khersonese (the Malay Peninsula) and Suvarnabhumi or 'Land of Gold' (probably the Malay Peninsula and the Malay Archipelago). Thus, no particular region of South Asia held a monopoly over trade with Malaysia. Conversely, it is probable that Malaysian traders also visited a wide range of trading centres in South Asia. However, South India, by virtue of its location on almost the same latitude as Kedah, was probably the most common point of departure and arrival for shipping crossing the Bay of Bengal to Malaysia.

South Indian merchant guilds began to play an important role in trade with Southeast Asia in the 9th century CE. In the 11th century CE, after the South Indian Cola Dynasty conquered Kedah and the rest of Srivijaya, an inscription was set up in Sumatra by one of them, the Tisaiyayirattu-Ainnurruvar. These guilds resembled later European East India companies. In addition to trade, they also conducted diplomacy, had substantial armed forces, and operated under royal charters. However, their appearance came at a rather late stage, and with the Muslim conquest of India and the rise of Chinese trade and settlement in Southeast Asia, their prominence was short-lived.

Little is known of early Indian shipbuilding. No artistic portrayals of the nature of the ships depicted on Borobudur in Java have been found in India. Indirect evidence, such as the peopling of Madagascar by Austronesians rather than South Asians, suggests that early Indian merchants travelled more often in Southeast Asian ships than in craft made in India.

South Indian influences

Discovered in the river bed near Site 4 in Kedah's Bujang Valley, this roof of a miniature bronze shrine (above) bears a striking resemblance to the wagon roof of a temple in Mahabalipuram, South India (above top). Similarities include the horseshoe-shaped gable window at each end of the roof, and the 'flowerpot' on the roof, although the shrine has only one of the latter compared to many on the Indian temple roof. Differences include the figure of a cross-legged *rishi*—suggestive of the Shaivite cult—at each corner of the shrine roof, which does not appear on the Indian temple. The openwork roof of the shrine could be a local Kedah adaptation modelled on temples which had roofs of perishable materials. The bronze shrine is believed to date from the 6th to the 7th century CE.

'Raja Bersiong's flagstaff'

Found at Site 24 beside the Muda River in South Kedah, this large sandstone object was known to the local inhabitants as the flagstaff of Raja Bersiong, a legendary ruler. Archaeologists have suggested that it could have been a stand for an image of a deity. Indian influences are apparent in the design of the cruciform depression on the top (top right) which bears a striking resemblance to the cruciform *mandapa* (porch) of a 10th-century temple (lower right) at Bhuvanesvara in Orissa, India.

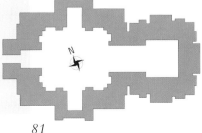

Chinese traders and pilgrims

Before the 10th century CE, the only known Chinese who came to what is now Malaysia were either officials or religious pilgrims en route to or from India. The burden of early Chinese–Malay communication was almost certainly borne by Malay diplomatic representatives to China who were also involved in commercial exchange. Some Southeast Asian sailors and traders, possibly including Malays, also began to visit China by the 5th century CE.

The earliest Buddhist pilgrim to leave an account of a journey passing through Malaysian waters was Faxian who travelled to India from China overland through Central Asia, returning by sea in the early 5th century CE. His voyage (see above) began in Sri Lanka. The boat was blown north to the Andamans by a cyclone, then it sailed through the Melaka Strait to Java or Borneo to await the change of monsoon before returning to China.

This terracotta image of a mother and child, identified as the Buddhist goddess Hariti, was discovered in 1980 by villagers digging an irrigation channel at Sungai Mas, Kedah. Yiqing, the Buddhist monk who visited Kedah in the 7th century CE, reports that Hariti worship was very popular in India. Measuring 22.5 centimetres in height, the Sungai Mas Hariti dates from the 7th to 9th centuries and is the only known Malaysian or Sumatran example in existence.

Dating from the Song/Yuan dynasty periods (960–1368 CE), this rare Qingbai ceramic vessel was unearthed at Sungai Mas in 1985. Archaeologists use ceramics to date sites and prove the existence of international traders.

The Chinese tributary system

Early relations were dictated by Chinese laws against unauthorized contact between Chinese and foreigners. From the Han Dynasty (206 BCE) until the Northern Song Dynasty (960–1126 CE), no Chinese could leave China without official permission, nor could foreigners travel freely within the country. Only religious and diplomatic contacts were permitted, and foreign merchants were only admitted to certain coastal areas.

According to official ideology, commerce was a lowly occupation. On the other hand, contact with foreigners was necessary as they provided the exotic commodities which were desired by the nobility. These included products from India and southwestern Asia, as well as from nearby Southeast Asia, which supplied pearls, kingfisher feathers, tortoiseshell, incense and fragrant woods.

The Imperial court was, however, keen to attract diplomatic envoys. According to Chinese belief, a virtuous emperor projected a kind of charisma which attracted distant countries to send representatives to present tribute and declare loyalty to the ruler. If many foreign countries sent such envoys, this would be a sign to the Chinese people that the ruler was indeed virtuous, thus fulfilling traditional expectations. As envoys were expected to bring tribute, emperors could acquire rare and precious commodities from foreign lands without the need to engage in the degrading activity of trading for them.

The Chinese offered two sorts of incentives to attract foreigners to make the journey to China: diplomatic recognition and 'gifts'—physical tokens of the emperor's 'regard' for foreigners who were submissive to him. In this way, foreign rulers obtained increased prestige within their own domains because the emperor of China recognized them as rightful kings. There is evidence that Southeast Asian rulers of the protohistoric period considered this recognition a useful tool in their internal contests for power. For example, in 430 CE, the ruler of He le dan, probably a kingdom in Java, sent a mission with tribute seeking such marks of Chinese approval.

The 'gifts' given to the foreign rulers were not trifling. It was customary to give gifts of slightly more than equivalent value in order to compensate visitors for the difficult voyage to China. This practice provided a material incentive for foreign rulers to send large quantities of tribute, secure in the knowledge that they would receive commodities of even greater value in return. This system of tributary relations was established over 2,000 years ago as a means of regulating relations with the troublesome nomadic groups along China's northern border.

In search of Southeast Asian exotica

The sea route brought to China many sought-after commodities. A source pertaining to the Han Dynasty, 2,000 years ago, states that officials from the Department of Eunuchs went in 'barbarian' (not Chinese) ships to buy pearls, gems and other rare items. This source mentions some places which may have been in what is now Malaysia, but none has been positively identified.

The Wubeizhi Chart

Depicting part of the east coast of the Malay Peninsula, this Chinese map is part of the Wubeizhi Chart which was published in the 1600s, but based on much older material. Some place names are Chinese descriptions, while others are transcriptions or translations of Malay names. Other inscriptions include sailing directions and names of local produce. Those which have been identified are as follows:

1. Terengganu (*Deng ga le*)
2. Kelantan estuary (*Ge lan dan kong*)
3. 'Produces incense wood' (*Chu Jiang xiang*)
4. Telubin (formerly Sai) estuary (*Sai gong*)
5. 'Produces incense wood' (*Chu Jiang xiang*)
6. Patani River (*Kun ha di*)
7. Langkasuka (*Long sai ga ti*)
8. Songkla (*Sun gu na*)
9. Pulau Bidong Laut (*Tu yuan su*)
10. Pulau Lang Tengah (*Shi shan*) 'Stone Mountain'(?)
11. Pulau Rhu (*Kun ha di (?)*)
12. Cat and Rat Island (*Mao shu xu*) (Koh Mu and Koh Gnu)
13. Pulau Redang (*Jiu yuan (?)*)
14. Pulau Perhentian Besar (*Yang xu*) 'Goat Island'(?)
15. Pulau Perhentian Kechil (*San jiu su (?)*)
16. Pulau Susu Darah (*Yan tun xu*) Beacon Island (?)
17. Sailing directions described a boat passing (out from?) a mountain
18. Unknown *Qiao li ma (?)*

In 220 CE, China entered a period of division when three main kingdoms, the Wu, Wei and Shu, contested for power. The Wu controlled the south coast, but were cut off by the other two from the Silk Road to the west. From 245 CE to 250 CE, the Wu sent envoys to a kingdom known as Funan, located in South Vietnam. Their original report has been lost, but fragments preserved in other sources contain the first detailed Chinese information about Southeast Asia.

In 581 CE, China was reunited under the Sui Dynasty (581–617 CE), and in 607 CE a new emperor sent envoys to establish relations with foreign countries. They passed Langkasuka, probably in Patani, now part of Thailand, and reached Chi tu, 'Red Earth Land' (see 'Chi tu: An inland kingdom'), where they proceeded to the capital of the kingdom located 30 days inland. Here, elaborate diplomatic rituals, including exchanges of rich presents took place. This capital may have been that mentioned in a 5th-century inscription from Kedah, or another kingdom of the same name on the east coast. People ate rice with fish, tortoise, pork, beef and mutton, and drank wine made from sugar cane.

Early Chinese visitors

For the early envoys, Southeast Asia was of less interest for its own attractions than as a region lying on the route to India. In 413 CE, the Chinese monk Faxian sailed from India to a place in Southeast Asia, the identity of which is so far undetermined but may have been in Java or Borneo. He stayed there for five months, then sailed to China. Both his voyages were undertaken in large merchant ships, neither of them Chinese. The passengers and crew of the ship which took him to China were mainly non-Buddhists, and apparently not Chinese.

The next place on the Peninsula to enter history is known by the Chinese transcription as Pan-pan. The Chinese first learned of its existence during the Sui Dynasty, and like Chi tu, it may have been in the Kelantan or Terengganu area. In 530 CE, 535 CE and between 666 CE and 669 CE, Pan-pan sent tribute to China, including pearls and perfume.

The most important Chinese description of protohistoric Malaysia was written by the Buddhist monk Yiqing who sailed from China to Srivijaya in southeast Sumatra in 671 CE. He stayed there for six months studying Sanskrit grammar, before sailing on to Malayu, also in southeast Sumatra, and then to Kedah, whence his ship voyaged across the Bay of Bengal to India.

Kedah had already appeared in a Chinese record in 638 CE, when it sent an ambassador to China, and it had already been an important trading centre for 200 years by the time it opened diplomatic relations with China. In 671 CE, during Yiqing's stay, Kedah was still an independent kingdom. Yiqing clearly stated that his voyages were all undertaken in ships belonging to Malay kings, underlining the active role of Malays in the commerce of this period. On his return voyage in 685 CE, Yiqing again stopped over in Kedah and reported that the port was then part of the Empire of Srivijaya.

Yiqing also mentions other monks who followed the same itinerary, one of whom died in Kedah. However, despite the importance of Kedah as a port of call for Chinese pilgrims en route to India, its name does not appear in the official history sources of the Tang Dynasty (618–906 CE). This suggests that Kedah was not visited by any other Chinese travellers. The golden age of Chinese commerce in Southeast Asia had yet to dawn. Some shards of late Tang porcelain have been found in Kedah, but they must have been brought there by other traders, possibly by local people.

During the period up to the 10th century CE few Chinese other than religious pilgrims visited Southeast Asia, and Chinese influence on the region was minimal. Only in the 12th century did this situation begin to change.

A green stone Buddha head discovered at Sungai Mas has lead historians to speculate that this site could have been where the Chinese pilgrim Yiqing stayed during his 7th-century sojourn in Kedah.

Archaeological researchers unearth ceramic shards from the foundations of architectural remains discovered at Sungai Mas, Kedah. This site, the oldest in the Bujang Valley, is believed to have been a Buddhist port settlement dating from the 5th century CE.

Bearing a moulded floral design, these Long juan celadon shards found in South Kedah originated from China during the Northern Song Dynasty (960–1126 CE).

The Xingjiao Pagoda in Xian was where Yiqing, the first known Chinese visitor to the Malay Peninsula, worked compiling his reports on his return to China.

Early Muslim traders

The expansion of early international commerce, which attracted Indian, Chinese and Southeast Asian trade to the Malay World, coincided with the growth of Muslim empires in the Middle East and greater use of land and sea routes linking the Arab heartlands with India and China. The extension of Muslim trading networks into the Malay Archipelago helped lay the basis for the spread of Islam.

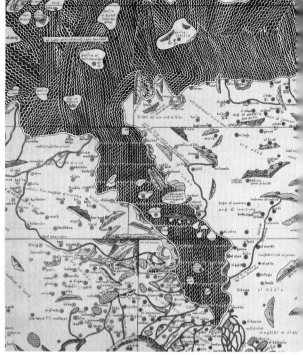

Drawn by the Arab prince Idrisi in 1154 CE, 'The Map of the World' consisted of 70 separate sections. The Middle East, shown above, is portrayed in the Arab cartographical manner which places south at the top of the map, making it appear upside down in Western tradition. Many geographical features and place names are discernible on this map, including the early Persian port of Siraf, the Hadhramaut, Oman, Aden and Mecca.

Chinese porcelain with Islamic designs became popular trade items throughout Southeast Asian Muslim communities during the Ming Dynasty (1369–1644).

The expansion of Muslim trade

From the late 7th century CE, the expansion of Islam in the Arab heartlands encouraged political centralization and the rise of urban centres at key points on the major trade routes. There were two channels for the transcontinental trade of Asia; one, entirely seaborne, went via the Red Sea, while a second combined a sea, river and overland journey from the Persian Gulf through Iraq and Syria. In 762 CE, the newly established Abbasid Caliphate moved its capital to Baghdad on the Tigris River. With both routes then under Abbasid authority, conditions were highly favourable for the expansion of commerce with the Chinese. Indeed, al-Mansur, the caliph who founded Baghdad, reportedly remarked: 'This is the Tigris. There is no obstacle between us and China; everything on the sea can come to us on it.'

Meanwhile, developments in China also favoured the growth of trade with the Middle East. The administrative unification and economic achievements of the Tang Dynasty (618–906 CE) encouraged links with foreign nations as well as territorial expansion westwards. Enhanced consumer demand for luxury items made the all-sea route to India and China increasingly attractive. The safety of the overland caravan routes also improved, leading to further expansion of the connections between China and the Arab and Persian areas. Chinese sources indicate that this trade peaked in the mid-8th century, declined with the unsettled conditions at the end of the Tang period, revived in the 10th century under the Song Dynasty (960-1279 CE), to continue into the Ming period (1369–1644).

The growing use of the maritime route to China brought Arab and Persian traders to Southeast Asia. With their navigational technology and commercial skills, they were well equipped to join Malay shippers as carriers of international cargoes between India and China. It has been suggested that the incorporation of Arab–Persian words into Malay, such as *nakhoda* (captain), *bandar* (port) and *syahbandar* (port official), may date from these times.

Ports known to Muslim traders

Until the 11th century, Arabic texts regarding the Malaysian region are largely composed of colourful sailors' tales or purportedly authentic reports that were, in fact. copied from earlier writings. Historians reconstructing early trade routes have had to exercise extreme caution when making use of such records. Nonetheless, it is apparent that certain places in the Malay World were well known to Arab traders. The most prominent of these was Zabaj, which has been identified with Srivijaya, believed to have been located in South Sumatra. Another frequently mentioned toponym is Kalah, which was probably located on the west coast of the Malay Peninsula. Although the exact location of Kalah remains a matter for debate, Arab sources specifically mention that tin was available there as well as jungle products. This reference to tin supports arguments identifying Kalah as Kedah, especially since other historical evidence has shown that Kedah was a major exchange and transshipment port for shipping between the Malay Peninsula and India. The view that Kedah was part of a Muslim trading network has been strengthened by the discovery in the state of two coins from the Abbasid Caliphate, one of

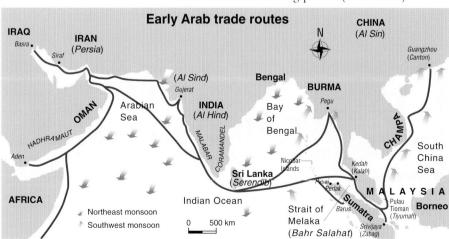

Early Arab trade routes

IRAQ
Basra
IRAN (Persia)
Siraf
OMAN
HADHRAMAUT
Aden
AFRICA
Arabian Sea
(Al Sind)
Gujerat
INDIA (Al Hind)
MALABAR
COROMANDEL
Sri Lanka (Serendib)
Indian Ocean
Bengal
Bay of Bengal
BURMA
Pegu
Nicobar Islands
Kedah (Kalah)
Pasai
Perlak
Barus
Sumatra
Srivijaya (Zabag)
Strait of Melaka (Bahr Salahat)
CHAMPA
CHINA (Al Sin)
Guangzhou (Canton)
South China Sea
MALAYSIA
Pulau Tioman (Tiyumah)
Borneo
N

 Northeast monsoon
 Southwest monsoon

0   500 km

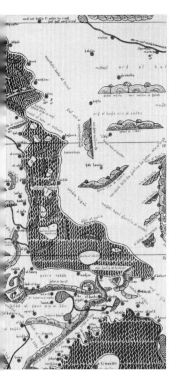

which is dated AH 234 (848 CE).

Another place which was well known to Arab sailors was Tiyumah, believed to be Pulau Tioman, in the South China Sea. Like Kalah, Tiyumah acted as a stapling port and a source of fresh water for ships sailing to China. In the 10th century, an Arab text also mentions 'Panhang' (Pahang). These place names provide a glimpse of the extensive commercial world in which early Muslim traders operated.

It is evident that the major maritime route followed by early Arab and Persian shipping went from Sri Lanka via the Nicobar Islands to Kedah, and then round the southern tip of the Malay Peninsula to the island of Tioman and north to China. By the 9th century CE, Muslim traders were apparently acquainted with the west coast of the Malay Peninsula as they sailed from Pegu, in present-day Myanmar, south to the Perak River. In these early stages, Malaysia was regarded primarily as a transitional area on the route to China, rather than a source of local products. However, by the 10th century, commerce with Malay areas was becoming more significant, with the port Kalah familiar to Arab, Persian and Indian traders. At times when the trading climate in southern China was unfavourable, as at the end of the Tang period, Kalah may have become the terminal point for Muslim shipping.

Declining Arab trade

Up to the 10th century, and even later, Arab ships and merchants sailed to China and back, stopping at intermediate ports along the way. However, this was an expensive voyage, and the absence of Malay place names in Arab texts from the 12th and 13th centuries suggests that Arab traders may have found it more profitable to focus their activities west of the Bay of Bengal. Another factor contributing to the decline of Arab shipping to Southeast Asia may have been instability in the Persian Gulf area as the control of the Abbasid Caliphate declined. The rise of the Fatamid Dynasty in Egypt in the latter part of the

Remnants of Middle Eastern glassware, such as this goblet stem, have been found at Kedah's Bujang Valley.

10th century brought about a commercial revival, but it appears that merchants working from the Red Sea region concentrated on the Indian and Sri Lankan coasts and rarely made excursions beyond South Asia. Maritime links between India and the Malay Peninsula were maintained by Indian and Southeast Asian traders.

The rise of Indian Muslim traders

Around this period, Muslim trading based in India became more prominent. Arab merchants had been established in Sind (present-day Pakistan) since the 8th century, and merchants from Siraf (Persia), and Oman and Hadhramaut (Arabian Peninsula) had settled on the west coast of India. Gujerat came under Muslim rule in 1287 and significant Muslim trading communities developed in Malabar, Coromandel and Bengal. From the 13th century, the commercial presence of Muslim Indians in the Malay regions was critical in introducing local societies to Islam. In 1292, Marco Polo mentions Muslims in Perlak, North Sumatra, and at nearby Pasai a royal gravestone dated 697 AH (1297) has been found.

Meanwhile, in China, trade with Persia and Central Asia had led to the growth of Sino-Muslim (Hui) coastal communities, notably at Canton (Guangzhou). From the 12th century, the closing of overland routes across Central Asia spurred the Hui communities to expand their ocean-going trade activities in Southeast Asia and Chinese Muslim settlements developed in Southeast Asia. Appropriately, when the Ming emperor sent an imperial fleet through the region in the early 15th century, he chose a Chinese Muslim, Zhenghe (Cheng Ho) (1371–1435), as his emissary.

Thus, though the sources are shadowy, it is nevertheless possible to reconstruct the growing involvement of Muslim traders from various cultures in the early Malay World. The wide-reaching commercial networks they established, and the knowledge of Islamic culture they helped convey are important factors when explaining the later appeal and popularity of the Muslim faith.

Evidence of West Asian trade in South Kedah

The whereabouts of the entrepôt known to the Arabs as Kalah has been debated for decades. However, based on archaeological research and geographical and historical evidence, current opinion is that it was located in South Kedah. At Sungai Mas, believed to be the earliest location of the Bujang Valley port kingdom, various artefacts have been found which originated from West Asia. These include shards (top and middle) of Islamic glazed pottery known as sgraffiate ware, typical of Iraqi and Persian Gulf ceramics of the 9th and 10th centuries CE, as well as glassware (right) of Middle Eastern origin.

This artist's impression is of Sinbad the Sailor, the legendary Arab adventurer of *The Thousand and One Nights*. He is believed to have been a composite of early Arab traders who voyaged to Southeast Asia in the 13th century.

Southeast Asian traders

For at least two millennia, Southeast Asian products have been sought-after commodities in the international trade arena. Spices from the Malay World reached Europe in the 1st century CE, and Malay ships were the dominant means of transport in the Indian Ocean during the early days of long-distance maritime trade. The strategic location of Southeast Asia at the nexus of the monsoons straddling the major East–West maritime trade route greatly contributed to its high trade profile.

This engraving by T. and W. Daniell (1820) shows a Malay prau passing Pedra Branca, a notorious landmark near the southern entrance to the Melaka Strait.

Still covered in barnacles from half a millennium spent under water, these Thai ceramics are part of the trade cargo of the 'Nanyang' shipwreck discovered off the coast of Pahang in 1995. The 14th-century vessel is a Chinese junk design with Southeast Asian features and was engaged in the ceramic trade between Thailand and Java.

From product collectors to international traders

Minor exchanges of forest and sea products probably took place in Malaysia during the Mesolithic period, perhaps from as early as 8,000 years ago. However, the first real evidence in Malaysia of exchange contacts with Southeast Asia emerged during Neolithic times, about 4,500 years ago. Around this time there was a significant increase in overland exchanges as evidenced by finds in Peninsular Malaysia of trade products from central and northeastern Thailand. Long-distance sea trade began during the Metal Age (500 BCE–200 CE) as shown by finds in Malaysia of Vietnamese and Cambodian bronzeware, as well as Indian and West Asian beads. With the increase in trade in Southeast Asia from about the 1st century CE, it is possible that long-distance sailors from Southeast Asia may have taken goods as far as India and Africa.

The rise of early kingdoms in Southeast Asia saw a subsequent rise in the volume of trade conducted in the region. Product collectors, who sometimes acted as primary traders, dealt in the raw products, while secondary traders acted as the middlemen between them and the tertiary traders who specialized in imports and exports, and conveyed external demand to the secondary traders.

At the ports, tertiary traders may have been in contact with Indian traders as early as 1,200 years ago as Indian beads have been discovered at the port site of Kuala Selinsing in Perak.

Early reports of Southeast Asian traders

From about the 5th century CE, local tertiary traders were trading with transient Southeast Asian and other overseas traders who were either private entrepreneurs or government-sponsored merchants on trading or tribute missions. Chinese texts frequently designate the Southeast Asian traders as Kun lun, which the geographer/historian Paul Wheatley identifies as 'peoples ranging from Malays around the coasts of the Peninsula to Chams along the shores of Indo-China'. The Kun lun are also believed to be the same people as the earlier seafarers who the Chinese had reported as controlling the maritime trade routes of the South China Sea. These Malay traders were also reported as reaching seaports in northwestern India. Arabic sources refer to the oceanic people who built and crewed the seagoing vessels engaged in international trade as Qumr.

More evidence of early Southeast Asian involvement in international trade comes from a 6th-century Greek account which mentions that Southeast Asian traders, probably Malays, exchanged their goods with Persians in Sri Lanka. The Chinese in 5th-century accounts called the Persians Bo se. However, they also gave this title to the Malays. Some historians believe that the early Persian traders only went as far as Sri Lanka and that their goods were then taken by Southeast Asian traders to their home ports.

By the 7th century CE, traders at Malaysian port kingdoms became involved in transient trade, visiting other ports to trade either as private entrepreneurs or on government-sponsored missions. The kingdom of Chi tu, probably in Kelantan (see 'Chi tu: An inland kingdom'), was involved in tribute missions. When the ruler's son accompanied a returning Chinese embassy to China in 607 CE, he took with him local products, including golden crowns and camphor.

Malaysia's oldest boat

The hull remains of an ancient boat (top left and right), radiocarbon dated to 60–293 CE, were discovered near Kuala Pontian in 1926. Pottery fragments in the boat, which date to about 200 CE, could have been trade cargo. The hull features planking fastened by wooden dowels and twine held together by ribs lashed to carved comb cleats (top right). The original remains, and a reconstruction measuring 20.04 metres in length (bottom left and right), are on display at the Pahang State Museum, Pekan.

The lure of rainforest exotica

The Chinese regarded Malaysia as a source of 'the strange and the precious'. Luxury goods coveted by the Chinese royal courts from the Nanhai (South Seas) included spices, such as nutmegs and cloves from Maluku (the Moluccas) and pepper from Java. Perfumed woods used for incense and as aromatics were in huge demand in China and many of these were sourced from the Malay Peninsula, including gharuwood from Langkasuka and camphor from Chi tu. The Nanhai was also a source of drugs, many of which were found in the rainforests of Malaysia, including the famed panacea, rhinoceros horn. Other local products brought to China by Southeast Asian traders included woven mats which were probably made in Malaysia from pandanus leaves, as they still are today.

During the Srivijayan period, trading activities were either in the hands of private entrepreneurs or were sponsored by kingdoms. Srivijayan traders had their own ships, and Yiqing, the famous 7th-century Chinese pilgrim who made a return journey from China to India via Malaysia, stopping over in Kedah, apparently used Srivijayan shipping.

Although the bulk of early trade between Malaysia and China was in the form of tribute missions, private Srivijayan entrepreneurs were given preferential treatment at Chinese ports in view of the special relationship that existed between Srivijaya and China. Their presence at Malay port kingdoms can be glimpsed from the Telaga Batu inscription from Palembang, dated 684 CE, which mentions a class of traders, known as *vaniaga,* who were probably the Srivijayan entrepreneurs.

Rulers and court officials were directly involved in trade as they sent their ships laden with goods to various ports to trade. The ships' captains, known as *nakhoda*, became the representatives of the shipowners in these trading ventures.

At the port kingdom site of the Bujang Valley in South Kedah, remains of trade products, such as Chinese ceramics, West Asian glass and ceramics, as well as Indian beads have been found. The shipment of these goods was once presumed to be mainly in the hands of Indian traders, but from current research and documentary and archaeological evidence it is now believed that Southeast Asians, particularly Malay traders, played a much larger role than was previously thought in the early international trade arena.

Originally published in the *Atlas Historique* (1824–44), this watercolour by Alphonse Pellion entitled 'Kora-kora from Gebe, North Moluccas, 1818', depicts an encounter with native shipping. These types of boats are capable of long-distance sea travel and were used to convey spices, especially nutmeg and cloves, to the entrepôts of Southeast Asia. About 2,000 years ago, Graeco-Roman sources report great trading ships coming across the Indian Ocean from the East carrying cargoes of spices. Evidence that these ships may have originated from Southeast Asia comes from reports of cloves reaching Roman markets by 70 CE. This commodity may have reached Mesopotamia as early as 1700 BCE, and has been confirmed in China 2,000 years ago.

Trade products of Southeast Asia
Some of the most popular local products traded by Southeast Asians include the following:

1. Gharuwood: an aromatic wood used for incense.
2. Camphor: an aromatic wood crystal used medicinally.
3. Kingfisher feathers: used for Chinese hair ornaments.
4. Tortoiseshell: hawksbill turtle shell used for ornaments.
5. Ivory: elephants' tusks used for carved ornaments.
6. Gold crowns: used as tribute to the Chinese court.
7. Nutmeg: aromatic seed used as a spice.
8. Dragon's blood: medicinal resin from a palm fruit.
9. Dammar: a tree resin used in lacquer and varnish.
10. Civet: a glandular secretion from civets used as perfume.
11. Cloves: dried unopened buds used as a spice.
12. Pandanus mats: woven mats from pandanus fibres.
13. Pepper: berry from a vine used as a meat preservative.
14. Rhinoceros horn: used in powdered form as a panacea.
15. Sandalwood: an evergreen wood used for incense.

Forms of money

Product exchanges probably dominated the early economy of Malaysia. However, as societies grew more sophisticated, certain objects became more valuable than others, which ultimately led to the creation of primitive money. Long before the first coins came into use in Malaysia, a diverse variety of objects were used for currency as well as for barter. These not only included precious metals such as gold and tin, but also cowrie shells, beads, ceramics and tin ingots cast in the shape of animals and mountains.

This Kenyah chieftain's skullcap is surmounted by a rhinoceros hornbill's head, beak and casque. Cowrie shells are sewn on the cap in the manner of beadwork. Although the Kenyah live in the interior of Sarawak, cowrie shells would have been obtained through barter trade with the coastal populations.

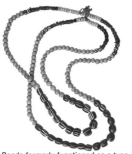

Beads formerly functioned as a type of currency in Borneo, and are much prized by Sarawak's indigenous people, including the Kelabit, Lun Bawang, Kenyah, Kayan and Bidayuh. Above all, the Kelabit value ancient bluish glass and stone beads, some of which are similar to beads produced in Damascus about 1000 BCE.

Currency from the sea

Cowrie shells (*Cypraea moneta*) were the earliest form of currency in Malaysia. These off-white, glossy seashells, measuring about 2 centimetres in length, have been popular as charms, ornaments and currency since prehistoric times. They are still used as currency in the remote coastal areas of the Philippines, on some Pacific Islands and along the coasts of Africa. Cowrie shells which have been found in archaeological sites in Kedah, dating from the 7th to the 13th centuries CE, have been identified as originating from the Maldive Islands of the Indian Ocean and from the coastal areas of Borneo. Despite the labour involved in boring, polishing and threading these shells, their intrinsic value is minute. Perhaps it was their natural beauty which originally made them so readily acceptable. In Sarawak, cowrie shells are also used to decorate heirloom clothing such as ceremonial vests and caps.

Beads used for barter

Glass or stone beads were another means of storing and displaying wealth, and continue to be valued by many ethnic communities in Sarawak and Sabah. Some of these are very old and were probably brought into the country over many centuries by Arab, Indian and Southeast Asian traders. Today, the beads are usually worn by women on ceremonial and festive occasions as an indication of social status and wealth. They are also prized for their mystical qualities. Beads were also used as a type of currency in exchange for goods, and have been found in many archaeological sites throughout Malaysia.

A large percentage of beads from Kuala Selinsing in Perak, and the Bujang Valley of Kedah, comprise dark red glass beads known as *mutisalah*, which are believed to have originated from southern India. These trade beads have been found throughout Southeast Asia. Other semiprecious stone beads found at both these sites include agates, carnelians, and rock crystals.

Miniature bronze cannons, often cast in the likeness of animals, such as this rare oxen-shaped specimen, were formerly used as currency and as wedding presents in Sarawak and Brunei. The art of brass-making was introduced to Brunei by craftsmen from Terengganu.

Beads found in graves and at archaeological sites are difficult to date. However, many scholars have suggested that some of these may have originated from Egypt, Greece, other Middle Eastern countries and India. Since there is an enormous variety of beads, particularly in Sarawak and Sabah where they are so prized, their value varies from one ethnic group to another. The most expensive are those known as *lukut sekala*. A century ago, one of these beads was worth the price of an adult slave, or half the price of a longhouse.

Heirloom 'dragon' jars

Glazed stoneware storage jars which have long been prized heirlooms and symbols of wealth in Sarawak and Sabah are known to the Iban, Melanau and Kelabit as *gusi* or *guchi*, or as *tempayan*, the Malay word.

They are also referred to as 'Song jars', as the earliest Bornean examples were manufactured in China during the 10th–13th century Song Dynasty. They are ovoid in shape with a short neck, sloping shoulders and lug handles to hold fibre or rope to facilitate carrying and to tie on the lids. The recurrent decorations on these vessels are dragons and floral scrolls. The jars are the subject of many legends which are intimately connected with the spiritual life of their owners. It is believed that if drinking water or rice are kept in the jars, the family will not die of thirst or hunger as the jars will keep replenishing themselves. The water stored in such jars is also believed to cure illness.

Miniature cannons and brass gongs

Before the advent of coins, miniature brass cannons were used as currency in areas of Borneo under the rule of the Brunei Sultanate, where the art of

Tin animal money

Believed to be first used by the royal courts of Peninsular Malaysia in the 15th century, these solid tin objects in the shape of animals were initially used as gifts to royalty and for magical rites associated with the opening up of new tin mines. Later they evolved into a form of currency and were used in Perak, Selangor and Negeri Sembilan. Tortoises, elephants, fish, crickets, beetles and other insects were depicted, but the most common shape for 'animal money' was the crocodile. This reptile features in many Malay legends and is considered particularly auspicious by magicians.

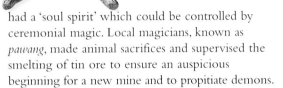

metal-casting was known from at least as early as the 16th century. These decorative cannons were greatly valued for bartering, payment of fines against the community, wedding gifts and as status symbols. Full-sized cannons were also prized and were used to fire salutes during weddings, births and visits by important people, and to drive away evil spirits. With the introduction of money in Borneo, cannons fell into disuse and many were melted down during World War II.

Chinese brass gongs were also valued currency in the hinterland of Borneo. The value of the brass object was calculated by the weight of the metal.

Metals used as exchange

In the early days of the Melaka Sultanate (1400–1511), merchants used gold dust and silver bars instead of coins in exchange for their purchases. The value was worked out in accordance with the value of the goods to the mutual

satisfaction of both parties. The ruler would only accept payments of gold dust and silver bars from the merchants. According to a 17th-century account by the Portuguese Emanuel Godinho de Eredia, 'the natives owned many *bâres* (bars) of gold'.

Blocks of tin wrapped in rattan baskets were also exchanged for goods from foreign traders. In the Melaka marketplace, the ordinary inhabitants used cowrie shells, rice and small scarlet weighing beans, known as *saga*, as currency.

After Parameswara, the first Sultan of Melaka, married a daughter of the ruler of Pasai (North Sumatra) in 1414 and converted to Islam, many Muslims then traded in Melaka, introducing Pasai coinage (see 'Early Islamic coins'). The first true Melaka coins so far recorded have been ascribed to the reign of Sultan Muzaffar Shah (1445–59) and bear his name. This tin coinage was die struck and was known as *pitis* or *casha*. It was withdrawn by the Portuguese soon after the capture of Melaka and melted down at the Melaka mint.

In Perak and Selangor, it was believed that tin

had a 'soul spirit' which could be controlled by ceremonial magic. Local magicians, known as *pawang*, made animal sacrifices and supervised the smelting of tin ore to ensure an auspicious beginning for a new mine and to propitiate demons.

The first tin from a new mine was cast into a pair of shell-backed ingots. In the course of time, these evolved into the shape of a tortoise with shell markings that represented a message from the spirit world. Eventually, other animal shapes were cast in the series and these were substituted for the live animal sacrifices. Their widespread popularity eventually led to their acceptance as a form of currency in Perak, Selangor and Negeri Sembilan, as well as in the border regions of neighbouring Malay states. In Selangor and Perak, they were presented as gifts to royalty.

Pyramid- or pagoda-shaped tin ingots were also used as currency in Perak and Selangor. Known as *tampang*, these were shaped into a four-sided pyramid with a flat top and a broad foot or plinth. The early tampang were crudely cast in hardened sand moulds. The actual value of the early tin tampang determined their face value. In Pahang, the earliest surviving tampang, issued in 1819 during the reign of Bendahara Sewa Raja Tun Ali, was equal to six and a quarter cents of a Spanish silver dollar. An improved variety, issued in 1846, was valued at four cents.

Official tampang were struck by the state, while private tokens were issued by Chinese clan associations, the latter for circulation within the tin-mining area around Kuantan. A one cent tampang was added in 1847. Tampang were issued until 1889 and remained legal tender until they were demonetized in accordance with Straits Settlements regulations in 1893.

'Mountain' money

Known to the Malays as *gunung-gunung* (mountains), these tin objects shaped to resemble mountains were found in Perak. They are of uncertain age, but the beliefs they symbolize predate the coming of Islam. In pre-Islamic belief, ancestors reside on sacred mountains, while Hindu belief accords Mount Meru as the axis of the universe. These tin objects also resemble the similar-named ornament found on the back of rulers' thrones, and the *gunungan*, a fan-shaped figure included in every shadow puppet play performance. Their exact use is unknown. It has been suggested that they could have served as a type of barter currency, or that they were used as mosquito net weights on Malay bridal beds.

Tin ingots, or *tampang*, also known as 'tin hat money', were used as currency in Pahang. They were cast in a brass mould (pictured).

ABOVE: Candi Bukit Batu Pahat ('The Temple on the Hill of Cut Stone'), also known as Site 8, is reconstructed on site in the Bujang Valley. The most famous of South Kedah's architectural remains, it is believed to date from the 11th century CE when Kedah was dominated by the South Indian Cola kingdom.

TOP FAR LEFT: Archaeological students excavate one of the Sungai Mas sites, believed to be the earliest entrepôt site of South Kedah dating from the 5th century CE.

TOP NEAR LEFT: Shown here *in situ* before it was reconstructed, the temple at Site 50, South Kedah, is of the South Indian *vimana–mandapa* style. Other Indian influences include the stone drain (centre) known as a *somasutra*.

BOTTOM FAR LEFT: This reconstructed Hindu temple at Site 19 in the Bujang Valley is believed to have been built in the 11th century. Artefacts found here include a stone Ganesa and a Siva trident.

BOTTOM NEAR LEFT: Site 11 in the Bujang Valley was reconstructed in 1974. However, scholars now agree that this reconstruction is not in accordance with other evidence. The temple dates from the 11th century.

INDIGENIZATION OF INDIAN CULTURE

Contacts between Malaysia and India may have begun by the 5th century BCE when Malay mariners—the first of the world's great, long-distance sailors—voyaged across the Bay of Bengal in search of metals, textiles and rare objects which served as status symbols. Communication between Malaysia and South Asia is recorded in Indian sources as early as the 3rd century BCE, as well as Graeco-Roman and Chinese records of the 2nd and 3rd centuries CE. The oldest signs of the adaptation of Indian elements into Malay culture date from the 5th century CE, and consist of statuary and inscriptions related to Buddhism. These traces of South Asian cultural elements indicate that northern Peninsular Malaysia was participating in the general phenomenon of Buddhist expansion along Asian trade routes.

Important centres of religious and literary activity were found in Bengal, Madras, Sri Lanka, and Gujerat, and the earliest inscriptions and statuary found in Malaysia display a familiarity with these various South Asian cultures, rather than a preponderant influence from any one region. This indicates that the Malaysian adaptation of Indian cultural elements followed a process of selective incorporation into the pre-existing civilization.

From approximately 680 CE to 1025 CE, the west coast of the Malay Peninsula was part of the Empire of Srivijaya. Although the Maharaja of Srivijaya resided in South Sumatra, the Chinese described the kingdom as a 'bipolar' polity. Kedah, which had the closest relations with India of any Southeast Asian port, was probably the northern 'pole', and Indian sources suggest that it enjoyed a substantial degree of autonomy and regional influence.

Although the Malay language borrowed some terms from Sanskrit, these were used to express a particularly Malay view of the proper relations between subject and ruler. South Asian vernacular languages had very little impact on Malay. Malaysian interest in South Asian culture was mainly stimulated by religious and philosophical concepts expressed in written form, rather than dissemination by personal contact.

In 1025 CE, Kedah was conquered by the Cola kingdom of South India, which seems to have exerted strong political and artistic influence over the Kedah region, as many South Indian-style Hindu shrines were built during this period. In the 12th century, the Cola kingdom declined and Kedah reasserted its independence.

Religious and artistic elements of South Asian culture attracted Malaysian attention. However, the major developments of this period were the results of indigenous factors. South Asian literature, architecture and sculpture are well represented in the archaeological and historical record because they were manifested in physical objects which have survived until now. But the dynamic developments of Malay culture which took place during this time were the result of Malaysian interaction with its nearest Southeast Asian neighbours, with South Asia providing a kind of international cultural milieu and language which facilitated rapidly intensifying regional communication.

This bronze Buddha image, weighing 393 grams, was discovered in 1978 by a farmer preparing to plant cassava at Kampung Pancing, near Sungai Lembing, Pahang.

Red glass *mutisalah* beads found at Kuala Selinsing, Perak, could have originated from India.

Transformation of indigenous religious beliefs

Former theories that the majority of the Malaysian population converted to Buddhism and Hinduism are now considered inaccurate. Current evidence suggests that early historic religious beliefs were a continuation of prehistoric traditions—emphasizing reverence for ancestors and mountains—which gradually incorporated imported religious concepts. These were introduced through trading contacts in the coastal entrepôts where indigenous courts combined with the foreign trading community to produce an internationalized form of politico-religious culture.

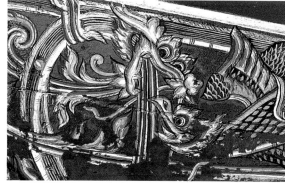

A fire-breathing *naga* painted on the hull of a traditional fishing boat in Kelantan derives from early beliefs in nature spirits.

Re-erected at the Perak Museum in Taiping, this granite cist or slab grave originates from the Bernam Valley of South Perak. Dates obtained from radiocarbon dating of similar graves range between the 1st and 7th centuries CE.

Known as *batu hidup*, 'living stones', because of a local belief that the stones 'grow', these megaliths are located at Tampin in Melaka. Little is known about these stone alignments found throughout Negeri Sembilan and Melaka, but they are believed to predate the coming of Islam in the 15th century.

Prehistoric burial practices

Religious beliefs are among the most abstract aspects of human culture. Without written accounts as a guide, it is difficult to understand the complex symbolic meanings which people attached to the meaning of life and death. Despite the uncertainty about attempting to portray prehistoric religious beliefs in what is now Malaysia, this task is necessary in order to evaluate the impact of South Asian cultures on Malaysian religion.

There is tangible evidence for early ideas about death and the afterlife. In the late prehistoric period, the dead were buried with grave offerings. The slab graves of South Perak and North Selangor indicate that some people, probably of an élite group, were given permanent memorials. Such practices suggest that religion and politics had acquired elaborate manifestations. In other areas, corpses were buried in jars. Secondary burial was also practised, as in recent times in Sarawak, where, at a certain interval after death, the buried bones of the deceased were exhumed, ritually cleansed, and reburied.

Another Sarawak custom practised up to recent times, where the deceased are interred in boat-shaped coffins and placed in caves, may also have been present in the Malay Peninsula in prehistoric times. Such burials in the Niah Caves, Sarawak, date from approximately 500 BCE. Also present are remains of cremations. Other prehistoric burials in Niah consisted of bodies laid out horizontally in trenches, wrapped in mats or cloth, and sometimes dusted with red ochre. This variability suggests that Malaysian religion in the late prehistoric period differed significantly from one area to another.

A particularly impressive site at Kampung Sungai Lang, Selangor, yielded two bronze drums of the Dongson type on a board. Dating between 500 BCE and 200 CE, they may have been part of a burial, as the objective of the entire structure was clearly religious. Other Dongson bronze drums discovered at Klang, Tembeling and Kuala Terengganu, as well as other late prehistoric ritual bronzes found at Klang and at Muar in Johor, indicate that these artefacts had special significance for late prehistoric Malaysians. Complex symbols on the drums suggest that they played roles both in religious ceremonies and as status symbols.

Megaliths and nature spirits

Alignments of stones in Melaka and Negeri Sembilan have affinities with prehistoric practices, but no firm evidence regarding their dates and functions has yet been found. The Kelabit of Sarawak still erected stone alignments as memorials to the deceased up until recent times. Malaysia was probably similar to other parts of Southeast Asia where prehistoric megalithic customs continued side by side with other practices connected with Hinduism and Buddhism.

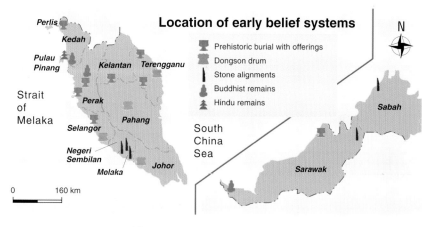

Location of early belief systems

Perlis
Kedah
Pulau Pinang
Kelantan
Terengganu
Strait of Melaka
Perak
Pahang
Selangor
Negeri Sembilan
Melaka
Johor
South China Sea
Sabah
Sarawak

N

- Prehistoric burial with offerings
- Dongson drum
- Stone alignments
- Buddhist remains
- Hindu remains

0   160 km

In the shadow puppet play, still popular in Kelantan, the 'tree of life', an indigenous religious symbol, is used for the 30-minute prologue after the ritual opening ceremony, when the play is introduced to the audience.

An important religious belief in late prehistoric Malaysia revolved around the idea that ancestor spirits could be invoked to protect the living. It is likely that these spirits were identified with high places such as mountain peaks.

Other important beliefs revolved around water, fertility, and serpent deities, usually termed *naga*. According to Yiqing, the Chinese monk who visited Kedah in the 7th century, the local Buddhists followed special customs. On religious feast days, priests prayed for the merit of their good acts to be shared with the spirits of the dead, the kings, and the nagas. Sponsors of feasts constructed 'wishing trees' to give to the priests. Yiqing does not specify the material of the 'wishing trees', but the practice is reminiscent of the *bunga mas* (literally 'golden flowers' shaped like trees), which Malay sultans presented as tribute to Thai rulers in the 19th century. Also, the 'wishing tree' is a symbol of 'heaven' in Indian mythology and was commonly used in Java as a temple decoration motif.

The tree as a symbol of life is a common motif in Malaysian arts and crafts. The *gunungan*, the tree symbol found in the shadow puppet play, may be another example of religious symbolism which has survived from prehistory.

Early Buddhist customs

Both epigraphy and statuary suggest that Mahayana Buddhism made converts in Malaysia by the 5th century, which accords with religious conversions in Sumatra in the same period. But the new religious beliefs and practices probably elaborated existing attitudes rather than creating a radical break with the past. The incorporation of prayers for ancestors, and nagas and 'wishing trees' into local religious festivals gives a glimpse into prehistoric beliefs.

Yiqing was also interested in the local Buddhist custom of chanting the *Jatakamala*, a collection of tales of the Buddha in his former existences before his final incarnation as Prince Siddharta around 500 BCE. At the time of Yiqing's visit, these tales were still unknown in China.

The great works of literature in South Asia were one of the most important sources of attraction which caused Malaysians and Southeast Asians to become Buddhists or Hindus. The high respect which Yiqing accorded to his Sanskrit teachers in Srivijaya suggests that the study of Indian literature was also avidly pursued in Kedah. Indeed, Yiqing states that one of the five greatest Buddhist teachers of his time lived in Srivijaya.

A mountain top temple
A popular early belief was the sanctity of high places. Malay legends abound with tales of sacred mountains but the first tangible evidence was revealed in the 1920s when archaeologists discovered the remains of what is believed to be a Hindu temple on the summit of Gunung Jerai, the 1217-metre-high peak behind the archaeologically rich Bujang Valley of South Kedah. Nine square stone foundations of what could have been hearths were found on the mountain top, leading some archaeologists to speculate that these might have been connected with the nine sacred planets of Hinduism, or Navagrahas. The remains are believed to date from the 7th century CE.

Imported religions merge with indigenous practices

Hinduism was also present in Malaysia during the protohistoric period, but was less influential. Most early religious shrines in Malaysia were devoted to Buddhism. Malaysian evidence for the worship of Hindu deities and construction of shrines for Hindu religious practices is only present for the period after the beginning of the 11th century CE.

It is commonly assumed that early Malays were attracted to Hinduism because of a supposed affinity between Hinduism and their prehistoric reverence for nature spirits. There is, however, little evidence for such a theory. Archaeological discoveries of South Asian artefacts in prehistoric sites indicate that the Malays were in contact with South Asia for centuries before any changes occurred. These were probably related to the incorporation of Hindu and Buddhist symbols into court rituals of sovereignty as Malay kingdoms became more complex. However, the use of South Asian architectural and sculptural motifs was rare outside royal circles. The population may have respected Hindu and Buddhist imagery, but evidence for the existence of these places of worship is restricted to only a few Malaysian locations. Thus, the old idea of an Indian cultural renaissance which transformed Malaysian beliefs is inaccurate.

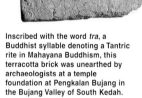

Inscribed with the word *tra*, a Buddhist syllable denoting a Tantric rite in Mahayana Buddhism, this terracotta brick was unearthed by archaeologists at a temple foundation at Pengkalan Bujang in the Bujang Valley of South Kedah.

This replica of the *bunga mas* tribute offering submitted by Kedah to Siam in the early 20th century is reminiscent of the 'wishing trees' remarked upon by the Buddhist pilgrim, Yiqing, in the 7th century.

Candi Bukit Batu Pahat at Merbok, South Kedah, features a *mandapa*, or 'closed-room', similar to Hindu temples from South India which used this space to house the image of the main deity. These temples are rare in Southeast Asia but the remains of at least 10 have been found in the Bujang Valley.

Candi architecture

The word candi *(pronounced 'chandi') is of uncertain origin. It is used in Indonesia and Malaysia to refer to any kind of permanent architecture constructed during the early historic period before the coming of Islam. However, its principal manifestation is the religious shrine. In Malaysia, only two regions have yielded confirmed examples of such remains: South Kedah and Santubong in Sarawak.*

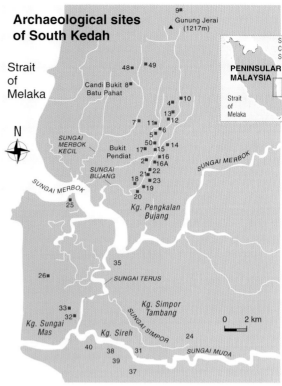

Archaeological sites of South Kedah

Strait of Melaka

Gunung Jerai (1217m)

Candi Bukit 8 Batu Pahat

PENINSULAR MALAYSIA

South China Sea

Strait of Melaka

N

SUNGAI MERBOK KECIL

Bukit Pendiat

SUNGAI BUJANG

SUNGAI MERBOK

SUNGAI MERBOK

Kg. Pengkalan Bujang

SUNGAI TERUS

Kg. Simpor Tambang

Kg. Sungai Mas

Kg. Sireh

SUNGAI SIMPOR

0   2 km

SUNGAI MUDA

This map of the Bujang Valley region shows the various archaeological sites indicated by numbers. This numerical system was established by the archaeologists D. C. and H. G. Quaritch Wales in the 1930s and is still in use. Remains of buildings dating from the 5th century CE, including *candi*, have been discovered at many of these sites.

Balinese temple roofs, designed to symbolize sacred Mount Meru, the Hindu conception of the universe, are believed by some historians to be similar to those which once roofed the *candi* of Kedah.

This spout for holy liquid which projects from the wall of the *vimana* at Candi Bukit Batu Pahat, Kedah, is evidence that the temple once housed a sacred Hindu deity.

The temple mount and foundations are all that remain of Candi Bukit Batu Pahat at Merbok, Kedah, also known as Site 8, which is believed to have been built in the 11th century.

Candi distribution and discovery

Examples of architecture from the pre-Islamic period have been reported from Kota Tinggi, Johor, and several locations in Pahang, but these reports have yet to be verified. South Kedah is the only part of Peninsular Malaysia to afford reasonably well-preserved examples. Encompassing an area of 350 square kilometres between Gunung Jerai and the lower Muda River Valley, this region was the focus of a centuries-long burst of intense activity aimed at building religious structures in conjunction with maritime trading pursuits. But despite the numerous ruins and artefacts which survive, many mysteries concerning their precise meanings and the identities of the builders remain unsolved.

Discovered by archaeologists in 1966, the candi at Bongkisam in the Santubong region of Sarawak forms part of a larger complex of archaeological sites, and like the Kedah candi, it was situated at a lively focus of communication. Despite the exposure to foreign cultural influences in both areas, the Malaysian candi exhibit features which can only be explained as a result of local beliefs and practices.

The candi at Bongkisam was constructed of rectangular stone blocks and may have been roofed with perishable materials. In the centre of the platform a pit was discovered containing an elaborate ritual deposit with a golden lingam (symbol of the Hindu deity Siva). The candi design was probably intended to form some kind of protected space or mandala, a purified area within which people could meditate and be initiated into higher levels of a religious hierarchy. This theme occurs in both South Kedah and Sarawak suggesting a basic commonality of belief.

Colonel James Low, of the East India Company, first reported 'undoubted relics of a Hindoo colony' in Kedah in the 1840s. He excavated but left no scientific reports as archaeological research was still in its infancy. Further studies followed in the 1920s and 1930s, but the first sustained excavations were carried out only in 1936–7. Since then, many archaeologists have continued researching this rewarding region, and work is ongoing. The Sarawak candi at Bongkisam was excavated in the 1960s by the archaeologists Tom Harrisson and S. J. O'Connor.

Historians speculate that Candi Bukit Batu Pahat was a Hindu temple with a multi-tiered roof supported by a wooden framework above the *vimana*. Inside was a sacred lingam, and on the terrace facing it (which was also roofed) was a statue of Nandi, 'the Bull'. The temple base was constructed from granite blocks quarried from the nearby stream bed of the Sungai Bujang.

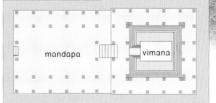

mandapa   vimana

Different types of candi

The candi of Kedah are concentrated in a coastal area near the northern entrance to the Strait of Melaka. All the ruins lie between the Muda River in the south and Gunung Jerai, a solitary 1217-metre-high mountain, 25 kilometres to the north. The only exception is a candi at Bukit Coras, 20 kilometres north of the mountain.

Within this area, 87 sites dating to the early historic period have been reported; 73 of these yielded remains of brick, laterite or stone buildings, and 60 are thought to have been religious shrines. Twelve are located on hill tops, a feature which may derive from prehistoric beliefs in the sanctity of high places. Of the sites south of Gunung Jerai, 22 cannot be assigned to a specific religion or period. A total of 16 candi can be dated to the period before 1000 CE, and of these, Buddhist sites (6) outnumber those known to have been Hindu (2), but half of the early candi cannot be definitely assigned to either religion.

Site 1, on Bukit Coras, dates from the earlier Buddhist phase before 1000 CE. Site 17, at Bukit Pendiat, is octagonal in shape, and could have been a base for a Buddhist stupa. Site 16A may have also been a stupa base.

The Hindu structures consist of two sections: a *vimana*, or enclosed sanctuary, where the main icon was kept, and a *mandapa*, or open-sided hall, with a roof supported on wooden pillars. The foundations were built of stone, fired bricks or laterite. The best preserved candi is at Site 8, Candi Bukit Batu Pahat ('Temple on the Hill of Cut Stone').

The mandapa are usually associated with stone bases used to protect the wooden pillars supporting the roof. This type of structure is identified with South Indian temples dedicated to the deity Siva. The Hindu sites probably date from the 11th century when Kedah was dominated by the Cola kingdom of South India. The Indian character of these sites is emphasized by the presence of a drain (*snana-droni*) to catch the sacred liquids used to bathe the main icon, and a spout (*jaladwara*) on the outside of the vimana where the liquid can be collected by worshippers. Such an arrangment is very rare in Southeast Asia, but common in India.

Multicultural and indigenous influences

The Kedah area probably had a cosmopolitan population in ancient times. The Malays were politically dominant, but the Mon people may have comprised a significant local element. Traders from the Malay Archipelago, Southeast Asia and India were frequent visitors from early times.

Despite foreign contacts, the Kedah candi display a particular local character. Permanent materials were used, but kept to a minimum, unlike on Java or Sumatra where some religious buildings were completely constructed of masonry. Foundation deposits suggest general continuity with contemporary religious practices in Java, Sumatra and Bali. Kedah architecture displays similar traits to several Southeast Asian areas, but the overall composition is unique.

Candi designs

Site 50, at Kampung Bendang Dalam, is a Hindu temple complex of the *vimana–mandapa* type containing an additional smaller structure thought to be a minor temple (pictured).

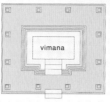

Site 21, originally sited at Pengkalan Bujang but now in the grounds of the Bujang Valley Archaeological Park, is a brick single-part structure of cruciform plan dated from the 9th to 10th century. Evidence suggests Buddhist influences.

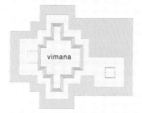

Site 19, at Pengkalan Bujang, is a unique vaulted-type Hindu temple made of brick in the 11th century. Iron nails found at the site indicate that a wooden structure probably originally supported the roof.

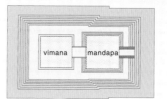

Religious sculpture

In the absence of grand architectural remains like Indonesia's Borobudur and Cambodia's Angkor Wat, archaeologists and historians studying Malaysia's early historical era place great importance on artefacts, particularly the finds of Buddhist and Hindu images . Dating from the 5th century CE, these sculptures have made a major contribution not only to the understanding of early Malaysian social and cultural life, but also to the role of religion and politics throughout South and Southeast Asia during that time.

Bronze Buddhist images

Hindu and Buddhist images made of bronze, terracotta and stone have been found at various Peninsular Malaysian sites, but the most numerous yields have come from the Bujang Valley of Kedah—believed to be the site of the ancient kingdom of Kedah—and from the Kinta Valley of Perak—speculated to have been the site of the mysterious kingdom of Gangga Nagara.

Images of the Buddha display postures, gestures, physical characteristics and robes which vary according to the period and artistic school of their creation. By studying these different aspects, scholars can ascertain the approximate date and place of manufacture.

The oldest bronze Buddhist image yet found in Malaysia was unearthed in 1941 by the archaeologist Dorothy Quaritch Wales from a ruined brick temple plinth at Site 16A in the Bujang Valley. The right hand of this image is in the position of *varadamudra*, one of the *mudra*, or hand gestures, which characterize the transcendent Buddhas of Mahayana Buddhism. This gesture is characteristic of the northern Indian Gupta style of the 4th–5th century CE which influenced other regions in India and Southeast Asia. The unfolded robe also derives from the Gupta style. However, the style of leaving the right shoulder bare comes from the Ajanta Cave temples of western India, which shows that Bujang Valley sculptors adapted both Gupta and Ajanta styles in their own interpretations.

Since 1908, a number of bronze Buddhist images have been dredged up during tin-mining operations in the Kinta Valley, which some scholars believe was the legendary kingdom of Gangga Nagara. Using the gestures and garment styles as a guide, scholars have dated the images from the 6th to the 9th century CE (see 'The Kinta Valley').

Another bronze Buddhist image was recovered from a fishing net near Pulau Ketam, Selangor. At 1.4 metres in height, this standing Avalokitesvara (one of the most renowned Bodhisattvas or 'enlightened beings' of Mahayana Buddhism) is the largest bronze image yet discovered.

Weighing 15.42 kilograms and measuring 52.5 centimetres in height, this bronze figurine found at Jalong, Perak, is dated to the 9th century CE. It is believed to have been cast in Malaysia, and may represent the Hindu figure Agastya—a priestly teacher.

Sculptures from Pengkalan Bujang

During the 1976 excavation of Sites 21/22 at Pengkalan Bujang in the Bujang Valley, various sculptures were discovered, including four terracotta Buddhist images and one of bronze. Their damaged condition makes dating difficult.

However, the style of the best preserved terracotta seated Buddha is similar to images of the 10th to the early 11th century CE during the period of the Cola Dynasty of South India. The most important evidence in dating this image to the Cola period is to compare the similar forms of the face, ears, hair, *usnisa* (cranial protuberance), shawl, placement of the legs and the gesture of *bhumisparshamudra*. Comparisons can also be made with the Buddha image of the same period discovered at Kota Cina in Sumatra. This dating is also supported by other artefacts found at Site 21/22, including ceramics and glassware imported from China and the Middle East during the 10th century CE.

Discovered in the Bujang Valley of Kedah in 1941, this bronze Buddha stands 21.6 centimetres in height and has been dated to the 6th–7th century CE.

The stylistic similarities of artefacts found at the various ports bordering the Melaka Strait, dating from the 10th to the early 11th century CE, are evidence of the strong political, trade and cultural relationships between this area and South India which culminated in the attacks by the Cola on the kingdom of Srivijaya—including Kedah and other ports on the Melaka Strait—around 1020 CE.

Cola influences are also evident in the style of the four-armed standing Bodhisattva image made of bronze which was also found at Sites 21/22. Although this badly eroded image stands only 8 centimetres in height, it has been identified as Bhrkutie, 'the threatening goddess', based on the conch shell held in her left hand and her style of clothing. The South Indian influences indicate a date from the 10th to 11th century.

The small terracotta seated Avalokitesvara found at the same site is reminiscent of Buddhist votive tablets made of clay which have been discovered in caves in Perlis and Kelantan. These are presumed to have been produced locally around the 9th or 10th century CE.

This small (4 cm) terracotta image of Avalokitesvara was made in the Bujang Valley, but the seating position, type of pedestal and hand gesture (*dharmachakramudra*) show stylistic similarities with 10th–11th century South Indian images.

Locations of religious sculptures

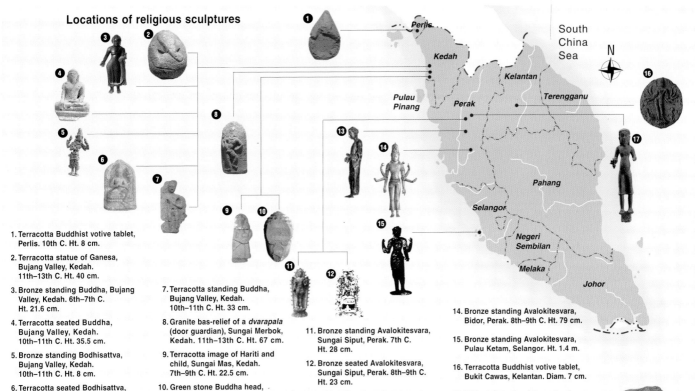

1. Terracotta Buddhist votive tablet, Perlis. 10th C. Ht. 8 cm.

2. Terracotta statue of Ganesa, Bujang Valley, Kedah. 11th–13th C. Ht. 40 cm.

3. Bronze standing Buddha, Bujang Valley, Kedah. 6th–7th C. Ht. 21.6 cm.

4. Terracotta seated Buddha, Bujang Valley, Kedah. 10th–11th C. Ht. 35.5 cm.

5. Bronze standing Bodhisattva, Bujang Valley, Kedah. 10th–11th C. Ht. 8 cm.

6. Terracotta seated Bodhisattva, Bujang Valley, Kedah. 10th–11th C. Ht. 4.5 cm.

7. Terracotta standing Buddha, Bujang Valley, Kedah. 10th–11th C. Ht. 33 cm.

8. Granite bas-relief of a *dvarapala* (door guardian), Sungai Merbok, Kedah. 11th–13th C. Ht. 67 cm.

9. Terracotta image of Hariti and child, Sungai Mas, Kedah. 7th–9th C. Ht. 22.5 cm.

10. Green stone Buddha head, Sungai Mas, Kedah. 7th–9th C. Ht. 30.5 cm.

11. Bronze standing Avalokitesvara, Sungai Siput, Perak. 7th C. Ht. 28 cm.

12. Bronze seated Avalokitesvara, Sungai Siput, Perak. 8th–9th C. Ht. 23 cm.

13. Bronze standing Buddha, Ipoh, Perak. 6th C. Ht. 46 cm.

14. Bronze standing Avalokitesvara, Bidor, Perak. 8th–9th C. Ht. 79 cm.

15. Bronze standing Avalokitesvara, Pulau Ketam, Selangor. Ht. 1.4 m.

16. Terracotta Buddhist votive tablet, Bukit Cawas, Kelantan. Diam. 7 cm.

17. Bronze statuette, Jalong, Perak. 9th C. Ht. 52.5 cm.

Buddhist images from Sungai Mas

Among the artefacts unearthed at Kampung Sungai Mas, South Kedah, is a terracotta image of a mother holding a child. It has been identified as the Buddhist goddess Hariti because the child is held in a similar way to a Hariti image from India. Hariti is believed to protect against cholera, as well as acting as a fertility symbol. Yiqing, the Chinese Buddhist monk who visited Kedah on his way to India and back in the 7th century, reported that Hariti worship was popular in northern India. No other Hariti images have been found in Malaysia or Sumatra, but there are depictions in Java and Bali. The Sungai Mas Hariti was probably made locally from the 7th to the 9th century. A green stone Buddha head, also discovered at Sungai Mas, is dated from the same period.

All the Buddhist images found in Peninsular Malaysia, dating from the 5th to the 11th century CE, are believed to have been produced locally using adaptations of Indian iconographic styles. This influence is evidence of the strong relationship between the Malay Peninsula and India during that era, while the finding of these images also shows the importance of the kingdoms in the Bujang and Kinta valleys. Religious expansion in both regions was closely linked with developments in Sumatra and South Thailand, probably because the leading power of the time, Srivijaya, was a well-known centre of Mahayana Buddhism from the 7th to the 11th century CE.

This bas-relief of a Hindu dancing *dvarapala* (door guardian), carved from a slab of rough granite measuring 67 centimetres in height, was found at Site 35/36 near the Sungai Muda in South Kedah. Although the image is damaged, the jewellery, hairstyle and broken club in her right hand show stylistic similarities with the Durga image discovered nearby, and with a bas-relief found on a temple at Padang Lawas, Sumatra.

Hindu images from South Kedah

From architectural remains and artefacts found in the Bujang Valley, archaeologists have deduced that Hinduism was the prevailing religion in that area from the 11th to the 13th century CE.

A granite image identified as Durga, the consort of Siva, triumphing over the Mahisasura (the bull-headed demon), was found at Site 4. She stands on a buffalo's head and holds a crescent-shaped knife and a club—both attributes of this deity.

Two damaged statues of Ganesa, the elephant-faced deity, have also been found in the Bujang Valley. The headless stone Ganesa from Site 19, Pengkalan Bujang, wears a string of pearls and armlets and is seated in a similar position to a Sathingphra image from Thailand. Ceramics found nearby have helped date this image to the late 11th century CE. The terracotta Ganesa found at Site 4 is crudely made, but the position of its feet is similar to a Javanese image, while the shape of the trunk resembles the Sathingphra image. This Ganesa is dated from the 11th to the 13th century on the basis of Song–Yuan ceramics found nearby.

Other Hindu images which have been unearthed in the Bujang Valley include a stone Nandi (sacred bull) head, a stone *dvarapala* (door guardian), a terracotta carved relief of an elephant, which perhaps formed part of a temple wall, and a recently discovered bronze image of the deity Visnu.

Carved from a mud-brick block, this eroded Buddha image unearthed at Pengkalan Bujang in the Bujang Valley is presumed to date from the 10th to the 11th century CE.

Hand gestures of the Buddha

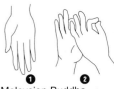

Malaysian Buddha images display various hand gestures known as *mudra*. These include (1) *varadamudra* (charity), (2) *dharmachakramudra* (preaching) and (3) *bhumisparshamudra* (earth-touching).

Concepts of kingship

According to older theories of Malaysian historical development, one of the main attractions of Indian culture was a well-developed theory of divine kingship. However, recent research has greatly altered this view. It is now believed that Malaysians did not attempt to imitate or directly transplant any Indian social structures, but rather, that communication between Malaysia and other parts of the ancient world acted as a catalyst to change, leading to the appearance of forms which were not found previously in either place.

A royal dais shaped like Mount Meru

A pyramidal tiered dais, known as the Balai Panca Persada, is used for the customary bathing ceremony at the installation of some Malaysian sultans. It is built in the shape of Gunung Mahameru, the Malay version of Mount Meru, the pivot of the universe in Hindu–Buddhist cosmology. This ceremony probably derives from the Southeast Asian idea that the king seated on the top of Mount Meru commands the waters of life to flow down so as to preserve the well-being of his subjects. The Perak royal dais (above top) was used at the installation of Sultan Azlan Shah in 1985. The photograph (above) depicts the enthronment of the Sultan of Selangor in 1939.

Evaluating South Asian cultural contributions

Earlier theorists believed that by adopting Indian trappings of statecraft, Malay rulers could increase their power, and by claiming to be incarnations of Hindu deities, they could acquire supremacy over their rivals. However, recent research has profoundly altered former evaluations of the relative importance of South Asian contributions to Malaysian culture, compared with the role played by the evolution of locally invented institutions. But this position does not negate the significance of historical interaction between Malaysia and South Asia, as Malaysian history would have evolved differently if there had been no link with India.

In South Asia 2,000 years ago, a process of 'Sanskritization' was under way. The Sanskrit language, already 'dead' in the sense that it was not spoken in everyday life, was used in a manner similar to Latin in medieval Europe. India did not yet exist as a unified political or cultural entity, although a particular type of social formation, which included the so-called 'caste system', was gaining acceptance across the subcontinent.

Ancient Hindu holy books, legal works and administrative manuals were written in Sanskrit, as were the early scriptures of Mahayana Buddhism, and this language exerted a major influence on early Southeast Asia, including leaving significant traces in modern Bahasa Malaysia.

The caste system had a limited impact on Southeast Asia. References to castes appear in ancient Cambodian inscriptions, but the system there bore little resemblance to the Indian form. Membership of castes was an honour awarded by the king, rather than a hereditary status. A modified version of this caste system also exists in modern Bali. There is no evidence that a caste hierarchy ever existed in Malaysia. Thus, one important component of an Indian concept of kingship—the hereditary *ksatriya* caste—never took root.

Symbolic armlets

Known as Pontoh Bernaga, these gold armlets in the shape of coiled serpent-dragons (*naga*) are part of the five items comprising the hereditary royal regalia worn by Perak's rulers. Sultan Azlan Shah, the 34th Sultan of Perak, is shown wearing the armlets at his installation in 1985. The serpent-dragon originally symbolized the waters of life which flow around the sacred peak of Mount Meru in Hindu–Buddhist cosmology. This symbolism occurs repeatedly throughout Southeast Asia and is a combination of Indian and Southeast Asian beliefs.

The silver mouthpiece of the royal Perak *nafiri* (trumpet) shows a tusked dragon with an uplifted tail ending in a lingam. This design, used in Javanese and Balinese art, blends Southeast Asian and South Asian symbolism.

Theories on royal deification

Early historians' ideas about ancient Southeast Asian kingship were influenced by an inscription found at Sdok Kak Thom, near the Thai–Cambodian border. This inscription discusses a cult connected with worship of a *devaraja*, a Sanskrit term meaning 'god-king'. Formerly, historians concluded that this 'god-king' was the human king of Cambodia who was deified, usually as the Hindu god Siva, or alternatively Visnu.

More recently, historians have pointed out that in India, kings were not worshipped. The institution of kingship was considered to be divine, and kings could be divinely inspired, but Indian kings were considered to be human, with the exception of heroes from the Hindu epics, such as Rama in the *Ramayana*. Thus, if early Southeast Asian kings had been divinized, this must be interpreted as a Southeast Asian custom rather than a belief imported from India.

The evolution of kingship in Malaysia

In Malaysia, at the dawn of the historic period, it is likely that the concept of inherited status had just begun to form. During prehistory, Malaysian societies were probably semi-nomadic groups characterized by egalitarianism, or semi-sedentary agricultural communities in which positions of leadership might be attained by exceptionally able individuals. Their positions would have depended on personal respect, which would not be inherited by their descendants. Thus, the large bronze Dongson (North Vietnam) drums of late prehistory, several of which have been found at various sites in Peninsular Malaysia, may have functioned as status symbols as they were apparently buried on the death of their owners rather than passed on to their successors or heirs.

The idea of inherited status may have formed as a result of the growth of maritime trade, as the possibility of acquiring high status through trade was probably the main motivating factor which led people to undertake the hazardous journeys required. Prowess in battle would have been a great asset, but since trading and raiding seem to have been equally esteemed occupations in early Southeast Asia, individuals would have needed the same qualities to be successful in either endeavour.

The kingdom as a mandala

The 7th-century Malay kingdom of Srivijaya in South Sumatra referred to itself as a 'mandala'. This Sanskrit word, meaning 'circle', came to symbolize the idea of a sacred order unifying a hierarchy of beings concentrically arranged at increasing distances from a central point. The space within this circular realm would be harmonious and protected from external evil by the spiritual power of the supreme being at the centre. Mandala often depict Mount Meru, the sacred mountain at the centre of the Hindu–Buddhist universe around which Hindu or Buddhist deities lived.

In India, the mandala was purely symbolic, but Southeast Asian rulers adopted it as an ideal structure for a kingdom. Each ruler vied with neighbours to attain a position of centrality, with those in surrounding territories acknowledging his moral superiority and paying tribute, both ceremonial and tangible, to him.

There is no evidence that the early kings of Southeast Asia claimed to be deified. However, by the 10th century, a transition began to take place. Inscriptions from Java and Cambodia indicate that kings were claiming to be, first, part divine, containing a 'divine essence', and, in following centuries, equal to Hindu or Buddhist deities. Some *candi* (temples) in Cambodia

and Java were built to contain statues which could be used as 'receptacles' into which souls of deceased rulers could be invited to descend in order that their descendants might invoke their supernatural assistance. It is possible that some of the candi in Kedah were used in this way.

The *Sejarah Melayu*, the court history of the Sultanate of Melaka, depicts the first Malay ruler as appearing on earth in a miraculous manner, but ruling thereafter as fully human, which suggests that Malaysian rulers were never deified. They probably utilized rituals to suggest that they had special qualities, and were divinely inspired, but such practices were nearly universal during the age of kingdoms. Malaysian rulers may have used Indian ceremonial elements to reinforce their positions, but their main concerns would have been to provide a stable centre which could link hinterland groups with other scattered groups, such as the Orang Laut ('Sea People').

Successful rulers would have attracted mobile people to enter into patron–client relationships based on economic redistribution between complimentary ecological zones which provided both local necessities and exotic items for long-distance luxury exchange.

In Malaysia, Indian symbols provided useful tools for forging greater unity than would have been possible without them. But, as current research has revealed, it would be most incorrect to view early Malay courts as small replicas of Indian kingdoms. It is evident that the economic, political, religious, social and geographic factors all varied significantly between the two areas.

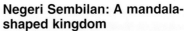

Negeri Sembilan: A mandala-shaped kingdom

The Peninsular state of Negeri Sembilan, which means 'nine states', is arranged in the shape of a mandala. This South Asian concept was originally symbolic of the universe, but in Southeast Asia was adopted as a blueprint for a kingdom.

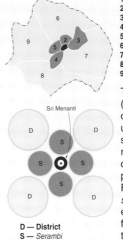

1. Sri Menanti—capital
2. Ulu Muar
3. Jempul
4. Gunung Pasir } Serambi
5. Terachi
6. Jelebu
7. Johol
8. Rembau } Districts
9. Sungai Ujung

D — District
S — Serambi

The schematic diagram (left) shows the organization of the nine-unit polity. Sri Menanti, the seat of the paramount ruler, was placed in the centre of the mandala—a protected spiritual sphere. Four regions, known as *serambi* (verandas), encircled this hub, while four larger districts formed the outer rim.

The *vimana*, or sanctuary, of Candi Bukit Batu Pahat in the Bujang Valley of South Kedah probably housed a statue or icon of a Hindu deity, but it is not known whether, as in some other parts of Southeast Asia, this deified statue was used to contain a deceased ruler's soul.

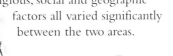

The shadow puppet play has been performed in Peninsular Malaysia for several centuries. In common with Cambodian and Thai versions, the Hindu epic, the *Ramayana*, provides most of the stories for the Malaysian plays. The royal hero, Sri Rama (far left), is deified as an incarnation of Visnu, which led former scholars to suppose that Southeast Asian rulers were also 'god-kings'. Rama's consort, Siti Dewi (near left), symbolizes wifely devotion, while Hanuman (centre) is the Hindu Monkey God.

Sociopolitics

The best information on the organization of early Malaysian political structures comes from traditional sources such as the Sejarah Melayu (Malay Annals), and inferences drawn from analogy with the period of early European contact. Early Malay polities were probably neither highly centralized nor autocratic. Rulers enjoyed great prestige, but had no organized bureaucracy to implement detailed regulations governing daily life. Rulers functioned more as reference points for rituals combining sacred and civil characteristics, and for exchange networks.

A typical Malay polity during the protohistoric period was three-tiered. The capital, the first tier, which was located by a coastal estuary, functioned both as the ruler's seat and the main trading port. The agricultural belt, the second tier, occupied the fertile river valleys; while the hinterlands, the third tier, provided rainforest products which formed the basis of the kingdom's trade.

This photograph of Tunku Muhamad, the Yang di-Pertuan Besar of Negeri Sembilan, with his retainers is from *Twentieth Century Impressions of British Malaya* (1908). His Minangkabau ancestors from Sumatra established the royal line of this state in the 18th century.

The nature of Malay royalty

Malay kinship is termed 'cognatic' by anthropologists, that is, descent can be traced in both the maternal and paternal lines. Traditional Malay kingdoms had no fixed rules of succession, such as primogeniture (the right of the eldest child as the successor). The normal practice for the earliest period of which there is evidence was for a group of influential people to gather when it was necessary to choose a new ruler. After a period of discussion, during which several suitable candidates were considered, one would be selected by consensus. Aristocratic descent was important, but it was only one of the variables considered.

Malay kinship is similar to that of their ancestral cousins, the Polynesians. In both instances, a family which did not intermarry with other families considered noble for several generations might cease to be considered royal. On the other hand, a person of unusual ability might find it possible to win acknowledgement of a claim to a noble relative several generations previously. Often, it seems, the appeal of such individuals struggling to revive royal status was made through the maternal rather than the paternal line.

It was common for a ruler to attempt to influence the choice of his successor by appointing a son as *raja mahkota*, or 'crown prince'. The rulers seem to have desired to install their favourites in a position which enabled them both to gain experience in government and build up a group of clients whose own positions depended on their patron's succession to the throne. In their later years, the rulers sought to retire from the public stage into a quieter life of religious contemplation. Thus, early European sources often refer to kingdoms with both an Old King and a Young King; these terms usually represented the father living in semi-retirement, and his son, who conducted the day-to-day affairs of the state.

This tactic did not always work. There are numerous instances in which elderly rulers came into conflict with their younger protégés. One of the best known of these occurred after Melaka was conquered by the Portuguese in 1511. The elder ruler, Sultan Mahmud Shah, had his own appointed successor, Sultan Ahmad, murdered and then he reassumed sole authority. This episode may have weakened Malay unity and facilitated the Portuguese conquest of the kingdom.

The first Malay ruler

The *Sejarah Melayu* describes the mystical appearance of the first Malay ruler on a hill named Bukit Seguntang in present-day Palembang, South Sumatra. One night, a bright light appeared on the hill where a rice field belonging to two old widows was located. The widows saw the light and hid under their beds in terror. The next morning they summoned courage, climbed the hill and found that the stalks of their rice had turned to silver and the grains to gold. A young prince then appeared whose name was Sri Tri Buana, a Sanskrit phrase meaning 'Lord of the Three Worlds'. This name is associated with Mahayana Buddhism, and is a reference to the heavenly realms of the gods, this world of humans and the lower world where demons dwell.

Sri Tri Buana was then conducted to the town where the chief, Demang (old Malay for 'village official') Lebar Daun (literally 'Broad Leaf') offered him the position of ruler. Lebar Daun then became Sri Tri Buana's chief minister. This arrangement was the occasion for a famous compact which is still influential in Malaysian governmental ideology. The people agreed always to be faithful to their ruler,

Tangible evidence of an inland polity

The location of the Buddhist kingdom of Chi tu, visited by a Chinese embassy in the 7th century, has long been thought to be in the interior of Kelantan. Although archaeological evidence has been lacking in the past, discoveries of Buddhist votive tablets (right), of a style popular a millennium ago, in a cave at Bukit Cawas, Kelantan (below), show that this region was the site of an early settlement.

PENINSULAR MALAYSIA

South China Sea

Strait of Melaka

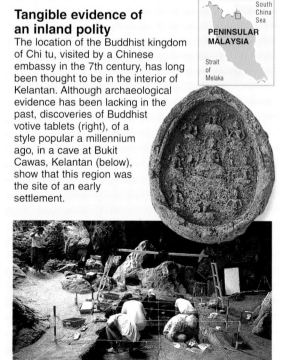

and never to commit *derhaka*. This word can be literally translated as 'treason', but it contains stronger overtones of immorality because it implies disloyalty to the ruler personally as well as to the abstract notion of community. In return, the ruler agreed never to shame his subjects. The condition of being ashamed, *malu*, was considered intolerable and the single greatest injustice.

The *Sejarah Melayu* can be read in several ways. In one reading, it is a cautionary tale for the rulers themselves, since it mentions several disasters which befell those who did not fulfil this obligation.

The structure of a Malay polity

The positive desire of Malays to place themselves under a ruler is well illustrated by the example of Negeri Sembilan. In the 18th century, this area still consisted of a loose confederation of polities. Without a court to focus on, the people of Negeri Sembilan felt insecure and lacking in status. They felt the need of a court for two reasons: to function as a ceremonial centre, and to provide a locus around which economic activity could be structured. A succession of princes from Sumatra was invited to rule over them, until eventually one succeeded in founding a royal line. Thereafter, the court acted as a point of contact between the people and the supernatural, and also with foreigners. The latter promised prosperity through the development of trade, but various problems could arise if communication with them was not structured correctly.

A typical early Malay polity had three main geographical components: a port, often at or near a river mouth; a zone of irrigated agricultural land along a river's middle reaches; and a hinterland which provided both sources of food and commodities useful in attracting foreign trade. One polity might comprise one or more river valleys, each with the same components.

In early modern times, the capitals were usually located near the river mouths and were thus conterminous with the ports, but there is evidence that in earlier times the capitals may have been far inland. Chinese sources mention a kingdom known as Chi tu, the capital of which lay at some distance from the sea (see 'Chi tu: An inland kingdom). Tangible evidence of this inland polity has been lacking in the past. But, in 1994, the archaeologist Adi Haji Taha of the National Museum, discovered Buddhist votive tablets, of a type popular around 1,000 years ago, in the interior of Kelantan. It is possible that these artefacts may relate to the 7th-century Chinese reports.

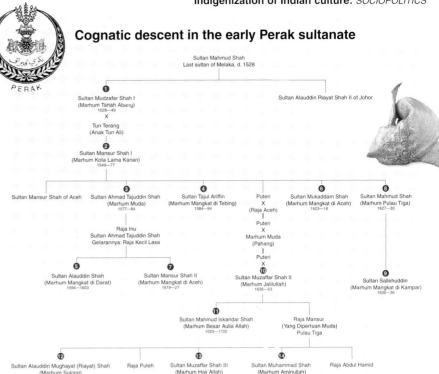

Cognatic descent in the early Perak sultanate

This diorama in the Cultural Museum, Melaka, depicts a 15th-century Chinese envoy presenting tribute to Sultan Mansur Shah in his throne room.

Royalty and trade

As the example of Negeri Sembilan illustrates, commercial factors may have been important in shaping the early Malay polities. The term *orang kaya*, which now means 'a rich person', was formally synonymous with 'noble'. However, this does not necessarily mean that success in trade could confer increased status; but, on the other hand, traditional sources indicate that power often flowed to those with wealth. Indeed, the main motive for engaging in trade in early times was probably not to amass wealth, for there was not a great deal to buy. Instead, the paramount goal of those who are now known as entrepreneurs, was to use the proceeds of their successful trading ventures to attract followers.

During the early kingdom period, the main criterion whereby a person could be judged rich was not the amount of property he owned, but the number of retainers he could command. Thus, the link between wealth and status was not direct; wealth was a means to an end, not the end itself.

Early Malaysian rulers did engage in trade. Indeed, they sometimes prohibited their subjects from undertaking trading ventures in order to prevent the possible rise of challenges to their own authority. On other occasions, they permitted certain favoured subjects to engage in foreign trade, contenting themselves with extracting customs duties and other charges.

The family tree of the first 14 sultans of Perak, from 1528 to 1750, indicates that although royal lineage is the most important criterion for succession, succession is not necessarily carried from father to son.

Chinese ceramics, such as these Song Dynasty (960–1279 CE) celadon shards (above) and the white Qingbai vase (below), were unearthed at Sungai Mas in the Bujang Valley of South Kedah. It is believed that ceramics were used as gifts from early Malaysian rulers to favoured subjects.

Language

Malay, in common with other great languages of the world, has a long history of absorbing and incorporating elements of other languages. This cosmopolitan mixing and merging of diverse components has strengthened the ability of Malay to meet the demands of its speakers. The history of the Malay language began with written texts carved in stone 1,300 years ago. Yet, even then, the incorporation of Indic language elements was already unmistakable.

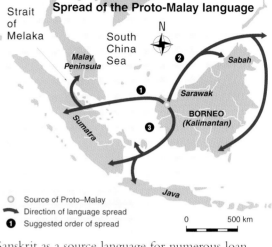

Spread of the Proto-Malay language

- ○ Source of Proto–Malay
- ➤ Direction of language spread
- ❶ Suggested order of spread

0   500 km

Sanskrit loan words in the Malay language were probably introduced by traders and religious pilgrims who imported Buddhist and Hindu ideas, such as Yiqing, the Chinese pilgrim who visited Kedah in the 7th century CE after studying at the famed Buddhist centre of Srivijaya in Sumatra. Buddhist remains, such as the small bronze Bodhisattva (above) discovered at Pengkalan Bujang, Kedah, have been dated from the 9th to the 10th century CE because of their similarity with South Indian images of that period. Hindu remains, such as this 11th–13th century Hindu temple (below), also in the Bujang Valley, are tangible evidence of early religious links between Malaysia, South India and other Southeast Asian centres.

The origin of the Malay language

The prehistory of Malay is indisputably linked to the diffusion of the Austronesian language family, of which Malay is a well-known member. The gradual dispersal of the Austronesian peoples from their homeland in Taiwan around 6,000 years ago, south through the Philippines, and then east and west from there to the islands of the Pacific and Southeast Asia, has been traced by archaeologists and linguists. Most scholars are confident that Malay, that is, Proto-Malay, the ancestor of all of today's Malay dialects, emerged within the riverine systems of western Borneo more than 2,000 years ago. From there, Proto-Malay speakers sailed to Sumatra, the Malay Peninsula, Java and eastern Borneo. Some of the earliest prehistoric sites of western Borneo display indications of far-flung international trade networks which brought Southeast Asian and South Asian cultural artefacts together. In some sites, Dongson drums from northern Vietnam and carnelian beads from India lay side by side.

Sanskrit influences in early scripts

The history of the Malay language begins with its oldest inscription dated to 682 CE. Seventh-century texts found in Sumatra and Bangka, and somewhat later in Java and even the Philippines, bear eloquent testimony to the close linkage between the so-called Old Malay language and Sanskrit, the sacred language of India. First, the orthography, or writing system, of the Old Malay inscriptions is an adaption of an Indic script, Pallava. Secondly, the texts themselves draw heavily from

Discovered over a century ago on a river bank at Kuala Berang, Terengganu, this inscribed stone, known as the Terengganu Stone, is not only the oldest extant evidence of the Malay language in Arabic script, but also the earliest record of the introduction of Islam to the Malay Peninsula. Dated 1303 CE, the inscription outlines Islamic laws couched in Sanskrit terms, such as *Dewata Mulia Raya* (The Supreme God), *adi-pertama* (the first), *tamra* (regulation) and *balanchara* (adultery).

Sanskrit as a source language for numerous loan words. Indeed, the opening lines and all the dates of these early inscriptions are in Sanskrit. However, the frequent omission of the inflectional endings of the Sanskrit loan words, as well as the occurrence of Malay grammatical markers, such as clitics and affixes, with Sanskrit words, already indicates the high degree of integration of Sanskrit elements into the Malay language. So, from the very first recorded appearance of Malay 1,300 years ago, Sanskrit—the pre-eminent cultural language of India—was already incorporated into the literary and court styles of the Malay language.

It is difficult to determine how widespread this Indic influence was in other more colloquial forms of Malay because only official court promulgations have survived from this period. But, it is relevant that many of the Sanskrit terms which appear in these, the oldest Malay texts, are now widely used in contemporary Malay, with few, if any, speakers guessing at their Indian provenance. Over the past 1,300 years, the meanings of many of these words have changed, but their semantic links to the earlier meanings are still clear.

It is important to observe that even during this early period Malay had borrowed not only specialized nouns related to religious practices, such as 'sin', 'incantation' and 'karma', but also verbs and nouns of emotion, such as 'betray', 'felicity' and 'success'. Perhaps more tellingly, Malay had already borrowed conjunctions and particles, such as 'when', 'while' and 'too'.

The introduction of religious concepts

Another point to emphasize is that, in the era when these early Malay inscriptions were produced, Sanskrit was no longer spoken in India as a daily language. It had already become a sacred language of the religious texts of Buddhism and Hinduism, in much the same way that Latin was supplemented by

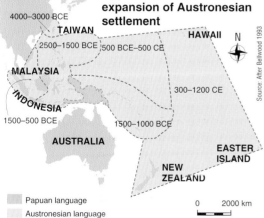

Approximate dates for the expansion of Austronesian settlement

CHINA
4000–3000 BCE
TAIWAN
2500–1500 BCE
500 BCE–500 CE
HAWAII
MALAYSIA
300–1200 CE
INDONESIA
1500–500 BCE
1500–1000 BCE
AUSTRALIA
EASTER ISLAND
NEW ZEALAND

Source: After Bellwood 1993

- Papuan language
- Austronesian language

0   2000 km

Dated 1380 CE, the tombstone of Minye Tujuh in Aceh, Sumatra, is inscribed with a Malay text written in a script derived from India.

basic religious concepts introduced through Indic languages in the pre-Islamic period have become so internalized within the Malay language that they have been retained in today's religious vocabulary. Examples of these include *dosa* (sin), *surga* (heaven), *puasa* (to fast), *neraka* (hell), *pahala* (religious merit) and *derma* (alms). This is not surprising because it is clear that Malay continued to be written in Indic writing systems well into the 17th century.

Early Malay inscriptions

One of the last known lithic examples is the Muslim gravestone of Minye Tujuh from northern Sumatra which is dated 1380. This carved stone bears a commemorative poem, apparently composed in a traditional Indic verse form (*Upajati*), written in Malay with Sanskrit and Arabic loan words and phrases. Even the oldest Arabic script inscription, known as the Terengganu Stone because of its place of origin on the east coast of Peninsular Malaysia, which is dated to the early 14th century, contains 29 different Sanskrit loan words besides Arabic terminology.

This pattern of Sanskrit, and later Arabic borrowings, linking and sustaining elevated literary and legal styles of the Malay language, can be detected even today. Although the early historical period of the Malay language marked a significant period in the incorporation of Indic elements in Malay, the process has been an ongoing and gradual one.

In much the same way as English and other European languages continue to borrow from Latin, Malay has continued to draw upon the resources of Sanskrit and other Indic languages to enrich and diversify its contemporary vocabulary.

SEMANTIC LINKS BETWEEN OLD MALAY AND MODERN MALAY

OLD MALAY	MEANING	MODERN MALAY	MEANING
bhakti–	submission	bakti	service
bhūmi	earth	bumi	earth
doṣā–	transgression	dosa	sin
drohaka	to betray	durhaka	traitorous
jaya	success	jaya	succeed
karmma–	karma	karma	karma
maharddhika	powerful	merdeka	independent
mantrā	formula	mantera	incantation
mūla–	beginning	mula	beginning
prakāra	sort	perkara	issue, case
rūpa	form	rupa	form
samiçrā–	mixed	mesra	intimate
sukha	felicity	suka	to like
tathāpi	also	tetapi	but
tatkāla–	that moment	tatkala	while
velā–	the moment	bila	when

The above diagram shows how numerous Sanskrit words which occur in Old Malay are still apparent in modern Bahasa Malaysia.

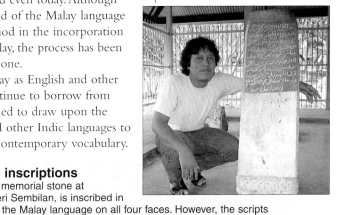

vernacular languages in Europe. The main channel of borrowing Sanskrit words may have been through these ritual, written texts because at that time (7th–8th century) Buddhist centres in Sumatra—particularly Srivijaya—were famous for their Sanskritic scholarship. As late as the 11th century, Chinese envoys collected Sanskrit books in Sumatra to take back to China. Nonetheless, in these 7th-century inscriptions the occurrence of Indic words which are not Sanskrit words, such as *curi* (thief), or Sanskrit words transmitted through some other language, such as *talāga* (lake) from the Sanskrit *tatāka*, suggests other lines of borrowing, not solely through sacred scriptures but also through the spoken Indic languages of the merchants, envoys and religious practitioners who travelled to the Malay-speaking world.

Religions change but words survive

Many other Indic words which appear in these earliest texts are, of course, no longer used in Malay. In particular, many words related to Buddhist and Hindu religious and philosophical doctrines have been lost. Technical terms, such as *jātismara* (memory of previous births) or *anuttarābhisamyaksamvodhi* (complete and highest illumination)—if they ever were in wide use—were probably displaced as Malay speakers embraced Islam. Nonetheless, many

Pengkalan Kempas inscriptions

This 15th-century Islamic memorial stone at Pengkalan Kempas, Negeri Sembilan, is inscribed in

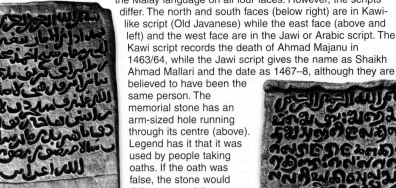

the Malay language on all four faces. However, the scripts differ. The north and south faces (below right) are in Kawi-like script (Old Javanese) while the east face (above and left) and the west face are in the Jawi or Arabic script. The Kawi script records the death of Ahmad Majanu in 1463/64, while the Jawi script gives the name as Shaikh Ahmad Mallari and the date as 1467–8, although they are believed to have been the same person. The memorial stone has an arm-sized hole running through its centre (above). Legend has it that it was used by people taking oaths. If the oath was false, the stone would tighten around the victim's arm.

THE PORT KINGDOMS

The early importance of the region now known as Malaysia was mainly due to its strategic location in the centre of the Malay Archipelago, midway between the sea and land routes linking India and China, as well as its highly desirable rainforest and sea products. Metals were among the most valued trade items, and as the world's most extensive tin deposits are located on the west coast of the Malay Peninsula, it is not surprising that Malaysia's earliest evidence of international commerce has been found there. Most sites uncovered by archaeologists were accessible from the sea or via navigable rivers, for maritime

This locally produced earthenware vessel was found at the entrepôt site of Pengkalan Bujang in Kedah.

trade was an essential element in the emergence of early polities. Between the 5th and 16th centuries, a number of places in Kedah and Perak appear to have functioned as exchange centres, particularly for Indian merchants, while finds of Chinese and Southeast Asian ceramics provide further evidence of a flourishing international trade. Other settlements, which served as feeder ports to larger entrepôts, played an important role in regional trade. Current interpretations suggest that Santubong in Sarawak supplied iron to larger centres nearby, and by this means established connections throughout the Archipelago and beyond.

The context in which these port kingdoms arose is difficult to reconstruct because of sparse evidence. Sites could have been overlooked owing to changes in coastal contours or river courses, while losses also occurred because significant discoveries were made before the introduction of scientific archaeological methods.

Throughout early history, one port would expand to become the dominant centre, while others operated as subsidiary markets. For example, at the height of Srivijaya's authority, local ports still flourished as long as they did not challenge their overlord. Similarly, after the founding of Melaka, Beruas accepted vassal status and continued to trade. This coexistence of a number of ports from which a leader periodically emerged has been called the 'rhythm' of Malay history.

Ports beside the Melaka Strait and in western Borneo shared the same cultural world. Some were located near mountains, which indigenous beliefs associated with powerful spirits, suggesting that ports developed at locations already enjoying prestige as centres of power. Such places acted as conduits for outside ideas, especially religion. Along the Peninsular west coast, interaction with India brought knowledge of Hinduism and Buddhism, as attested by temple remains and statuary. Similarities between Malaysian and Sumatran sculptures, and stylistic links between gravestones in Aceh and Beruas, indicate that this was a culturally interactive environment which survived despite the rise and fall of political and economic centres. Local legends reinforce the sense that a common store of myths and heroes developed in the region. Perhaps the most important cultural element was the successful adaptation of outside ideas to fit the local culture, an ability which has always been one of the strengths of Malay culture.

This bronze Buddha image found in Kedah is dated from the 6th to the 7th century CE.

The Bujang Valley

In Malaysia's richest archaeological region, the Bujang Valley of South Kedah, archaeologists have unearthed evidence which proves the existence of an ancient polity from the early centuries of the Christian era. It was probably the kingdom of Qie zha mentioned by Yiqing, a 7th-century Buddhist pilgrim from China, and the same as that known to the Tamils as Kadaram, Kidaram or Kalagam, called Kataha in Sanskrit.

The most prominent Hindu temple excavated so far is the 11th-century Candi Bukit Batu Pahat (Site 8) which is made from cut sandstone obtained from the adjacent Sungai Merbok Kecil. It was the first monument in the Bujang Valley to be comprehensively excavated and reported.

At Sungai Mas (Site 32), Chinese ceramics from the Tang Dynasty and West Asian ceramics and glassware have been found.

The evolution of the kingdom

The Bujang Valley extends from Gunung Jerai in the north, to the Sungai Muda in the south and the Strait of Melaka in the west. Its principal rivers are the Merbok and the Muda, while Gunung Jerai, at 1217 metres, is the highest land form in the area. Settlements were located on ridges and natural levees along the rivers, and on the foothill slopes, while the main temples were built on elevated land.

The discovery of prehistoric sites at Guar Kepah provides evidence that the kingdom evolved from local settlements. Presumably, these merged together under a strong leader who established a landfall port for traders from India and China. Buddhist inscriptions found in the valley are proof of Indian contacts from the 5th to the 6th century CE. As a result of increased trade in the Strait of Melaka, the Bujang Valley developed into a collecting centre for the products of the Malay Peninsula, and by the 7th century it had evolved into an entrepôt.

Sungai Mas: The original capital

Evidence for the Bujang Valley's entrepôt status is provided by trade products found in the Sungai Mas area, believed to be the centre of the kingdom from the 5th to the early 11th century. Sungai Mas was eminently suitable for a capital as this area today is one of Kedah's major rice-producing regions. In addition, it had the ability to provide shippers and traders with landfall port facilities.

Based on the evidence of religious inscriptions, statuaries and temples, the religion at Sungai Mas was Buddhism. Apart from the Sungai Mas area, Buddhist monumental sites were located at Bukit Pendiat (Site 17), Bukit Meriam (Site 26), Bukit Coras (north of Gunung Jerai) and Sites 14 and 21/22 in Pengkalan Bujang.

Pengkalan Bujang: A later entrepôt

By the end of the 10th century, the area around Pengkalan Bujang became prominent. Evidence of this is based on the density of West Asian and Song Dynasty ceramic deposits, as well as imported glass and beads discovered in the region. These wares were mixed with the products of Thailand and Indochina. The very cosmopolitan nature of the deposits led archaeologists to conclude that Pengkalan Bujang was an entrepôt. Further evidence which suggests its importance from the end of the 10th century is the large number of temples, artefacts and images associated with Hinduism. The rich variety of artefacts indicates a prosperous and innovatory culture during this period. Local materials were used in temple construction, and tiles, pottery and gold and silver reliquary ornaments were produced locally.

The kingdom in the Bujang Valley evolved earlier than Srivijaya, but came under Srivijaya's influence around 670 CE.

However, the kingdom was allowed to retain entrepôt status as long as it did not challenge Srivijaya. At the end of the 11th century, when Srivijaya declined, the Bujang Valley became powerful again. It was still in existence in the 14th century, as evidenced by finds of Ming Dynasty ceramics, but declined with the coming of Islam and the rise of Melaka as an entrepôt.

The Hindu temple at Site 50, Bendang Dalam, has been reconstructed near the Bujang Valley Archaeological Museum.

The Hindu temple at Site 19, Pengkalan Bujang, has been reconstructed on site.

Archaeological sites of the Bujang Valley

The site numbers shown on this artist's impression of the Bujang Valley follow the system established by the archaeologists H. G. and D. Quaritch Wales in the 1930s. Other prominent locations are marked as follows:

A. Sungai Mas Archaeological Project
B. Sungai Muda
C. Guar Kapah
D. Sungai Merbok
E. Pengkalan Bujang
F. Bujang Valley Archaeological Museum

Bujang Valley

South China Sea

PENINSULAR MALAYSIA

Strait of Melaka

The Kinta Valley

The location of Gangga Nagara, an ancient kingdom mentioned in the Sejarah Melayu—the court annals of the 15th-century Melaka Sultanate—has long been the subject of historical debate. Various sites have been suggested, including Beruas in Perak and the Bujang Valley in Kedah. However, historians now agree that Kedah was the ancient kingdom of Kadaram, and while the early Islamic settlement at Beruas is believed to be the last capital of Gangga Nagara, the Kinta Valley in Perak is now being considered as the earlier site of this lost kingdom on account of several Buddhist bronzes which have been found there.

This late 19th-century print shows Chinese coolies working in a Kinta Valley tin mine. All of the Buddhist bronzes found in this region have been unearthed during mining operations which have greatly altered the original environment. and probably destroyed the remains of any early settlements.

This old photograph is the only evidence of the seated bronze Avalokitesvara found at Sungai Siput in 1938.

This four-armed bronze Avalokitesvara from Sungai Siput holds the *aksamala* (rosary) in the upper right hand, and the *kalasa* (water vessel) in the upper left hand. The lower right hand is in the *varadamudra* (charity gesture), and the lower left hand probably held the *padma* (red lotus).

Evidence unearthed from tin mines

Because Gangga Nagara was described in the *Sejarah Melayu* as standing on a hill 'at Dinding on the other side of the Perak River', Beruas has always been considered the most likely site because of its location. However, none of the remains and artefacts from Beruas correspond to those of the 8th–9th century Srivijayan era when Gangga Nagara was at the height of its power. This leads to speculation that perhaps the original capital was further inland—in the Kinta Valley—and that gradually it moved downstream to Beruas as the rivers silted up.

The Buddhist bronzes found in the Kinta Valley are believed to date from the 6th to the 9th century CE, and were unearthed during dredging or were washed out of open cast mines where they had been buried many metres under alluvium. Other than the bronzes, no evidence has been found to establish an exact settlement site for the Kinta Valley. As these artefacts have been found in various regions of the valley, the capital could have changed its location, as was the case in Kedah.

Environmental factors probably played a major role in the changing nature of early Kinta settlements. During the British colonial period, the Kinta Valley was one of the world's major tin-producing regions, and centuries before, early tin miners had also worked the valley, resulting in not only heavy siltation but sometimes causing rivers to completely change their course. Malay legend, early European maps and geological evidence show that the Sungai Perak, the state's major river, formerly entered the Melaka Strait much further north, at the present Sungai Dinding estuary. When this river mouth

Location of Buddhist bronzes found in Perak

N

• Taiping
Kuala Sepetang
Kuala Kangsar
Sungai Siput Utara
SUNGAI PERAK
Tanjung Rambutan •
Ipoh •
Beruas
• Batu Gajah
KINTA VALLEY
Pulau Pangkor
• Lumut
Kampar •
• Sungai Siput
• Kampung Gajah
Bidor •
SUNGAI PERAK
• Teluk Intan

South China Sea
PENINSULAR MALAYSIA
Strait of Melaka

0   2 km

🧍 Buddhist bronzes

silted up, the waterway changed course to empty into the Strait further south, near Teluk Intan, its present position. The Sungai Kinta is now a tributary of the Sungai Perak but previously it had entered the Strait independently and was presumably a much larger river than it is today. The towns of Bidor and Beruas, and the city of Ipoh, are now further inland than these sites would have been in early historic times, leading scholars to speculate that it was feasible for these areas to have supported a port kingdom such as the legendary Gangga Nagara.

The bronze standing Buddha images

Archaeologists and historians base much of their speculation of a Kinta Valley kingdom on the discovery of several Buddhist images. However, the present whereabouts of all but one of these is unknown. The first of five Buddhist bronzes

South Asian influences
The Pengkalen Buddha found near Ipoh displays various influences. The wearing style of the robe (1) reflects the earliest Buddhist art of Gandhara (1st–4th century CE), from Peshawar, Pakistan. The thinness of the cloth, which clearly shows the shape of the body (2), indicates similarities with the Gupta School (4th–5th century CE) from Sarnath, India, while the hairstyle (3) and *usnisa* (cranial protuberance) are characteristic of images from South India (2nd–3rd century CE) and Sri Lanka. From the incorporation of these varying styles there is a strong possibility that the standing Buddha from Pengkalen was produced in Malaysia during the 6th century CE.

holds is the *aksamala* (rosary), *dhanu* (bow), *kartri* (knife), *danda* (staff) or a broken *ankusa* (goad), *kalasa* (water vessel) and *padma* (red lotus). Stylistically, it resembles the Pala School of North India (9th–12th century CE) but it is believed to have been produced locally in the 8th or 9th century CE.

A shared iconography with Srivijaya
Malaysia's finest and most important Buddhist bronze discovered to date is the eight-armed Avalokitesvara in the Tantric form of Amoghapasa unearthed at Bidor in 1936. The identifiable symbols it holds include an aksamala, *tridandi* (trident), *pustaka* (book), *pasa* (noose), padma and kalasa. Scholars believe that it dates from the 9th century CE mainly on the basis of its unusual iconography—a tiger's skin loincloth. This iconographic symbol is unknown in Indian images of this deity, but it occurs in similar images discovered at Palembang (Sumatra), in Java, at Satingphra and Chaiya (southern Thailand), and in Tibet—all believed to have links with the development of Srivijayan religious art.

Perhaps this iconography was linked with the Hindu deity Siva who also wore the tiger's skin. In Southeast Asia during the Buddhist and Hindu period before the coming of Islam, such images may have been representations of the ruler. The idea of identifying rulers with images of deities most probably originated from the region of Srivijaya. During the 7th century CE, this idea was popularized in Palembang, and by the 8th century CE, it had spread to southern Thailand and Java.

Documentary evidence also supports this practice. The historian O.W. Wolters noted that the kings who preceded the Melakan Sultanate, such as Sri Tri Buana, the King of Palembang, were identified as incarnations of Avalokitesvara. This was the traditional practice during the Srivijayan period, and Bukit Seguntang in Palembang was seen as Mount Potala, the traditional sanctuary of Avalokitesvara.

While there is very little hard evidence for suggesting that the Kinta Valley is the site of Gangga Nagara, the Buddhist images which have been unearthed over a large area of the valley are definite evidence of the existence of more than one Buddhist settlement during the Srivijayan era.

discovered in Perak was dredged up from a tin mine at Pengkalen, near Ipoh, in 1931. This standing Buddha image, measuring 46 centimetres in height, went missing during World War II, and all that remains is a photograph.

Dredged up at the same time from Pengkalen was a bronze throne believed to have been for a Buddhist image. Measuring 21.5 centimetres, the throne was dated in 1940 by the archaeologist H. G. Quaritch Wales as being produced no later than the 6th century CE. He based this date on the style of other Buddha thrones from Southeast Asia.

Published in 1908, *Twentieth Century Impressions of British Malaya* contained a photograph of a bronze standing Buddha which had been discovered 18 metres deep in a tin mine at Tanjung Rambutan. Although it is difficult to identify, the image is similar to the bronze Buddha discovered in Kedah's Bujang Valley which was influenced by the Gupta School, but made locally. Archaeologists believe the Tanjung Rambutan image was also produced locally no later than the 6th century CE.

The bronze images of Avalokitesvara
In 1908, a Buddhist bronze image was discovered in an open cast tin mine near Sungai Siput. Standing 28 centimetres in height, the image is of a four-armed Avalokitesvara, one of the most important Bodhisattvas, or 'enlightened beings', of Buddhism. It was discovered together with a pottery vessel containing gold ornaments, but the present whereabouts of these and the image is unknown. This Avalokitesvara is stylistically similar to Pallava images, leading scholars to date it to about the 7th century CE.

Three decades later, another bronze Avalokitesvara was discovered in the same mine. This eight-armed image is seated on a bronze throne, and among the iconographical symbols it

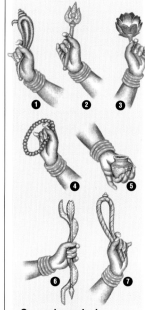

Sacred symbols
The symbols held in the hands of Buddhist images are important clues in the identification of the various Buddhas or Bodhisattvas ('enlightened beings'). Some of the symbols which occur in the Kinta Valley bronzes are as follows:
1. goad (*ankusa*)
2. trident (*tridandi*)
3. red lotus (*padma*)
4. rosary (*aksamala*)
5. water vessel (*kalasa*)
6. bow (*dhanu*)
7. noose (*pasa*)

Presently in the collection of Muzium Negara (the National Museum), this eight-armed Avalokitesvara wears a tiger's skin loincloth—an iconographic symbol which began in Srivijaya and was influenced by local beliefs. Later, the iconography spread through the Srivijayan Empire to Malaysia, and it is believed to have even reached Tibet with the return of Atisa, the Tibetan Buddhist reformer, who is thought to have studied in Srivijaya in the 11th century CE.

Beruas

Ancient royal graves at Beruas in southwestern Perak are tangible evidence of a 15th–16th century Islamic kingdom, while documentary accounts confirm that during this time Beruas was the paramount power of Perak. On account of its geographical situation—mentioned in the Sejarah Melayu (Malay Annals)—Beruas has long been the favoured site of the legendary Gangga Nagara, an earlier Indianized kingdom. However, archaeologists have so far failed to find any substantial evidence in support of this theory.

Progress has bypassed the present-day town of Beruas in southwest Perak, the site of an Islamic kingdom which thrived as a contemporary of Melaka during the 15th and 16th centuries CE.

Tin ingots
Discovered at Beruas, these tin ingots are remnants of the kingdom's tin trade. Originally cast as shell-backed ingots, they later developed into animal shapes, such as tortoises, and were used as an early form of currency. The casting of ingots was supervised by a *pawang* (shaman). The animal-shaped ingots are believed to have been a substitute for animal sacrifices.

Reports of Beruas are found in the 15th-century *Sejarah Melayu* (Malay Annals), which is pictured above showing the title page of a copy written in Melaka in 1873.

A 15th-century port kingdom

The oldest documentary mention of Beruas is found in the *Sejarah Melayu*, which relates that in the 15th century CE, the king of Beruas went to Melaka to seek military support from Sultan Mahmud Shah (1488–1511) in his war with neighbouring Manjung. The sultan bestowed the ruler of Beruas with the title Tun Aria Bija Diraja, and dispatched a war party to Perak. Manjung was subsequently defeated and placed under the rule of the Melaka Sultanate, but Beruas was given royal consent to govern it.

Beruas was mentioned by the Portuguese apothecary, Tomé Pires, in his *Suma Oriental* (1512). He writes that Beruas was an important port with a busy harbour much frequented by trading ships. It supported a large population, and although the majority were rice farmers, Beruas was well-known for its merchants who traded at the Peninsular ports of Melaka and Kedah, at Pasai and Aceh in Sumatra, in Thailand, and as far afield as Gujerat and Bengal in India. During the time of the Melaka Sultanate, Beruas was ruled from Melaka by an Orang Besar (a dignitary) and every year the settlement sent 6,000 calains (a tin ingot used as currency) to Melaka. Recent discoveries of tin ingots could represent the remnants of the Beruas tin trade.

The villages along the banks of the Sungai Beruas mentioned by Tomé Pires could have been Kampung Pulau Meranti and Kampung Kota. These two villages are the location of ancient graves, as well as the sites where tin ingots, tin animal money and Chinese blue-and-white wares from the Ming Dynasty (1368–1644) have been found.

Mysterious royal graves

Makam Raja Beruas ('the graveyard of the Rajah of Beruas') at Kampung Kota contains most of the graves, while a few have been found at Kampung Pulau Meranti. They are marked by carved Islamic gravestones known as Batu Aceh, which were usually reserved for royalty and dignitaries. Similar gravestones are found at other Peninsular Malaysia sites, and in Aceh, where it is believed they originate from—hence their name. The gravestones date to the 15th and 16th centuries CE and are presumed to be those of the rulers and their families although their identities remain a mystery.

The origin of the ruler of Beruas

There are four different stories depicting the origin of the founder of Beruas. One source mentions that the ruler, Ganji Sarjung, came from Kedah in the 5th century CE. Another source, *Riwayat Negeri Perak Darul Ridzuan*, states that after the death of Raja Shah Johan (?), Beruas was without a ruler for a long time until the arrival of a princess named Mesoka of unknown origin. She was made chief until Tun Saban ibni Tan Chendera Panjang Ibni Laksamana Tan Panjang Melaka arrived in Beruas. He was a descendant of Raja Iskandar Shah, the first ruler of Melaka, and together with his family had escaped from Melaka when it fell to the Portuguese. On his arrival, Mesoka appointed him as an administrator of Beruas. After the death of Mesoka, Tun Saban decided to invite a prince from Kampar, Sumatra, to take over as ruler. At that time, Kampar was ruled by Sultan Mahmud Shah of Melaka, who sent his son, Mudzafar Shah, to become the new ruler of Beruas.

Another version, from the *Hikayat Raja-Raja Pasai*, states that the first ruler of Beruas came from Aceh. He was Malik (?)-al-Mansur, the younger brother of Sultan Mahmud Azzahir (c.1455–77), who, together with his royal entourage, arrived in Beruas in about 1456.

Oral histories from Aceh also stress the role of the Acehnese in the foundation of Beruas. Prominent rulers of Acehnese descent included Daik Ismail and Syamsul Baharin, who both died during a war with the Thais. After that time, Beruas came under Thai and later Melaka rule. According to the *Sejarah*

Melayu, Beruas was still in existence after Melaka fell to the Portuguese in 1511. After the exiled Sultan Mahmud Shah set up court in Bintan, he sent an emissary to 'the Western territories' (Beruas and Manjung) to summon their ruler, Tun Aria Bija Diraja, who had not paid his respects since the fall of Melaka. The ruler of Beruas subsequently sailed to Bintan with a fleet of 30 ships to pledge allegiance to the sultan.

The legendary Gangga Nagara

Prior to the 15th century, the name of another Perak kingdom appears in the *Sejarah Melayu*, namely, Gangga Nagara. In the past it has been assumed that this was another name for Beruas because of its location as described in these annals: 'Now this city stood on a hill: and though from the front it appeared to stand at a great height, it was quite low at the back. Its fort still stands to this day, at Dinding on the other side of the Perak River.' It goes on to relate the tale of Gangga Nagara falling after a great battle against the Cola who raided the ports of the Melaka Strait in the 11th century CE.

Archaeological researches in Beruas have failed to find the site of an earlier kingdom, although the discovery of a celadon bowl dating from the Song Dynasty (960–1279 CE) is evidence of earlier occupation. However, it is probable that there was an Indianized kingdom somewhere in Beruas before the 15th century CE. On the basis of archaeological finds it is now believed that the capital of the 15th–16th century Islamic kingdom of Beruas was most probably located at Kampung Kota, although Kampung Pulau Meranti is another possibility.

The decline of Beruas

The discovery of tin ingots and tin money in Beruas confirms the literary evidence that Beruas was a tin producer in the 15th century CE. Tin was exported from Beruas via Melaka during the Melaka Sultanate.

After the fall of Melaka in 1511, Beruas was probably trading independently. However, its stature as a kingdom diminished with the

This Batu Aceh gravestone is one of several at the graveyard known as Makam Raja Beruas, located at Kampung Kota, Beruas.

Makam Raja Beruas

All the Batu Aceh gravestones found in the two royal graveyards known as Makam Raja Beruas 1 and 2 at Kampung Kota are undated and unnamed, but are believed to date from the 15th and 16th centuries CE. They were probably imported from Aceh, Sumatra, and are inscribed with phrases from the Qur'an or the Hadith, which are written in the Kufi script, the oldest form of Arabic calligraphy. Other decorative motifs include rosettes, flowers and geometric patterns. Some scholars speculate that the curling shoulders (1 and 2) indicate women's graves, whereas those without (3 and 4) are of males. Panels (5) often contain the Kalimah Shahadah, the Islamic declaration of the faith, which also occurs on shoulders (6). The lotus motif (7) derives from both Indian and Egyptian sources, while the meaning of the geometric side panels (8), known as 'ladders', is unclear.

establishment of the Perak Sultanate in 1528. The silting up of the river was also a major factor in the kingdom's decline.

The present-day town of Beruas is located near the old watercourse of the same name. Local legend and scientific surveys show that the river was much larger in earlier times, and that it has changed course several times during the historical period. A geo-hydrological survey in 1962 showed that the Perak River once flowed past Beruas to drain directly into the Strait of Melaka. A subsequent sea rise caused the enlargement of the Sungai Dindings estuary which captured the Perak River. It is believed that this estuary then extended all the way to Beruas where ships could anchor. The survey also revealed that a later changing of the Perak River course to south of the Dindings caused the Sungai Beruas to silt up. This occurred around the 16th century when the kingdom of Beruas declined. No doubt, the lack of a proper harbour would have been disastrous for a trading kingdom such as Beruas which was dependent on maritime links for its existence.

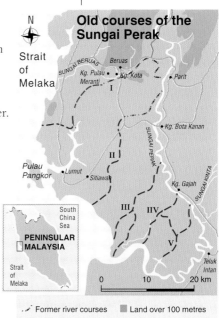

Old courses of the Sungai Perak

N

Strait of Melaka

Sungai Beruas   Beruas
Kg. Pulau Meranti   Kg. Kota   Parit
I

Kg. Bota Kanan

SUNGAI PERAK

Pulau Pangkor   II
Lumut   Sitiawan
Kg. Gajah

SUNGAI KINTA

South China Sea

PENINSULAR MALAYSIA

Strait of Melaka

III   IV

V

Teluk Intan

0   10   20 km

Former river courses   Land over 100 metres

Santubong

Legends abound about Santubong, Sarawak's richest protohistoric archaeological region, where evidence has been found of an ancient seaport and iron-smelting centre, the remains of a Buddhist stupa and associated artefacts, Chinese trade ceramics from the Song and Tang dynasties and mysterious rock carvings.

Rising 823 metres above sea level, Gunung Santubong, pictured here in the 19th-century lithograph 'Santubong Entrance' by W. Brierly and G. Hawkins, has acted as a beacon for South China Sea navigators for at least a millennium.

Discovered at Bukit Maras, this stone Buddha is similar to 7th-century Buddha images from the Indian Gupta School. Other artefacts found at this site include a stone tile decorated with a charging elephant, beads, and a finial, believed to be from a stupa.

Legends associated with Santubong

Santubong generally refers to the area around Gunung Santubong, a distinctive solitary peak located on a peninsula in the delta of the Sarawak River. Kampung Santubong, a traditional Malay fishing village, is situated at its foot next to the river.

There are numerous theories as to the origin of the name 'Santubong'. In the local Malay and Iban dialects it means 'coffin', in Chinese it generally means 'mountain visible a long way off', or specifically, in the Kheh dialect, 'king of the jungle', and in Hokkien, 'the mountain of the wild pig'.

There are two main local legends associated with Santubong. The first tells of two beautiful princesses who descended to Earth from Kayangan, the heavenly abode of people endowed with mystic powers. The older princess, Puteri Santubong, was an accomplished weaver, while her younger sister, Puteri Sejinjang, was an expert paddy pounder. They lived and worked harmoniously together, vowing not to quarrel, until they fell in love with the same man. They then began arguing and eventually came to blows. As a result of breaking their vow, they were petrified and turned into Gunung Santubong and Gunung Sejinjang, the two mountains which face each other at the entrance to the Sarawak River. Legend has it that the peculiar features of each mountain were caused by blows from the implements of trade which the princesses used as weapons. The face of Santubong was gashed by Sejinjang's pounder, while Sejinjang's head was flattened by a blow from Santubong's spindle.

The second legend concerns Datu Merpati, a Malay nobleman and adventurer, also from mystical Kayangan, from whom the local Malays trace their descent. Originally known as Radin Depati, he fled to Johor with his brother, Radin Urei Sri, after

losing a battle. In Johor, Radin Depati married the ruler's daughter, Dayang Suri. While voyaging to Santubong they encountered a fierce storm and were forced to land at Sambas (Kalimantan) where Radin Urei Sri married the ruling queen. Continuing their journey they reached Tanjung Datu, in present-day Sarawak, where Radin Depati changed his name to Datu Merpati and that of his wife to Datu Permaisuri. They eventually arrived at Santubong after being attacked by crocodiles during their journey. However, Datu Merpati killed the crocodile leader and placed its head at a spot marked by a large boulder, known today as Batu Buaya (Crocodile Rock).

After further adventures involving the courts of Brunei and Johor, Merpati and Permaisuri retired to Tanjung Datu, while their son, Chipang, ruled at Batu Buaya.

In another interpretation, Santubong and Sejinjang were said to be the daughters of Datu Merpati. Although these legends are vague and fanciful, they have parallels in Malay court histories, such as *Salasilah Raja-Raja Brunei* and *Tarsilah Raja-Raja Sambas*, which also mention that the royal families of Johor, Sambas and Brunei were linked by marriage.

An ancient port and iron-smelting centre

Although there is no concrete literary proof that Santubong was once a trading port engaged in iron smelting, there is ample archaeological evidence.

At Sungai Jaong, a site located beside a creek about 2 kilometres from Kampung Santubong, dense reefs of iron slag, together with numerous shards of Tang Dynasty

Carved in low relief on a boulder at Sungai Jaong, Sarawak, this spread-eagled, half life-size human figure is known locally as Batu Gambar, literally 'rock picture'.

Santubong sites

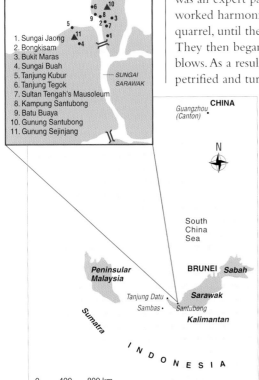

1. Sungai Jaong
2. Bongkisam
3. Bukit Maras
4. Sungai Buah
5. Tanjung Kubur
6. Tanjung Tegok
7. Sultan Tengah's Mausoleum
8. Kampung Santubong
9. Batu Buaya
10. Gunung Santubong
11. Gunung Sejinjang

SUNGAI SARAWAK

CHINA
Guangzhou (Canton)

N

South China Sea

BRUNEI Sabah

Peninsular Malaysia

Tanjung Datu Sarawak
Sambas Santubong
Kalimantan

Sumatra

I N D O N E S I A

Java

0   400   800 km

Legend has it that the face of Gunung Santubong was disfigured by a blow from a stone paddy pounder.

(618–906 CE) and Song Dynasty (960–1279 CE) ceramics and earthenware, as well as glass beads, were recovered. Also at this site, about 10 sandstone boulders in the vicinity are engraved with anthropomorphic and geometric figures. The quantity and distribution of the iron slag debris and shards are evidence of a substantial habitation site where iron smelting was carried out from about the 10th century CE.

Excavations at the Bongkisam site revealed a similar mixture of artefacts and iron slag. The most unusual find at Bongkisam was a paved stone platform, which could have been a Buddhist stupa, and a ritual deposit box. More Buddhist artefacts were found at Bukit Maras on the slope of Gunung Santubong, overlooking Bongkissam.

The site of Sungai Buah, across the river from Santubong, yielded the remains of an iron foundry and many shards of Song Dynasty ceramics. Other sites in the Santubong region include Tanjung Kubur, a cemetery with predominantly Song ceramics, and Tanjung Tegok, another earlier cemetery site.

Based on archaeological evidence from the six related sites, Santubong may have played a part in the international trade network linking West Asia, Southeast Asia and China. The Buddhist and Hindu relics found in Santubong indicate that this region of Borneo, known as Tanjung Pura, was in minor contact with India or with other 'Indianized' states in Southeast Asia. It is quite likely that the southwestern region of Borneo was part of the 7th–13th century Srivijayan Empire of South Sumatra, as well as being part of the succeeding 14th–15th century Javanese Majapahit Empire.

Iron production at Santubong

The presence of iron slag intermixed with other dateable finds from the Santubong sites indicate that the manufacture of iron was carried out from about the 10th to the middle of the 14th century.

There are two schools of thought as to the type of iron working that was carried out. The original excavators, Tom Harrisson, Stanley J. O'Connor and Cheng Te-Kun, assumed that the iron industry was conducted on a large scale and was export oriented. They posited that the Chinese or Indian method of production was employed because they believed that the fragments of earthenware cylinders found there were crucibles. They also believed that the iron ore was obtained from the hinterland, that foreigners were employed in the industry, and that the iron produced at Santubong was exported mainly to China during the Tang and Song dynasties.

The other theory, by J. W. Christie and F. E. Treloar, is that the so-called crucibles are actually tuyères, and that the method used was the primitive bloomery process still practised by the Kayan and Kenyah people of Sarawak. Christie argues that the iron slags were probably concretions of natural iron, and that Santubong supported a medium-sized local industry situated at the source of its raw material. It is posited that the iron produced at Santubong was used in the hinterland and at other feeder ports along the coast. It is possible that the industry declined when the iron workers moved upriver to richer ore deposits. Whichever theory is correct, it is evident that Santubong was an ancient trading centre engaged in iron working to some degree.

One confirmed historical fact concerning Santubong is that an old grave near Bongkisam is that of Sultan Tengah, the first and last Sultan of Sarawak, who was murdered at Batu Buaya in 1641. He was appointed by his stepbrother, Abdul Jalilul Akbar, the 10th Sultan of Brunei, in 1598. His grave is marked by a mausoleum built in 1995.

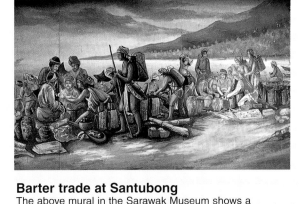

Barter trade at Santubong

The above mural in the Sarawak Museum shows a cosmopolitan group of traders bartering on the beach at Santubong. Formerly, scholars believed that Santubong attracted international traders. However, current opinion differs. Unlike the Bujang Valley sites in Kedah, there is no evidence to suggest that the Sarawak River Delta sites had direct international trade links with China. Sarawak trade goods, which included rhinoceros horn, spices, edible birds' nests, dammar and other jungle produce, were probably first shipped from Santubong to another regional entrepôt. In return for these goods, local traders received Tang and Song Dynasty ceramics (below), and glass beads and coins similar to those found at Kuala Selinsing in Perak. These artefacts have been found in profusion throughout the Santubong sites, offering proof that a thriving seaport existed here from at least the 10th century CE, ending around the 13th century.

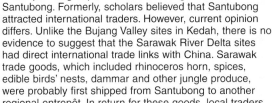

The Bongkisam shrine

Excavated in 1966 by Tom Harrisson of the Sarawak Museum and Stanley J. O'Connor of Cornell University, this stone platform at Bongkisam in the Santubong region could date from the 10th century CE. The architecture is similar to Buddhist–Hindu temple remains in the Bujang Valley of Kedah (see 'Candi architecture') and is the only one so far found in Sarawak. Buried in a vertical shaft under the structure (marked by the white card, left) was a ritual silver deposit box (below). The spherical, three-piece box consists of a lid, decorated on the interior with a sunburst pattern, a dish-shaped bottom, and a divider surmounted by a solid gold lingam. When the box is closed the lingam is directly beneath the sunburst, suggesting a spiritual link, perhaps a representation of the Hindu–Buddhist universe. Scattered around the ritual box were semiprecious stone beads and 142 gold objects. The latter (above right) included gold foil shapes symbolic of both Hindu and Buddhist faiths. The snake could be a *naga* or a hooded cobra, the crescent moon was worn by both Siva and Manjusri, the lotus is found in sacred deposits through Southeast Asia, the elephant is revered in Hindu–Buddhist cosmology, as is the tortoise. The seated male figure is in a meditation posture and is not readily identifiable with either Buddhist or Hindu iconography.

The best preserved architectural remains in the Bujang Valley are those of Candi Bukit Batu Pahat (The Temple on the Hill of Cut Stone). In 1960 (left) it was excavated and reconstructed by the archaeologist Alastair Lamb.

ABOVE TOP: An artist's impression of Kedah's Bujang Valley, the most famous of Malaysia's early entrepôts, at the height of its power in the 11th century. Ships from China, India, Southeast and West Asia stopped over, as evidenced by finds of trade products. Some architectural remains are believed to have been Hindu–Buddhist temples.

ABOVE: Ceramics, textiles and beads on display at the Sarawak Museum in Kuching comprise some of the trade items imported through early Malaysian entrepôts.

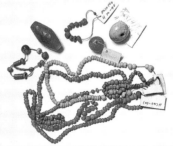

ABOVE: Beads of glass and semiprecious stones, including a 3-cm-long carnelian bead (top left), were found at the port site of Kuala Selinsing, Perak, where trade products dating from 200 BCE to 1100 CE have been discovered.

ABOVE: Archaeological finds from Kuala Selinsing include this earthenware pot which is believed to have been of local manufacture.

RIGHT: This 14-cm-high bronze statue, perhaps dating from the 14th century, was found near Pekan, Pahang. The basket was a later addition.

FROM PORT KINGDOMS TO ENTREPÔTS

Before the emergence of the Melaka Sultanate in the early 15th century, Malaysian ports ranged from minor supply depots to large entrepôts specializing in international trade. The formation of small ports began during the Bronze Age, as evidenced by finds of bronze drums and bells, believed to originate from North Vietnam, at Malaysian sites, including Kuala Terengganu, the Tembeling River Valley of Pahang, Klang and Kampung Sungai Lang in Selangor, and Muar in Johor. These ports emerged because their hinterlands provided minerals, such as tin, which was necessary in the production of bronzeware. Traders probably travelled to the Malay Peninsula expressly for this mineral.

Thai celadon recovered from the 14th–15th-century 'Nanyang' shipwreck discovered off Pahang.

Over time, some supply ports grew into large trading ports handling the trade of early Malay kingdoms, and eventually they evolved into port kingdoms involved in East–West trade between India, China and West Asia. According to Chinese sources, port kingdoms such as Qie zha (Kedah), Ji lan dan (Kelantan), Fo-lo-an (Kuala Berang, Terengganu), Deng ya nong (Kuala Terengganu), Pang geng (Pahang) and Le yue (Johor) were already in existence in the 5th century CE. During this port kingdom period, other small ports which may have been founded by then, include Kuala Selinsing in Perak, Jenderam Hilir in Selangor, the Bernam Valley of Perak/Selangor and Karimun Island in the Riau Archipelago.

The pace of long-distance and international trade heightened during the 7th century bringing large-scale change to port kingdoms strategically located along the East–West trade route. Some of these ports became increasingly stronger and wealthier as almost all vessels plying the route would call in to trade and stock up on supplies of firewood, water and food before continuing to their destinations in China or India. Because of the volume of trading vessels in these ports, other merchants from neighbouring ports also came to trade, thereby eliminating the need to wait for vessels to call on their ports.

From the beginning of the 7th century, the port kingdom at Sungai Mas in Kedah's Bujang Valley had begun to expand its operations into entrepôt trade, as did other port kingdoms in the north of the Malay Peninsula, including Takuapa on Thailand's west coast, Chaiya, Nakhon Si Thammarat and Patani on Thailand's east coast, and Santubong in Sarawak. Evidence of these changes comes from finds of imported porcelain, beads, glass, mercury and amber which indicate the level of international relations and the entrepôt role of such ports from the 7th until the 14th century. In Borneo, Santubong acted as an entrepôt, supplying imports to other smaller Borneo ports and the interior. Imported goods, such as bronzeware, pottery, beads and textiles, were exchanged for rainforest and sea products which were highly sought after by traders from South and West Asia, as well as from China. The lists of products produced by the various areas in Southeast Asia were recorded in Chinese documentary sources and included aromatic woods, resins, spices and pharmaceuticals. Because this entrepôt trade also involved local traders, Malay ships were a familiar sight on the East–West trade route.

Entrepôts along the Melaka Strait

Documentary sources indicate that there were already several entrepôts on the west coast of the Malay Peninsula 2,000 years ago, but archaeological research has not yet established their exact locations. However, it has been verified that 1,500 years ago there were at least two entrepôts: one was sited in the Bujang Valley of South Kedah, and the other at Kuala Selinsing, Perak. They possessed several common features, including a heterogeneous population which fluctuated in size with the rhythm of the monsoons.

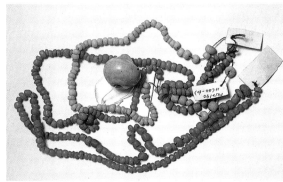

Thousands of beads, including an unusually large bead made of yellow glass, have been discovered at the entrepôt site of Kuala Selinsing in Perak, which dates from about 200 BCE to the 10th century CE.

Pillar bases from South Kedah

Various stone pillar bases found at sites in the Bujang Valley are on display at the Archaeological Museum inMerbok, Kedah(above).They are believed to have been bases for wooden pillars which supported the tiered, thatched roofs of Hindu–Buddhist temples. Associated artefacts (5th–12th century CE) suggest that this architecture was prevalent during the time when the Bujang Valley was an international entrepôt.

Shell jewellery

A number of shell bracelets and rings, as well as *Trochus niloticus* shells used in their manufacture, were found at the early entrepôt of Kuala Selinsing, Perak.

Wind patterns dictate trade movements

The relatively consistent monsoons led to a predictable pattern in the Melaka Strait. In January, ships sailed southwest from China to the Malay Peninsula, then from June to August they sailed back. Ships going to South India left the Peninsula with the southwest monsoon (April to August), or the northeast monsoon in December, while those heading towards the Strait from northwest India sailed in March, or from August to September. Other seasonal patterns governed the shipping movements from the southeast of the Peninsula.

Ports along the Strait of Melaka came into existence because of this climate, as it was impossible to make the journey from China to India in one season. Ships could only hope to sail to a halfway point in the Strait. At this port, goods and passengers would be unloaded, and ships would refill their holds with cargo from the other end of the route, which had been stored here to await their arrival. The reversal of the monsoon would carry them back the other way. At these emporia, shippers found safe harbours, a population accustomed to dealing with foreigners according to an international code of conduct, and dependable institutions for exchanging their cargoes for other profitable commodities.

Mode of business at the entrepôts

Transactions along the Asian sea trade route followed a standard pattern. Upon arrival in a port, ships were boarded by representatives of the local rulers, the cargo was valued and duties were levied. Duties were variable: some goods were more heavily taxed than others, while 'gifts' to the king or other authorities might secure a reduction in tax. Some imports were claimed as monopolies by local rulers.

The mode of exchange varied. In many cases, no bargaining was allowed. Instead, goods were exchanged for others at fixed rates. In other cases, after monopolized goods and duties were taken, the shippers were allowed to deal with designated traders. In yet others, a freer exchange might take place. In all cases, exchanges were moneyless.

An important figure in the system was the official known during Melakan times as the *syahbandar*. This word is usually translated as 'harbourmaster', but his duties went far beyond those associated with this position today. The syahbandar was often a foreign merchant who had acquired the trust of the ruler, and had been given the task of mediating between merchants of his home area and the ruler.

Malaysian rulers sometimes engaged in trade directly, but more often they delegated the conduct of their commercial affairs to the syahbandar. Although foreign ships did not remain long in Malaysian ports, the foreign merchants did, while awaiting the change of the winds, and the syahbandar was in charge of this transient foreign merchant community.

The prosperity of entrepôts in the Strait depended on their ability to create favourable trade conditions. One of the most important was the ability to keep piracy within limits. By attracting the allegiance of the Orang Laut, nomadic boat dwellers who comprised a significant proportion of the population, Malay rulers achieved this objective, and simultaneously obtained the services of a force of skilled seafaring manpower. A similar set of relations existed with hinterland dwellers—the ancestors of the present-day Orang Asli. Bonds of personal loyalty between Malay rulers and gatherers of forest products such as dammar and rattan, brought both commercial and military benefits.

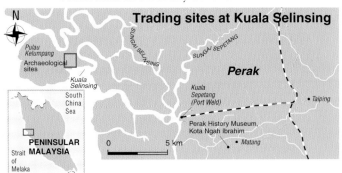

Trading sites at Kuala Selinsing

N

Pulau Kelumpang
Archaeological sites

Kuala Selinsing

SUNGAI SELINSING

SUNGAI SEPETANG

Perak

Kuala Sepetang (Port Weld)

Perak History Museum, Kota Ngah Ibrahim

• Taiping

• Matang

South China Sea

PENINSULAR MALAYSIA
Strait of Melaka

0   5 km

Documentary evidence

It is believed that the earliest maritime trade route was that between the Strait of Melaka and India. A 2,000-year-old Greek manuscript mentions huge ships coming to India from the East, probably from the Strait of Melaka, with rich cargoes. Another Greek text written around 100 CE mentions several emporia along the Strait of Melaka. Indian texts written about 2,000 years ago also contain references to the 'Land of Gold' (Suvarnabhumi), which the Greeks called the Golden Khersonese, believed to be the Malay Peninsula.

Kedah enters history in the 5th century CE, when a 'great sea captain', Buddhagupta, inscribed a prayer for a safe voyage on a rock in the Bujang Valley. Other verifiable events in the rise of Kedah as an entrepôt include a mission sent to China in 638 CE, a stopover by the Chinese pilgrim Yiqing in 671, and his return visit in 685 when Kedah had been placed under the suzerainty of Srivijaya.

Indian and Arab sources from the 8th and 9th centuries mention places with names such as Kalah or Kataha, referring to Kedah and the adjacent coast of South Thailand. Kedah retained commercial importance, although Takuapa further north also possesses archaeological evidence of important entrepôt activity during this period.

Archaeological evidence

It has been speculated that the Kuala Selinsing area of Perak was the location of an early entrepôt, as sites there have yielded artefacts of widely varying age. A stone inscribed in Indian-style script may date from 500 CE, and shards from the Northern Song Dynasty (960–1126 CE) suggest that the site was in existence during that time. Although no remains of permanent architecture have been found, there is evidence that imported glass was being recycled to make beads. Scholars believe that Kuala Selinsing may have been a secondary collecting point for hinterland produce, rather than an international entrepôt.

In South Kedah, in addition to approximately 60 sites of architectural remains spanning the long period 500–1300 CE, several concentrations of imported ceramics have been discovered. Around 1000 CE, Chinese porcelain became an important article of trade, providing archaeologists with much useful data on Southeast Asian commerce. However, for the preceding centuries, few trade goods have survived to mark the exact locations of entrepôts.

One of the most important centres of early trade in South Kedah is Kampung Sungai Mas which has yielded important ceramic remains, including Chinese and Vietnamese wares of the 9th–13th centuries, Middle Eastern wares of the

Trading sites of South Kedah

Sungai Mas—Kedah's earliest entrepôt

Brick and laterite architectural remains, together with ceramics dating from the 7th centuy CE, have been discovered at Kampung Sungai Mas, which is believed to have been an early entrepôt. The most recently excavated site (No. 32, top right) has yielded a large number of shards, including those of the Tang Dynasty (618–906 CE) (shown *in situ* centre right), local earthenware with bound-paddle decorations (right), and Qingbai wares made during the Song (960–1279 CE) and Yuan (1280–1368) dynasties.

11th and 12th centuries, fragments of Middle Eastern glass vessels, and glass beads, possibly made locally. At nearby Kampung Simpor Tambang, 10th-century Chinese and 11th–12th century Middle Eastern ceramics were found, as well as signs of bead-making. Other significant accumulations of imported ceramics, including large quantities of Chinese wares of the Song period, have been found at Pengkalan Bujang and Kampung Sireh. Shards found at Pengkalan Bujang belong mainly to the Song or early Yuan Dynasty (1280–1368), with a few Middle Eastern shards, but many remnants of glass and glass beads. At Kampung Sireh, ceramics of the Song, Yuan and Ming (1369–1644) dynasties, mixed with Thai and Vietnamese wares, have been reported in stratified layers. These have been exposed over a distance of 80 metres along the bank of a stream.

Archaeological evidence suggests that numerous crafts were conducted in the coastal entrepôts. In addition to bead-making, clay, bronze and iron may have been worked.

The entrepôt sites of South Kedah and Kuala Selinsing, Perak, seem to have been abandoned around 1300 CE. The reason for this is unclear, though it may have been related to several factors, including the extension of Thai influence into the Strait, the restrictive trade policy of the Ming Dynasty, which came to power in 1369, and the changing economic climate associated with the introduction of Islam. Melaka, founded in about 1400 CE, represented a continuation of the ancient port kingdom tradition.

An earthenware bowl excavated from Sungai Mas, Kedah.

Raw glass materials, of a type used for bead-making, have been found at the archaeological sites of Kuala Selinsing, raising the possibility that some of the glass beads found there in abundance were manufactured on site.

Objects of horn, bone and ivory have been found at Kuala Selinsing, including a bone tool (lower right), and an unfinished knife handle made from deer horn (lower left), which was excavated from the Kelumpang 6 site. The estuarine settlements are believed to have existed from about 200 BCE to the 10th century CE.

Srivijaya

In the 7th century CE, the appearance of numerous inscriptions in South Sumatra signalled the birth of Srivijaya, the first great Indonesian kingdom, which attained dominance over the Strait of Melaka, the main artery of maritime trade between India and China, and controlled the port kingdoms of both the Malay Peninsula and much of Sumatra. Srivijaya was the paramount power in the region until its decline in the 11th century.

The bustling waterfront of Palembang, South Sumatra, is a reminder of the days when the city was the capital of the Srivijayan Empire, during its 7th–11th century reign as the dominant maritime entrepôt of Southeast Asia.

This stone Ganesa found in the vicinity of Palembang provides more evidence that the capital of Srivijaya was located there.

Evidence from inscribed stones

The whereabouts of the powerful maritime kingdom known to the Chinese as Shi li fo shi, and to the Arabs as Sribuza, had puzzled scholars until 1918 when the historian George Coedès identified them as Srivijaya, the same kingdom mentioned in various 7th-century stone inscriptions located in South Sumatra (see map). He also identified Srivijaya as the kingdom where the Chinese Buddhist monk Yiqing stopped over on his travels from China to India and back in the years 671–85 CE. When Yiqing arrived in Srivijaya, it was already a well-established kingdom and the recognized Southeast Asian centre of Sanskrit studies.

It is believed that Srivijaya extended its authority over Malayu (Jambi), Qie zha (Kedah) and other kingdoms in the Strait of Melaka from the 7th century. A century later, it controlled Ligor, Takuapa and the rest of the kingdoms in the northern part of the Malay Peninsula. This expansion was made possible with the support of a 20,000-strong army which included the sea warriors known as the Orang Laut. At the same time, Srivijaya had family links with the rulers of the Sailendra Dynasty of Java. This is based on the evidence of the Ligor and Kalasan inscriptions (see map), the Pala Copper Plate (Nalanda, India) and the Cola inscription of 1025 CE (Tanjore, India).

A hub of Buddhist learning

The dominance of Srivijaya as the Southeast Asian centre for Buddhist studies is evident from Yiqing's mention in 671 CE that those who wanted to go to Nalanda (the Buddhist centre in India) must try to study Sanskrit in Srivijaya. The kingdom continued its pre-eminence as a centre for learning until about the 12th century as reports mention that Atisa, the great Tibetan Buddhist reformist, studied at Srivijaya from 1011 to 1023 CE. The ruler of Srivijaya, Raja Dharmapala, also presented a book to Atisa.

Numerous references to Srivijayan rulers being patrons of Buddhism are found in the stone inscriptions which also mention their strong diplomatic ties with India and China. The Karang Berahi inscription describes how a ruler of Srivijaya donated a park to his people. The Ligor inscription of 775 CE tells how the ruler of Srivijaya ordered his royal monk Jayanata to build three Buddhist temples at Chaiya (southern Thailand). According to the Nalanda inscription, dated about 850–60 CE, a temple was built at Nalanda upon the request of Raja Balaputra of Srivijaya. In 1006 CE, another Srivijayan ruler had a temple built at Nagapattinam, India. Further, in the 11th century, Raja Diwakara of Srivijaya donated some money for the upkeep of the Tao temple at Guangzhou (Canton).

Control of the Strait of Melaka

Srivijaya was able to become a powerful maritime power at the end of the 7th century CE because the areas it controlled had products which the East–West traders sought. Moreover, under Srivijayan control, the Strait of Melaka and the east coast of the Malay Peninsula became pirate free, offering safe passage for shipping. By controlling Kedah, Chaiya, Takuapa and other ports, Srivijaya

The Empire of Srivijaya

ANDAMAN SEA

Aninditapura

SOUTH CHINA SEA

Kuah
Pan Pan
Chaiya
Takuapa
Ligor
Grahi
Tambralinga
Langkasuka?
Kelantan
Kedah
Ch'ih-t'u
Kuala Tan-tan
Selinsing
Lamuri
Kota Cina
Barus
Tenderam
Hilir
Po-lu-shih
Panai
Panai
Kampar
MALAY PENINSULA
Lo-yuen
Pulau Tioman
BORNEO
Pontianak
Sambas
Pochi

INDIAN OCEAN

SUMATRA
Malayu
Malayu
Bangka
Srivijaya
Srivijaya

JAVA SEA

SUNDA STRAIT
Sunda
JAVA
Mataram

Srivijaya Inscriptions:
1 Bangka
2 Talang Tuwo
3 Telaga Batu
4 Kedukan Bukit
5 Palas Pasemah
6 Karang Berahi
7 Ligor
8 Takuapa
9 Lubok Tua
10 Kalasan

Realm of the Sumatran Sailendras, 9th-10th centuries
Empire of Srivijaya c. AD 1000
Extension of empire c. AD 1082
Voyage of Yiqing, AD 689-95

was able to promote itself as the most prominent entrepôt in Southeast Asia. At the same time, Srivijaya controlled trading activities at other ports along the Strait of Melaka and on the Peninsula. However, Srivijayan hegemony did not destroy existing trade patterns as these ports were allowed to continue with their trading activities as long as they did not challenge Srivijayan control. Besides the port kingdoms which acted as secondary entrepôts, there were also feeder ports, such as Jenderam Hilir and Kuala Selinsing in the Malay Peninsula, and Panai, Kampar and Kota Cina in Sumatra. These ports and kingdoms had established relationships with Indian, Arab and Chinese traders, as well as the inland societies from which they obtained rainforest products, but at the same time they had to maintain peaceful relations with Srivijaya.

At the port kingdoms under Srivijayan control, foreign traders, such as Tamil merchants, were given their own areas to live in. Evidence of their presence is found in stone inscriptions. Dated 1088, the Lubuk Tua inscription of northwest Sumatra, mentions the presence of about 1,500 Tamil traders, while the Takuapa inscription of southern Thailand indicated that a Tamil merchant guild was represented at Takuapa in the 9th century CE.

It is apparent that Srivijaya enforced its authority over other ports and kingdoms which had long-established administrative systems, religious practices and trade patterns. Peninsular Malaysian kingdoms, such as Pan-pan, Langkasuka, Chi tu, Malayu and Kedah, are mentioned in Chinese records from the 2nd century CE. At the end of the 7th century, Srivijayan ships were used to carry traders, travellers and monks to India and China, stopping off at Malayu and Kedah. The list of names became longer

This lithograph by J. Nieuhof, dated 1732, depicts the City of Palembang under attack by the Dutch fleet in 1659. This is one of the earliest European views of the city which most scholars believe was the hub of the Empire of Srivijaya.

as centuries went by: Takuapa on the northwest coast appeared in about the 9th century CE, and in the 10th century, Tioman Island was mentioned in Arab records.

A regional centre for rainforest products

Srivijaya acted as the main supplier of Southeast Asian trade products and as the major distributor of trade products from West Asia, India and China to other ports in Southeast Asia, including those of northwest Sumatra, the Malay Peninsula, western Borneo (Sambas and Pontianak) and the Irrawaddy coast of Burma. Forest products which Srivijayan shippers took to China included benzoin, camphor and dammar, which were used to make pharmaceutical products and incense, as well as spices, aromatic woods, ivory, tin and gold.

Srivijaya was able to sustain its role as the dominant entrepôt in Southeast Asia because it possessed the necessary sociopolitical and administrative organizations, as well as providing attractive port facilities. The Telaga Batu inscription mentions administrators appointed by the ruler who were in charge of the various bureaucratic functions necessary in the day-to-day running of the empire. It recounts that Srivijaya was a *kedatuan* (kingdom) which controlled many other regional kingdoms. Its territories were divided into a number of *mandala* (administrative districts), each administered by a *datu* (headman).

Srivijaya's power began to wane from the 12th century CE. Its belligerent relationship with the Cola rulers of South India resulted in the Cola attacks on kingdoms under Srivijayan rule along the Strait of Melaka during the 11th century. This resulted in Kedah becoming independent from Srivijaya, while Panai and Kampar also distanced themselves. In 1088, Malayu became more powerful than Srivijaya, and Srivijaya's power base shifted there. By the first quarter of the 13th century, other kingdoms, such as Chaiya and Tambralinga, were no longer under Srivijayan rule.

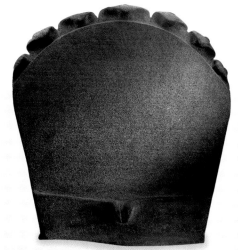

The Telaga Batu inscription
Found near present-day Palembang in South Sumatra, this inscribed stone describes how the various rulers in charge of the kingdoms and districts under the control of Srivijaya gave allegiance by drinking a special 'oath water'. This water was poured over the stone which was carved in the likeness of a seven-headed cobra. After flowing over the inscribed oath, the water was collected from the spout at the bottom. The inscription mentions the consequences to those who broke the oath, and the happiness for those who obeyed.

Discovered at Bukit Seguntang, Palembang, the legendary hill where the first of the Malay rulers appeared, this stone Buddha image is over 2 metres in height. It bears similarities to Buddhist sculptures from the 7th to the 8th century CE found in Nalanda, North India, where an inscribed stone tells of a temple built there by a ruler of Srivijaya.

The Cola attacks

In the early 11th century, the Tamil-controlled Cola kingdom of South India, a large maritime power of the time, embarked on a policy of imperial expansion in the northern Strait of Melaka. After conquering all the main Srivijayan centres, the Cola established their colonial capital at Kedah, which was viewed in ancient India as a significant commercial and political centre. Tamil influence over Kedah lasted no longer than a century, but Tamil cultural and religious influence left a strong imprint on Malay memories.

Hindu motifs of lotuses and stepped pyramids symbolizing holy Mount Meru decorate this sandstone lintel fragment from India, which is now at the Bujang Valley Archaeological Museum in Kedah. These motifs, imported during the Cola period, appear in Malaysian designs from that time onwards.

The importance of Kedah in ancient Indian writings

Kedah, under various names, including Kalagam and Kataha, is mentioned in several works of Indian literature written nearly 2,000 years ago. A Tamil poem, 'Pattinappalai', depicts lively commerce between India and Kalagam, and the term 'Kataha-dvipa' appears in Indian writings earlier than the famous 'Suvarnadvipa' (Sumatra). Kataha-dvipa was later one of nine major *dvipa*, the main units of Bharatavarsa or Greater India—the entire world as known to early Indians. The ancient Tamil work, *Kathasarit-sagara*, contains several stories portraying Kataha as an important and rich country near Suvarnadvipa. In one, a princess from Kataha is shipwrecked near Suvarnadvipa during a voyage to India; in another, a merchant sails from India to Kataha, pursued by his wife. In yet another, a man sought his son and his younger sister in Kataha-dvipa, Kar-pura-dvipa (probably North Sumatra), Suvarnadvipa, and Singhala-dvipa (Sri Lanka).

According to a Chinese report, 'Srivijaya is a double kingdom and the two parts have separate administrations'. Most scholars agree that Palembang, Sumatra, was the southern base of the empire, but speculate as to the whereabouts of the centre of the northern kingdom. Evidence, however, points to Kedah, as Indian and Arab sources from the 8th to the 11th century called the king of the Strait of Melaka 'ruler of Srivijaya and Kataha'. The latter was considered as one of the two 'poles' of Srivijaya. Some Indian writers even called the ruler of the Strait of Melaka 'Raja of Kataha'.

More information on Kedah comes from a South Indian inscription called the Larger Leiden Plate (1025 CE), which contains the information that King Rajaraja granted the revenues of a village to support a Buddhist temple in a monastery then under construction by Culamanivarman, king of Kadaram, at Nagapattana. It adds that this village was granted to the monastery built by Sri Maravijayottunggavarman in the name of his father Culamanivarman, and that the former was of the Sailendra family, rulers in Srivisaya [*sic*], who had extended the rule of Kataha. From this inscription it is apparent that the Cola viewed the Sailendra as rulers centred in the Malay Peninsula, whose authority stretched to Srivijaya.

Kedah conquered by the Cola

The relationship between Kedah, Srivijaya and India was harmonious in the early 11th century, but 20 years later the situation changed drastically. An inscription from Tanjore, the Cola capital, says that in 1025 CE the Raja of Kadaram was captured by the Cola, his great war gate was seized, and his treasury stolen. It also lists other Srivijayan territories which were defeated.

Several historians have concluded that the Cola conquest of Kedah, and the rest of Srivijaya, was a momentary event of no lasting significance. However, reconsideration of the evidence suggests otherwise. In 1068 CE, something happened in Kedah which involved both the Cola and Srivijaya, but exactly what transpired is a mystery. The Inscription of Perumber (1069–70 CE), says: 'Having conquered Kadaram, (he) was pleased to give (it) (back) to (its) king who worshipped (his) feet (which bore) ankle-rings.' The simplest explanation would be that Kedah revolted against Srivijaya, but was put down by the Cola king and

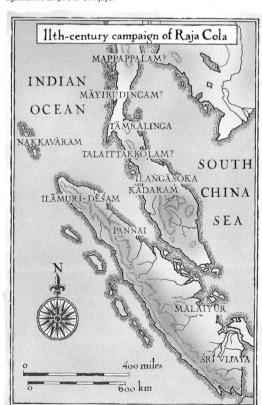

Discovered at Site 24 in the Sungai Muda Valley of South Kedah, this pedestal for a religious sculpture features a drainage spout for holy water used to lustrate the deity. It is similar to those in South Indian temples indicating close cultural links between the Malay Peninsula and the Cola kingdom.

The place names mentioned in the campaign of Raja Cola in 1025 CE are taken from an inscription found on a temple wall in Tanjore, South India, which describes a raid against the Empire of Srivijaya.

11th-century campaign of Raja Cola

MAPPAPPALAM?

INDIAN OCEAN

MĀYIRUDINGAM?

 TĀMRALINGA

NAKKAVĀRAM

TALAITTAKKŌLAM?

SOUTH CHINA SEA

ILANGĀSOKA

KADĀRAM

ILĀMURI-DĒSAM

PANNAI

N

MALAIYŪR

SRI VIJAYA

400 miles

600 km

then returned to Srivijayan rule. However, later information casts doubt on this theory. In 1070 CE, Kulottungga became raja of the Cola kingdom. In Chinese sources he was called Di-hua-jia-luo, probably a transcription of Diwakara. According to the Sung shi, in 1077 CE, two ambassadors came to China from India. Another inscription from Canton mentions that from 1064 CE to 1067 CE the king of Srivijaya was named Diwakara, adding that in the same year mentioned by the Sung shi, he sent two emissaries to China whose names were also the same as those of the Cola ambassadors.

Inscriptions from early in Kulottunga's reign describe how he was 'gently raised, without wearying (her) in the least, the lotus-like goddess of the earth residing in the region of the rising sun'. This region could have been Kedah. Kulottungga's link to Kedah is mentioned in two other sources. According to the Smaller Tamil Leiden Grant (1089–1090 CE), he donated a village to the Sailendra monastery at the request of several envoys from the king of Kidara (Kedah). The other reference in a 12th-century Tamil poem mentions Kulottungga's destruction of Kadaram.

Speculation as to Kulottungga's role in Kedah is ongoing. The historian Coedès concluded that he had been a high official in Kedah before becoming the Cola king in India. O.W. Wolters, another historian, disagreed. He believed it was coincidence that the name of Srivijaya's king was identical to that of the Cola king. However, the puzzle remains, as the Chinese in 1068–77 CE thought that the Cola kingdom was a vassal of Srivijaya.

It is currently thought that he served as an apprentice viceroy in Kedah before returning to India to assume the throne. In view of the report that the king of Kedah had become king of the Cola kingdom, perhaps the Chinese wrongly concluded that the Cola had been conquered by Kedah. Whatever the case, the Tamil connection with the Strait of Melaka remained close throughout the 11th century as Tamil inscriptions of that time have been found in Sumatra. Cola power declined in the early 12th century, and after that date Indian sources seldom mention Kedah.

South Indian architectural links

Architectural remains, known as *candi*, are the main source of data on links between Kedah and the Cola kingdom. Many examples of Kedah's ancient architecture consist of a *vimana* (closed room) housing an icon, and a *mandapa* (pavilion). This architectural style is unknown in Indonesia except for a site in North Sumatra which possibly dates from the same period. In the rest of Southeast Asia it is only found in 12th–14th century Buddhist sites of central Thailand

Cola influence on temple designs
Originally sited at Kampung Bendang Dalam on the west bank of the Sungai Bujang, but since reconstructed at the Bujang Valley Archaeological Park, this Hindu temple complex known to archaeologists as Site 50 features a *vimana*, or closed room for housing a deity, and a *mandapa*, or pavilion. The structure to the right is believed to be a minor temple as Hindu sculptural fragments were found inside it. This type of complex is rare in Southeast Asia, but common in South India, and is dated to the 11th century when the Cola Empire attacked Kedah.

The drain for holy liquid found at two sites in Kedah is also rare in Southeast Asia. Both the drainage system and the vimana–mandapa structures are common in South India. Therefore, it is highly likely that the presence of these architectural elements in Kedah is a mark of strong and long-standing links with South India.

According to the archaeologist Nik Hassan Shuhaimi, candi in Kedah can be divided into a Buddhist phase from the 5th to the 10th century, south of the Merbok River, and a Hindu phase, from the 10th to the 13th or 14th century, north of the river. The rise of Hinduism at this period indicates a heightening of South Indian links in the 11th century. Hindu sculpture with a strong South Indian influence also forms an intrusive element in southern Thai art during the 9th to 11th centuries. Such strong artistic influence may well reflect equally as vigorous political contacts.

Another intriguing piece of evidence of Tamil influence comes from the *Sejarah Melayu* (Malay Annals), the history of the 15th-century Melaka Sultanate. It traces the origin of the Srivijayan royal house to a prince whose name, Raja Chulan, is probably a thinly disguised version of Raja Cola.

Believed to be part of a lingam, a representation of the Hindu deity Shiva, this stone fragment was discovered at Site 13 in the Bujang Valley, South Kedah.

Hindu reliquaries found in Kedah
Hindu cultural and religious influence over the Malay Peninsula during the 11th-century campaign of Raja Cola included the practice of burying reliquaries under the foundations of Hindu temples. At Candi Bukit Batu Pahat, believed to have been built in the same century, stone reliquaries (1) measuring 18 centimetres square have been unearthed. A bronze pot was found in the central chamber surrounded by eight smaller chambers (2). Gold and silver foil relics, which include a female divinity holding a lotus flower and a trident (3), a Nandi bull (4), and inscribed foil discs (5) were found in both the pot and the chambers. Semiprecious gemstones, including rubies and sapphires, possibly imported from India or Sri Lanka, were also found.

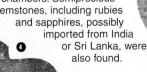

From Srivijaya to Temasek to Melaka

From about the 5th century CE until the coming of the Europeans in the 16th century, control of the strategic Strait of Melaka, the major maritime artery for East–West trade, has been a significant factor in the rise and fall of several important Malay entrepôts, including Kedah, Malayu, Srivijaya, Temasek and Melaka—the most prosperous of all the trading kingdoms.

Early historic Malay trading kingdoms

This 1856 lithograph of Singapore shows Fort Canning Hill (Bukit Larangan), the former residence of the rulers of Temasek (ancient Singapore), topped by a flagpole, in the far mid-distance.

The rise and fall of Srivijaya

Between 400 CE and about 650 CE, several important Malay kingdoms, including Kedah and Malayu (Jambi), evolved along the Strait of Melaka. However, by the late 7th century, they were eclipsed by the powerful Empire of Srivijaya, headquartered near modern Palembang. Evidence for this comes from the account of Yiqing, the Chinese monk who studied Sanskrit in Srivijaya before travelling to India. On his return from India in 685 CE, he wrote that Kedah and Malayu had 'become Srivijaya', implying that they had been subjugated by Srivijaya. Indeed, neither Malayu nor Kedah sent any diplomatic missions to China for the next several hundred years. Chinese depictions of Srivijaya as a 'double kingdom' with one capital in the south (Palembang) and another in the north (Kedah) suggest that the two rulers who controlled the two entrances of the Strait had close relations but exercised considerable local autonomy.

In 1025 CE, the Cola kingdom of South India launched a successful naval invasion of Srivijaya (see 'The Cola attacks'). According to archaeological remains, the ports along the Strait did not suffer as a result of this invasion. Indeed, they may have become more prosperous as Srivijaya's centuries-long policy had been to monopolize all international contacts (see 'Srivijaya'). Evidence from Srivijaya for the period from 1050 to 1300 CE has revealed fewer trade goods than at Kedah, Jambi (South Sumatra), Kota Cina (North Sumatra) and sites in the Riau-Lingga Archipelago. This suggests that Srivijaya went into decline, but its former subjects, freed from Srivijayan overlordship, became much more affluent.

Ceramics from a Ming Dynasty shipwreck off the coast of Pahang were probably made by Thai potters in the late 14th century. During this era, Malay ports suffered from declining trade due to the Ming emperor's ban on international trade.

The Buddhist temple site of Muara Takus, upriver from present-day Jambi, shows evidence of building activity during the 12th and 13th centuries when Jambi became the most prominent of the Sumatran trading kingdoms.

The re-emergence of Jambi

The Chinese continued to use a term, 'the Three Vijayas', for the main trading centre in the Strait. However, the overlord of the 'Three Vijayas' was probably living in Jambi, which reversed its formerly subordinate position in the late 11th century. In 1225, a Chinese writer recorded that Pahang, Terengganu, Langkasuka and Kelantan were vassals of the Three Vijayas, and that the chief of Fo-lo-an (now identified as Kuala Berang, Terengganu), was directly appointed by Jambi who sent a prince there each year to burn incense in a temple. Fo le an was quite prosperous; its temple had a roof of bronze and its annual tribute to Jambi consisted of gold and silver bowls.

In the late 13th century, Jambi was subjugated by the eastern Javanese kingdom of Singasari. In 1292, Singasari also fell, but its successor, Majapahit, soon restored Javanese control over the Sumatran port kingdoms.

The monolith from Temasek

This stone fragment, probably inscribed in Old Malay, is all that remains of a monolith which originally stood by the mouth of the Singapore River. It may have been erected by the Majapahit conquerors of Temasek (old Singapore) in the 14th century. Munshi Abdullah, scribe to Thomas Stamford Raffles, the founder of modern Singapore, was witness to its destruction by British engineers in the 1830s. He was appalled that the stone was lost before it had been deciphered. 'We Malays have a proverb,' he wrote. 'What you cannot replace you should never destroy.'

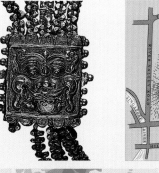

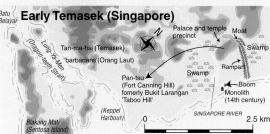

Early Temasek (Singapore)

Evidence of Temasek

In the early 19th century, the ramparts and moat of the original Malay kingdom of Temasek could still be discerned (top right map). Their location, as well as landmarks referred to in 14th-century Chinese sources, are marked on the above map. The gold armlet (top left) bearing a Javanese *kala* head (a highly conventionalized lion's head design) was found on Fort Canning Hill and has been dated to the Majapahit period of the mid-14th century.

Temasek and Chinese trade

The growing prosperity of Malay ports was due to the increased freedom granted by the Chinese government to private merchants, who, for the first time, were allowed to voyage to Southeast Asia. New ports appeared, including Temasek, located on the site of modern Singapore, which grew from a minor port in the 13th century to a place of importance by the early 1300s. In the 1320s, the Mongol government of China sent a mission to Long ya men, 'Dragon's Tooth Strait' (probably the western entrance to Keppel Harbour), to acquire elephants. The port reciprocated by sending a diplomatic mission to China. By the 1330s, Temasek traders were mentioned in a Vietnamese source. The Chinese merchant Wang Dayuan who visited Temasek at that time described it as a place of honest traders where some Chinese merchants lived, but where pirates lurked in the surrounding seas. A few years earlier, he said, Temasek had been attacked by the Thais, but the city's defensive walls had succeeded in holding off the besiegers.

By 1365, Temasek had become a vassal of Majapahit. Three years later, the Mongols were overthrown by the Ming Dynasty who restored the old policy forbidding Chinese merchants to go abroad, and only permitted exchange under the guise of tributary trade. Archaeological evidence shows that the Malay ports suffered as a result. Also, as Javanese vassals, the Malays were not permitted to have direct relations with foreign countries, and thus were excluded from the trade with China.

Parameswara conquers Temasek then founds Melaka

In 1389, when the king of Majapahit died, Parameswara, a Malay prince of Palembang, attempted to use this opportunity to regain independence from Java. As an independent ruler, he would be permitted to send an official trading mission to China, but the Javanese retaliated by attacking the island of Bangka where the bulk of his seafaring subjects lived. He fled to Bintan Island, and then to Temasek where he assassinated the local ruler and established a new kingdom.

Parameswara then attempted to create a new political and economic centre from which the southern entrance to the Strait of Melaka could be controlled—a successor to Srivijaya. He resided at Temasek until 1397 when he was driven away either by the Javanese or the Thais.

Parameswara escaped and after living in the forest with his followers for three years, made his third and most successful attempt to establish a new power base in the south of the Strait. This time he selected a location further north and called it Melaka. Backed by his loyal 'navy' of Orang Laut and his impeccable Malay pedigree, he was able to establish a port which quickly became the most prosperous trading city in Southeast Asia. The news of Melaka's meteoric rise to fame spread to China, all around the Indian Ocean and to the shores of the distant Mediterranean. Chinese envoys visited Melaka in the early 15th century and the entrepôt was given the monopoly on Chinese goods, a right which quickly attracted international traders. When Parameswara embraced Islam and became the first Sultan of Melaka, the growth of the kingdom accelerated, and its commercial success reinforced the spread of Islam throughout the Malay World. Melaka's dominance over the Strait of Melaka continued until 1511 when the Portuguese successfully attacked the city, marking the beginning of Western domination in the Malay Archipelago.

Taken from Middleton's *Complete System of Geography* (1770), this engraving of Melaka mistakenly depicts the town in reverse. St Paul's Hill, topped by the church of the same name and surrounded by the fortifications of A Famosa, should be located on the right side of the river, and vice versa. Prior to the Portuguese conquest, this hill was the location of the sultan's palace and mosque.

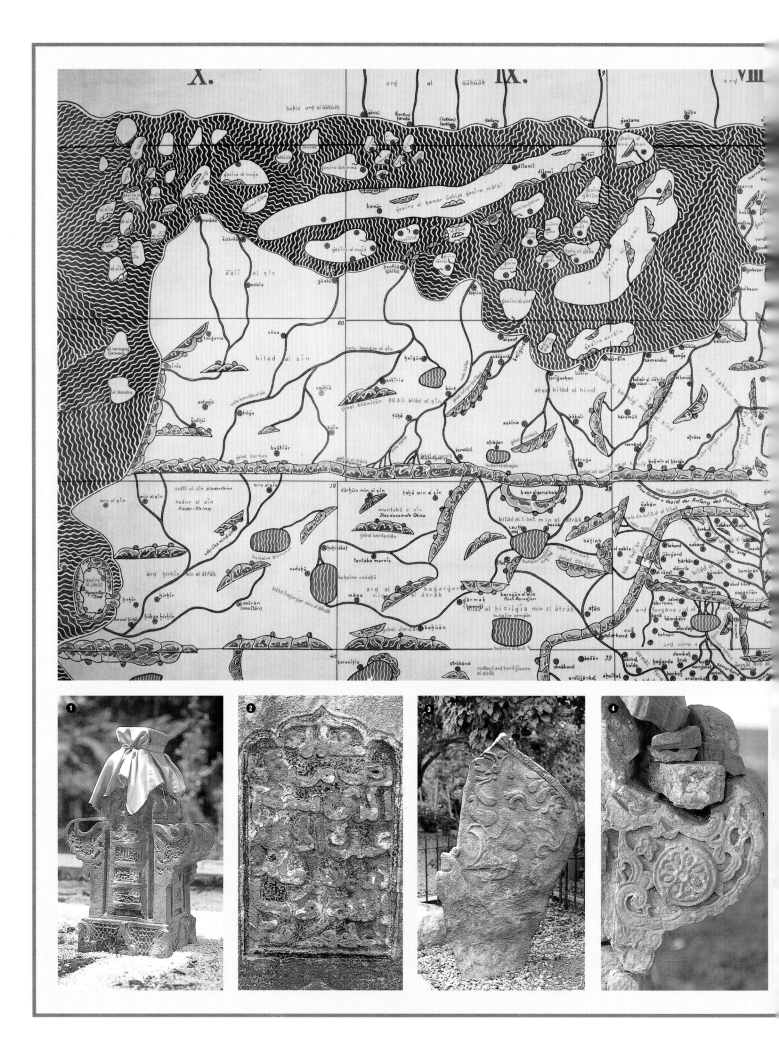

THE EARLY ISLAMIC PERIOD

The arrival of Islam in the late 13th and early 14th century CE, and its consequent acceptance by much of the Malay World during the 15th and 16th centuries, was an important historical event which greatly influenced the Malay lifestyle and culture. The integration of Islam into everyday life is an ongoing process in Malaysia even today.

A Kijang coin from Kelantan, c. 1400.

While the conversion of the Sultan of Pasai, North Sumatra, in the late 13th century, and the acceptance of Islam by the Melakan Sultanate in the early 15th century are both well documented in Malay and European sources, the process of Islamization, particularly in Malaysia, is not very clear. Evidence of the spread of Islam before the Melakan period consists of Arab, Persian and Chinese textual sources, together with gravestones and pillars inscribed with Arabic script which have been found along the trade routes. However, these sources do not indicate the first Malaysian location to receive Islam, or provide evidence as to the role of the local people in its propagation. Academics agree that trade was the major factor in spreading the religion, but they are divided as to whether Islam arrived via West Asia, India or China.

Although Islamic inscriptions dating to the 11th century CE have been found in Vietnam, Brunei and Java, and artefacts, including Arabic coins bearing dates from this same century, have been found in Malaysia, the earliest confirmed evidence of the introduction of Islam to Malaysia comes from the stele known as the Terengganu Stone, discovered in the state of the same name. The inscribed Islamic proclamation, dated 1303 CE, is the oldest extant Malay text in the Arabic script, and is proof that Islam had been introduced to the east coast of the Peninsula a century before the conversion of the Melakan ruler. The use of some Sanskrit religious terms has led some scholars to speculate that the inscription was produced during the transitional period when the population was in the process of conversion.

Melaka's conversion to Islam was a watershed event which contributed greatly to its meteoric rise as the region's most powerful commercial centre. During its 15th-century heyday, Melaka was renowned as a hub of Islamic studies and was responsible for the Islamization of its dependencies on the Malay Peninsula, the southern archipelagos and Sumatra. Islamic coinage was introduced to the Melakan Sultanate by Pasai and was later adopted by other Malay sultanates.

Other evidence of early Islam includes a 15th-century tomb and inscribed pillar at Pengkalan Kempas, Negeri Sembilan, and many elaborately carved gravestones known as Batu Aceh, which are found in most Peninsular states. Their shapes and inscriptions provide important indications of the history of the early Islamic period and the extent of the Islamization of the Malay World.

Above: The Southeast Asian section of the 'Map of the World' drawn by the Arab prince Idrisi in 1154 CE, which follows the early Arab style of placing south at the top of the map, shows the Malay Peninsula as the long island of Kamar-Malai.

1. A yellow cloth, symbol of royalty, protects this gravestone in the royal graveyard at Teluk Bakong on the Perak River. Some scholars believe the stone marks the grave of the wife of Sultan Muzzafar Shah I (d.1549), the first Sultan of Perak.

2. Qur'anic inscriptions adorn the headstone of Sultan Muhammad Shah I, the first Sultan of Pahang who died in 1475 at Dusun Tua near Pekan, the royal town of Pahang.

3. This cement replica of 'The Rudder', a carved megalith of unknown date from Pengkalan Kempas, stands in the gardens of the Negeri Sembilan State Museum in Seremban.

4. A rosette surrounded by vines on this Batu Aceh gravestone at Makam Chondong, Pekan, Pahang, is similar to those found on 15th–16th century mosques throughout the Middle East.

The gravestone of Derma Taksiah, also known as Tok Subang (1528–49), is located by the Perak River at Sayong, Perak.

The arrival of Islam

The date when Islam first arrived in Malaysia, and the identity of those responsible for its introduction, will probably never be known with certainty. Arab and Chinese documentary sources, archaeological investigations and inscribed stones provide clues, but debate continues as to whether the propagators of Islam were of West Asian, Indian or Chinese origin. The only theory which most scholars agree on is the important role that trade played in the Islamization of the Malay World.

The grave of Pahang's first Muslim ruler, Sultan Muhammad Shah I (d.1475), bears a footstone and a headstone inscribed with his name, descent, date of death and Qur'anic quotations.

Malaysia's earliest dated royal grave

Exiled from Melaka by his father for stabbing a nobleman, Raja Muhammad was installed as Sultan of Pahang in 1470. The headstone (above top), at Langgar near Pekan, Pahang, records his death on 17 September 1475. The panel on the footstone (above) is part of Surah 2: 255 from the Qur'an: 'God! There is no God but he, the Living, the Self-subsisting, Eternal. No slumber can seize Him nor sleep. His are all things in the heavens and on earth. Who is there can intercede in His presence except as He permits? He knows what appears to his creatures as before or after or behind them.'

Early Muslim traders in Southeast Asia

The best evidence that the Malays first came into contact with Islam through trade routes comes from Arab sources. Even in the 5th century CE, prior to the Islamization of Arabia, Arab and Persian traders were living in some of the major southern ports of China, especially in Guangzhou (Canton). There is a possibility that they stopped over in the Malay Archipelago for fresh water and other necessities required on their sea journeys.

With the rise of Islam in the 8th and 9th centuries CE, the Arab lands became the centre of a united, wealthy and powerful empire, and thus, an important commercial centre for the products of India, China and Southeast Asia. By the beginning of the 9th century, Arab and other Muslim merchants had begun to dominate the Nanhai, or Southeast Asian trade arena.

In 878 CE, an important event involving foreign merchants took place in Canton. The rebel leader Huang Chao sacked Canton and, according to reports, massacred thousands of foreign merchants. Following this incident, Muslim traders left China and flocked to a Peninsular Malaysian port known to the Arabs as Kalah, probably Kedah, or perhaps Takuapa (southern Thailand), which then became the major entrepôt of Arab trade and possibly their easternmost base. Kalah is mentioned in the *Kitab al-masalik wa'l mamalik* of Ibn Khurdadhabih (c. 850 CE) as being famous for tin mines and bamboo plantations, but no mention is made as to whether Islam was then propagated. Pulau Tioman, the landfall port off the coast of Pahang, was also known to the Arabs, as was possibly another port in Johor.

Two other Arab authors, Abu Zaid and Mas'udi, who met in 916 CE, furnish more detailed reports of the Malay Peninsula. Kalah is reported as the rendevous of Muslim vessels from West Asia and entrepôt for Southeast Asian trade, while a 10th-century report by the Egyptian Muhallabi describes Kalah as 'a prosperous city . . . inhabited by Muslims, Hindus and Persians'. Further evidence of a Muslim settlement in Kedah during this era comes from

archaeological evidence found in the Bujang Valley, including Middle Eastern glass fragments, Arabic coins dated 848 CE, and a stone slab inscribed with an Arab name and the date 850 CE. However, evidence of Islamization of the local population at that time is lacking.

Arab, Persian, Gujerati (Indian) and other Muslim traders did not found colonies for their mother countries, but simply established trading communities for the merchants who had to remain at the ports for some length of time to await the movement of ships dependent on the monsoons. Because of the existence of these trading communities, some scholars believe that Islam came to Malaysia from West Asia or from India.

The earliest Islamic evidence

The first confirmed evidence of the arrival of Islam in Southeast Asia comes from Phan Rang, in South Vietnam (formerly Champa), where an Arabic-inscribed pillar recording laws, dated 1035 CE, and a Muslim gravestone, dated 1039 CE, have been found. These two stones testify to the existence of an 11th-century Muslim settlement in Champa, although the presence of Muslims in this region was first reported by Ibn Rusta about 900 CE.

More evidence of early Islamic expansion comes from a Muslim woman's gravestone found in Brunei (1048 CE), and another from Leran, East Java (1082 CE). The existence of these graves could indicate that Muslim settlements in these places were well established. As Muslim traders did not journey with their families, the women commemorated by the gravestones were probably local women who had married the traders during their long periods of stay while awaiting the change of winds.

The most important evidence of Islam arriving in Malaysia, and that which is most accepted by academics, is the inscribed stone known as the Terengganu Stone, dated 1303 CE, which was found at Kuala Berang, Terengganu (see 'The Terengganu Stone').

This mysterious gravestone found near Pekan, Pahang, is dated 1028 CE, but as the style of the script is 14th century, some scholars believe it could have been made then to replace an earlier stone which may have been for a Muslim trader.

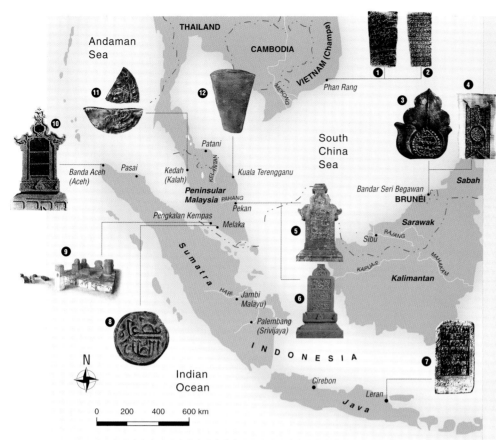

The earliest evidence of Islam

Inscribed pillars and gravestones, and artefacts such as coins found along the major trade routes provide evidence of early Muslim settlements and the spread of Islam.

1. Pillar at Champa (South Vietnam) inscribed with Kufi calligraphy, dated 1035 CE. The inscription is difficult to decipher, but mentions a 'Sultan Mahmud' of unknown origin and perhaps a Muslim craft guild.
2. Gravestone at Champa of Abu Kamil, believed to have been a Shi'ite Muslim from Persia, dated 1039 CE. The chiselling of the Kufi script shows a high degree of workmanship similar to the Fatimid style of North Africa.
3. Gravestone at Brunei of Sulaiman bin Abdul Rahman bin Abdullah Nurullah, dated 1418/19 CE.
4. Gravestone at Brunei of Putri Makhdarah binti Ali, dated 1048 CE. This highly decorative gravestone style is found nowhere else in the Malay Archipelago.
5. Gravestone of Sultan Muhammad Shah I of Pahang, the first Sultan of Pahang, dated 1475 CE, is located near Pekan.
6. Unknown gravestone at Pahang in 14th-century style script, dated 1028 CE (?). This date is the earliest-known mention of Islam in Malaysia, but scholars have yet to verify it.
7. Gravestone at Leran, East Java, of Fatimah binti Maimunbin Habatallah, dated 1082 CE. The origin of this woman is unknown.
8. Tin coin from the reign of Sultan Muzaffar Shah of Melaka (1445–59 CE). This is the oldest, indigenous Islamic coin as yet found in Malaysia.
9. Inscribed pillar and tomb of Ahmad Majanu (or Sheikh Ahmad Mallari) bearing a Jawi script (1467/68 CE) and a Kawi script (1463/64 CE) at Negeri Sembilan.
10. Gravestone of Sultan Malik-al-Salih of Pasai, Sumatra, dated 1297 CE. The conversion of this ruler to Islam is recorded in the *Sejarah Melayu* (Malay Annals).
11. Arabic coins dated 848 CE found in the Bujang Valley, Kedah. These coins are proof that Muslim traders visited the early kingdom of Kedah.
12. The Terengganu Stone inscribed with laws, dated 1303 CE. This is the earliest confirmed evidence of Islam in Malaysia.

The inscription in Malay was done on the command of the ruler and features a series of Islamic-style laws. As both the Terengganu Stone and the inscribed stones from Phan Rang occur along the Chinese trade route, some scholars believe that Islam first came to Malaysia via China.

Along the Melaka Strait, Arab merchants' colonies were established at Kalah (Kedah), Zabaj (Srivijaya [Palembang]) and Lamuri, northern Sumatra. These settlements facilitated the expansion of Islam during the 13th century when Muslim missionaries, mainly Sufis from West Asia, travelled to these ports to reinforce Islam among the traders. By the end of the 13th and into the early 14th century, Islamic influence became very pronounced.

The earliest dated gravestone of a local Muslim ruler is that of Sultan Malik-al-Salih of Pasai, North Sumatra (d. 1297 CE), who, according to the *Hikayat Raja-Raja Pasai* (the oldest known history in the Malay language), converted to Islam in the 1250s. Pasai was known to Indian Muslim traders, particularly those from Gujerat, as Samudra, a name that later became Sumatra. Gujerati influence is apparent in the design of early gravestones (see 'Early Islamic gravestones'), lending support to the theory that Islam arrived via India. Pasai's influence as an Islamic centre spread over North Sumatra to Aceh and later to the Malay Peninsula and Java, but was eclipsed by Melaka in the early 15th century.

The shoulders of this gravestone from Pekan, Pahang, are of an Acehnese flower design known as *awan si tangke*.

Islam and the Melakan Sultanate

There are various accounts of the conversion of the ruler of Melaka. Afonso de Albuquerque, the conqueror of Melaka, relates that Parameswara, the founder of Melaka, married a daughter of the Sultan of Pasai and converted to Islam. However, the *Sejarah Melayu* (Malay Annals) records that it was his grandson who became Sultan Muhammad Shah after a dream instructed him to follow the actions of a traveller from Jeddah who disembarked from a ship and performed his prayers on the shore. After this miraculous occurrence, 'the Bendahara and the chiefs embraced Islam; and every citizen of Malaka was commanded by the Raja to do likewise.' In 1413, the Chinese traveller Ma-Huan visited Melaka and reported that the ruler and his people 'revered the doctrines of the Muslims'.

After the conversion of Melaka, wealthy Muslim traders flocked there and it became a renowned centre of Islamic scholarship. It was during the 15th-century 'Golden Age' that Islamic ideals became incorporated into Malay culture, a process which was so successful that even today a convert to Islam is said by Malays to *masuk Melayu*, or 'become Malay'.

During the 15th and early 16th centuries, Islam spread to other areas under Melaka's control, including Pahang and Perak. But after Melaka fell to the Portuguese in 1511, Muslim merchants abandoned Melaka in favour of Aceh which took over as the new Malay centre for Islamic studies.

This gravestone is one of several at Makam Chondong, Pekan, Pahang, believed to be those of Pahang royalty who were abducted to Aceh, Sumatra, after that kingdom conquered Pahang in the mid-17th century. The stones were brought from Aceh and the *Bustan-al-Salatin*, a historical source of the time, describes the event: 'The stones were carried in procession accompanied by musical instruments, hundreds of umbrellas, standards, banners and pennons.'

The Terengganu Stone

The most important evidence so far uncovered in the quest to ascertain where Islam first appeared in Malaysia is the text inscribed on the granite stele known as the Terengganu Stone. Dated in the Muslim Lunar year of 702 AH, which corresponds to 1303 CE, the stone inscription is not only the oldest Malay text in the Arabic script in existence, but is the earliest record of the introduction of Islam into the Malay Peninsula. The inscription is also significant in terms of the development of writing and the Malay language.

How the stone was found

Measuring 84 centimetres in length, with a maximum breadth of 53 centimetres and an average depth of 24 centimetres, the stone weighs 214.8 kilograms. It was unearthed from a river bank in 1887 where it was exposed after a flood, and placed at a *surau*, or prayer house, in Kampung Buluh near Kuala Berang, a river junction settlement about 40 kilometres upstream from Kuala Terengganu.

In 1902, Syed Hussin bin Ghulam Al-Bukhari, an Arab-Malay trader from Riau Lingga who was travelling upriver to prospect for tin or gold, came ashore to do his midday prayers. While he was taking the ritual wash before prayer, he noticed that the stone placed by the steps of the surau, where the worshippers stood while performing their ablutions, was inscribed with Arabic letters. According to Engku Pengiran Anum, his assistant, who was 15 years old at the time, when the dirt was washed off some of the letters, they recognized the name of the Prophet Muhammad inscribed on the stone.

Realizing its importance, Syed Hussin had the stone carried to his boat, and on his return to Kuala Terengganu it was presented to the Sultan of Terengganu, Sultan Zainal Abidin, who placed it at the old fort of Bukit Puteri which overlooks the mouth of the Terengganu River. The stone remained there until the 1920s when it was sent to the Raffles Museum in Singapore. In the 1960s, it was brought to the National Museum in Kuala Lumpur where it remained until it was finally returned to Terengganu. It is presently on display in the Terengganu State Museum.

Panel A

Translation of the inscriptions

Panel A: *The Messenger of Allah (Prophet Muhammad), together with those who have faith in the Supreme God (Allah), have been enslaved to implant the religion of Islam; with truth they have spoken of the Laws binding upon all the servants of the Supreme God here in my domain. The arbiters of the faith of the Messenger of Allah (peace be upon him) are the King Mandalikas who speak the truth on the side of the Supreme God here on earth. To decide on the right knowledge is statutory upon all the Muslim King Mandalikas, in accordance with the decrees of the Supreme God who speaks the truth; that the correct way for the two determiners of knowledge is to be in solitary seclusion. Thereupon, I, Seri Paduka Tuhan declare that this edict be erected in this country of Terengganu on Friday, in the month of Rejab, year 702, in the era of the Messenger of Allah.*

Panel B: *[F]amilies in distant lands give those who come. Fourth Law: Debtors must never take . . . where have you lost the gold. Fifth Law: Whosoever must never take the mould for the making of money, if he takes then he must forfeit his gold. Sixth Law: Whosoever . . . of trouble makers, be they male or female, as decreed by the Supreme God, if they are free persons and bachelors then give them 100 strokes of the cane. If they are free persons with wives, or women with husbands, then bury them up to the waist and stone them to death. If they revolt then torture them; if the bachelor son of a chieftain then . . . .*

Panel B

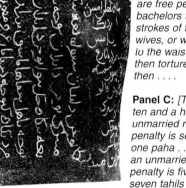
Panel C

Panel C: *[T]he penalty is ten and a half sagas. If an unmarried minister, the penalty is seven tahils and one paha . . . half a saga. If an unmarried headman the penalty is five tahils . . . seven tahils and one paha goes into the Treasury . . . If . . . a free person. Seventh Law: A woman who wants . . . has not got a husband, if she causes trouble . . . .*

Panel D: *[N]ot true, the penalty is one tahil and one paha. Ninth Law: Seri Paduka Tuhan punishes those who fail to prepare the fine . . . if my son, or my playmate, or my grandchildren, or my family, or child . . . this edict, and whosoever ignores its contents shall be damned by the Supreme God, cursed by the Supreme God, all those who disregard the articles of this ordinance.*

Panel D

Deciphering the inscriptions

The inscription records an order to put into effect certain laws; a proclamation ordering the ruler and his ministers to expound and uphold the Muslim faith and the teachings of Prophet Muhammad; and, most importantly, the date which predates the conversion of the first ruler of Melaka to Islam by at least a century. Attempts have been made by some early historians to disclaim this date—Friday, 4th of Rejab, 702 AH (Friday, 22 February 1303 CE). However, it is now accepted by most scholars that this date is correct.

The inscription on the Terengganu Stone is similar to those on stones found in the territory of Phan Rang, or Champa, in today's South Vietnam, although they are dated much earlier, to the 11th century CE. Based on textual similarities between the stones, historians believe that the inscriber of the Terengganu Stone copied the Arabic-type script from that used by the people of Champa. However, the Terengganu Stone is the first instance of Islamic writing, or Arabic, in the Malay language (known locally as Jawi) found in the Malay Archipelago.

The stone on which the inscription was chiselled has flat faces on the front, back and sides, which permitted the composing of the edict. The top part has been broken off and is missing, thus affecting the inscriptions on the lateral sides (Panels C and D) which are incomplete. The inscriptions on the front and back (Panels A and B) are essentially unaffected by this breakage.

According to some scholars, the phenomenon of writing Malay in the Arabic script implies that there was already a growing consensus early in the 14th century to discontinue the use of Tamil, Nagari or Kawi which appear on earlier inscriptions. The Naskh style of Arabic calligraphy, popular with writers, was chosen probably because of its clarity. However, the skill with which the inscriber chiselled a pen technique onto hard granite is impressive as the resulting script retains much of the flowing quality of handwriting.

Islam is introduced

The inscription hints at a literary tradition centred at the court which was concerned with preserving the old Hindu–Buddhist traditions of the powerful Javanese kingdom of Majapahit, the current ruling power of the region, as well as adopting the new religion of Islam. However, based on linguistic evidence, Terengganu was probably Islamized by Muslims from Sumatra rather than from Java. As the Terengganu Stone was written in the Malay language, this shows links with the kingdom of Malayu, based in Jambi, Sumatra. As seen by the inscriptions, the ruler was promulgating the basic teachings of Islam to the newly converted population. These laws, which prohibited people from stealing, fornication and rebellion, are reminiscent of Islamic laws, but are couched in a number of Sanskrit terms, such as Dewata Mulia Raya (the Supreme God), Mandalika (man of the rules), *derma* (fine, penalty), *balanchara* (adultery), *adi-pertama* (the first) and *tamra* (regulation). As many historians point out, the evidence of the Terengganu Stone shows that the introducers of Islam to Terengganu used language which was obviously adapted to the understanding of a population educated in Sanskrit religious terms. However, as the Arabic script was used as the medium for this message, substituting earlier Indian scripts, this proves that Islam was already well established in the Malay Peninsula during the time of the inscription.

Location of the Terengganu Stone

Location of insribed panel

The discovery of the Terengganu Stone

This artist's impression of how the inscribed stone was found is based on documentary and oral sources including an account by Engku Pengiran Anum, who assisted in the discovery at the age of 15. His account in *Malaya in History*, Vol VII, 1961 appeared when he was 76.

In 1902, he accompanied Syed Hussin bin Ghulam Al-Bukhari up the Terengganu River. When 'we went ashore to say our midday prayer' Syed Hussin realized that the stone he was standing on while making his ablutions 'was inscribed with words in the Jawi script'.

The Pengkalan Kempas inscriptions

One of the most important sites relating to the introduction of Islam to Malaysia is the group of inscribed stones at the Pengkalan Kempas Complex in Negeri Sembilan. Formerly known as Keramat Sungai Udang, the site contains a group of standing carved megaliths of unknown date, and the 15th-century tomb and inscribed tombstone of Ahmad Majanu, a mysterious character who, according to the inscription, is variously described as a saint and a traitor, although current opinion favours the former.

Location of inscribed stones

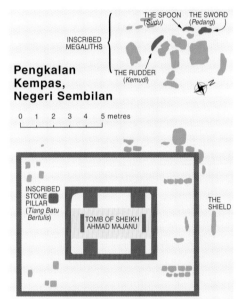

Pengkalan Kempas, Negeri Sembilan

THE SPOON (Sudu)   THE SWORD (Pedang)

INSCRIBED MEGALITHS

THE RUDDER (Kemudi)

0 1 2 3 4 5 metres

INSCRIBED STONE PILLAR (Tiang Batu Bertulis)

TOMB OF SHEIKH AHMAD MAJANU

THE SHIELD

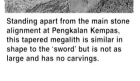

Standing apart from the main stone alignment at Pengkalan Kempas, this tapered megalith is similar in shape to the 'sword' but is not as large and has no carvings.

A sacred site

The inscribed stones are located near the village of Pengkalan Kempas, an old river port beside the Sungai Linggi about 35 kilometres north of Melaka town. The tomb, commonly believed to be that of a 'saint', was a place of pilgrimage in the past. However, scholars believe that the megaliths, which probably predate the tomb, are indications that the site has been considered sacred since ancient times and that over the course of time cult objects were placed there.

The site was first excavated by I. H. N. Evans in 1921 who placed the megaliths in their current position. Further study was conducted by D. V. van Stein Callenfels in 1927 and J. G. de Casparis in 1980. The inscriptions on the quadrilateral pillar facing the tomb provide contrasting evidence as to the deeds or misdeeds of Ahmad Majanu, and have been the subject of much academic speculation over the years. The pillar is made of a type of sandstone not found in the general area, which is similar to that used for Batu Aceh gravestones, and like them is believed to originate in Aceh, Sumatra. Running through the centre of the pillar from the north to the south side is a hole, the size of an arm, which may have been made to insert a pole to carry it to its present location. Local legend has it that the hole was used to determine if a person making an oath was telling the truth or not. If a false oath was sworn, the hole would tighten causing intense pain. However, no inscriptions mention this use of the stone and it was probably a later practice in response to the convenient arm-sized hole.

The 15th-century tomb and the inscribed pillar which describes the deeds or misdeeds of Ahmad Majanu.

The puzzle of the inscriptions

The inscriptions, in the Malay language, are found on all four faces of the pillar. However, they tell conflicting tales. The north and south faces are in Kawi or Old Javanese script, while the east and west faces, which are identical, are in Jawi or Arabic script. The Jawi inscription reads: 'In the name of Allah, the merciful and compassionate. This abode of peace is a place of goodness. The grave of Sheikh Ahmad Mallari bin . . . .' Following this is the Islamic date of 872 Hijrah, which corresponds to 1467/68. The inscription concludes with a mention that his death took place during the reign of Sultan Mansur Shah of the Melakan Sultanate.

The Kawi inscriptions, on the other hand, tell a different tale. The north side is freely translated: 'Allah, the merciful and the compassionate. (?) (This tomb) belongs to Ahmad Majanu, who carried out a stratagem. Ahmad fell with his wife Balat and his son. While Ahmad was fighting (?) they all fell.' The south side reads: 'Allah, the merciful and the compassionate. Ahmad Majanu the first to emerge on the road at the time when the princess, together with Tun (?) Barah Talang, were taken captives. Subsequently he fell.' This is followed by the Islamic date corresponding to 1463/64.

Despite deciphering attempts by numerous scholars over the years, the inscriptions are still a puzzle. Why do different inscriptions report on the same person? Why is the Kawi date four years earlier than the Jawi date? How did Ahmad Majanu in the Kawi became Sheikh Ahmad Mallari bin . . . in the Jawi? Other unanswered questions include the whereabouts of the Sheikh's death. Did he die where the shrine is located, or elsewhere? And who were his slayers?

Various theories have been put forward. Van Stein Callenfels concluded that

Ahmad Majanu was a traitor who was executed after unsuccessfully attempting to kill Sultan Mansur Shah. However, R. J. Wilkinson believed that Ahmad Majanu was killed while leading a group of Proto-Malay protesters against the chief who controlled the fiefdom of Sungai Ujung. De Casparis, however, believes that the Jawi inscriptions do not indicate any treacherous act or dishonourable element in Ahmad Majanu's conduct. He points out that it was not possible for a traitor to be given the title of a saint whose grave subsequently became a pilgrimage site, and that when a revolt fails the victors rarely erect a monument in memory of the leader of the losing side. De Casparis believes that Ahmad's stratagem was not directed against the sultan but at his enemies, implying that his brave action saved the princess but cost him his own life. He also notes that it is feasible that the stele is a memorial stone which was placed at the scene of the battle a few years after the event.

As to the different names and dates, some scholars believe that these could have been inscribed by two different scribes, and that during the period in question the militant hero Ahmad Majanu became the saintly Sheikh Ahmad Mallari. The historian Zakaria Ali believes that the inscriptions were carved in memory of a hero who died a martyr. The differing dates could have been the result of a mistaken calculation from the Indian to the Islamic system of chronology. It is also probable that they were carved at different times.

The mysterious megaliths

Apart from smaller standing stones, the other major sculptures at the site consist of three carved and dressed granite megaliths which, on account of their shapes, have been nicknamed the 'sword', the 'spoon' and the 'rudder'. Apart from the carvings, they are similar to many other megaliths which have been found throughout the states of Melaka and Negeri Sembilan. These are commonly known as *batu hidup*, literally 'living stones', which gives the impression that they were originally sanctified. They are generally believed to be of much greater antiquity than the Sheikh's tomb and stele. However, the difficulty in dating the stones at Pengkalan Kempas comes from the inscribing of the word 'Allah' on the 'sword', which otherwise resembles a phallus. The gland, the three bands marking circumcision (which was also a pre-Islamic local practice), and the curling hairs are unmistakable phallic representations. Beneath are three discs of uncertain symbolism, then what could be the head of a Kala, a mythical Hindu animal, and the outstretched wings of a plumed Garuda, the Hindu bird-deity. Some scholars believe that the word 'Allah' was carved later to sanctify a Hindu sculpture. However, most believe that it was contemporaneous with the rest of the carving. This is problematic because it is difficult to reconcile the carving of anthropomorphic motifs with Islamic scripts as the former are prohibited in Islam.

The designs sculpted in low relief on the 'rudder' include a horse, a bird-like creature, possibly a peacock, and a discoidal object. The carving on the upper edge of the stone has been compared to an elephant's trunk, while the object at the bottom left has been described as the head of a horse or bull. As with the 'sword', the meaning of these sculptures is a mystery.

The 'spoon' is devoid of any sculptural motifs, and its status as a sculpture is only because of its arched top which suggests that it has been carved. It is relatively crude and unadorned, but as it forms part of the trio which constitutes the most prominent megalithic display at Pengkalan Kempas it is considered an important element.

Other granite and laterite stones at the site include a circular stone facing the foot of the tomb. Known as the 'shield', it is engraved with geometrical patterns. From the number of stones found around the Pengkalan Kempas site, and the past popularity of the shrine with pilgrims, it is believed that this was a sacred site certainly from pre-Islamic times, and perhaps even dating from pre-Hindu times.

The main collection of megaliths at Pengkalan Kempas is surrounded by smaller laterite and granite stones which were also placed there according to some unknown religious ritual. The 'sword' stands at the right, the 'spoon' in the centre, and the 'rudder' on the left. Historians believe that the surrounding stones were also significant, but to date no studies have been undertaken on these.

Among the unexplained standing stones of Pengkalan Kempas is this arched megalith which has a carved crenulate edge. It stands near the bottom left-hand corner of Ahmad Majanu's grave and faces west towards the group of standing megaliths. The historian John Miksic has reported similar stones in West Sumatra which were used as ceremonial back rests in the 14th century.

Early Islamic gravestones

Present-day Malay culture owes an inestimable debt to the part played by the region in the ancient East–West maritime trade. The impact of imported cultures was obviously profound, as many foreign elements left evidence that can be recognized and appreciated today as part of Malaysia's cultural heritage. Early Islamic gravestones, commonly known as Batu Aceh, are one example.

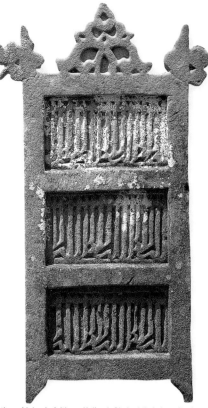

The declaration of Islamic faith, or Kalimah Shahadah, is inscribed on the front panel of this early 16th-century grave known as Makam Raja Beruas, at Beruas in Perak, believed to be the site of a lost ancient kingdom.

This tear-shaped panel on a royal grave at Teluk Bakong in the Perak River Valley bears a Qur'anic inscription.

Legend has it that this Batu Aceh, known as Makam Tok Subang, located near Sayong opposite the Perak royal capital of Kuala Kangsar, is the grave of Derma Taksiah, a wife of Sultan Mudzafar Shah I, who was wrongly executed for adultery.

Mysterious graves

The term 'early' refers to dated gravestones used in the Malay Peninsula from the 15th to the 19th century, as well as to two gravestones discovered in Pahang and Kedah which belong historically to the 10th and 11th centuries, but stylistically to the 15th and 17th centuries, respectively.

These gravestones are unique in style, shape and design. Made in pairs from sandstone, some are highly ornamented, while others bear inscriptions of Arabic calligraphy from the Qur'an. The exact origins of these gravestones, especially those at Beruas in Perak, in Kedah, and in Perlis, are still a mystery. It is not known who were buried there, although these facts have already been established for the gravestones found in Pahang and Johor.

Indian and Acehnese origins

Previously, it was not known whether these gravestones originated from Aceh in northern Sumatra, or from India, or were of local creation. The assumption that they were from Aceh is due to the designs, which are similar to those found on the grave of Sultan Malik al-Salih of Pasai (d. 1297).

Some early scholars thought that similar gravestones found in India, Java, Sumatra and the Malay Peninsula all originated from India. It was also assumed that the gravestones at Pasai were brought by Indian traders from Cambay, a trading port in India. Other scholars, however, believed that the gravestones known as Makam Chondong in Pahang were not from India but from Aceh.

Historians now conclude that the pre-Melakan gravestones of Peninsular Malaysia were brought directly from Cambay, via Aceh, while those made in Aceh were imported during the 17th century when Aceh was the major regional power. It was common practice for wealthier people to order goods from abroad, and it was probably through this custom that the gravestones from Aceh found their way to the Malay Peninsula.

Early Kedah gravestones

Very little is known about the history of early gravestones in Kedah and Perlis except for those on a group of early 16th-century graves known as Makam Langgar near the Merbok River. From their elaborate designs, historians suggest that they were erected for members of royalty or other important persons. There are no inscriptions, but from the shapes of the stones, two of the graves are believed to be those of females and two of males. The female gravestones are of the flattened 'Chinese lantern' type, their outline probably being based on a lotus bud viewed from the side. The lotus motifs on the stones show Hindu influence.

Evolution of tombstone design

1400 CE   1500 CE   1600 CE   1700 CE–1800 CE

On Pulau Langkawi, this type of early 17th-century gravestone can be seen in Kampung Ulu Melaka, a village inhabited mostly by people of Aceh descent. In neighbouring Perlis, only one pair of this kind of 15th-century gravestone has been found, at Kampung Tok Paduka near Kangar. They are now kept in the Bujang Valley Archaeological Museum, Kedah. These gravestones seem to be of similar antiquity to those known as Makam Raja Beruas at Beruas, Perak, although the latter are more highly inscribed.

Design and decoration

In order to analyse the different types of gravestones and interpret the meanings of their decorative motifs, it is necessary to look at various Malay and international Islamic arts, as well as to make a comparative study of the styles and decoration that derive from the arts of neighbouring civilizations, particularly India and China. The great contribution of Islam to world culture, in general, and to that of Malaysia, in particular, has not received sufficient recognition, mostly because regional historical studies have concentrated on Indian and Chinese civilizations. This lack of exposure of the Islamic arts, however, is partly due to the teachings of Islam itself, and the unresolved debate over commemorating the dead with elaborately ornamented gravestones. Although some people believe that this practice is contrary to the teachings of Islam, the Hadith (traditional teachings of Mohammad and his followers) is silent on the matter. In Islam, anthropomorphic designs are prohibited because of their association with idolatry.

Islamic burial derives from local practices modified by Islamic ideas. In pre-Islamic societies, the tomb symbolized the unity of life, death and eternity. Primitive beliefs associated with kingship gave the royal tomb a mysterious significance, which survived in the subconscious even when the king was recognized as being mortal. This explains why early Islamic gravestones in Malaysia are unique as their shapes and decorative motifs are a combination of Islamic themes and un-Islamic influences, thus distinguishing them from similar arts in other Muslim countries.

After Othman Yatim (1988)

gunung-gunung pattern

Kalimah Shahadah panel

curly shoulder

rosette

panel text

ladder

lotus

spider web

What the shapes mean

Although no certainty exists, some scholars believe that the shapes of early Islamic gravestones differ according to gender. Those for men are peg-shaped and prism-like, with four, six or eight angles, which perhaps evolved from phallic symbols. Some narrow towards the base, while the side surface resembles a trapezium. Foot pieces and ornamental tops are of various forms, and the entire surface is incised with fine patterns similar to those of the mangosteen calyx. Women's gravestones are narrow, and the back and front broad. On both side are projecting spiral ornaments, called *subang* (earrings) by the Acehnese. The words of the Muslim profession of faith are usually engraved on the stones.

The upper part of some gravestones resembles the ornamentation on Malay rulers' thrones known as *gunung-gunung* or 'mountains'. The adoration of mountains was one of the most popular early beliefs throughout the pre-Islamic Malay World. The principal motif derived from the 'tree of life', which symbolizes the highest unity in the Hindu pantheon. In Hinduism, the heavenly abode of the gods, known as Mount Meru, is described as a high mountain top surrounded by four lower levels—similar to the appearance of the gravestones. This design also occurs in the roof shapes of early mosques, such as Masjid Kampung Laut in Kelantan.

The motifs on Islamic gravestones are not only decorative but contain meanings derived from Islamic theology, philosophy and mysticism. Quotations from the Qur'an act as reminders of the word of God—an affirmation of faith. The specific passage usually selected evokes the key Islamic idea that all creation and acts occur only by the will of God (Allah).

Significantly, these types of Batu Aceh gravestones are found only in Perak, Kedah, Perlis, Melaka, Pahang and Johor, which were all briefly conquered by Aceh in the 17th century, although Acehnese traders frequented the region somewhat earlier.

By studying the distribution of these early and foreign Islamic tombstones in Malaysia, historians can gain insight into the pattern of early trading contacts and the effect of regional political upheavals.

The decorative rosette on the 16th-century grave of the wife of Sultan Mudzafar Shah I of Perak is believed by some scholars to denote a female tomb, while others attribute its shape to religious symbolism as this design is frequently found in Middle Eastern mosques. The gravestone is located in the royal graveyard at Teluk Bakong in the Perak River Valley.

A popular design of lotus and spider web patterns on the foot of this mysterious royal grave at Beruas borrows symbolism from Sufi, Egyptian and Southeast Asian sources. Sufi poems likening the world to a spider's web—'perishable' and 'not everlasting'—have been found inscribed on early gravestones in Pahang, Melaka and Pasai in Sumatra.

Location of Batu Aceh

South China Sea

ACEH → PENINSULAR MALAYSIA

Indian Ocean

Perlis
Kangar
Alor Setar
Pulau Langkawi
Kedah
Merbok
Kota Bharu
Kuala Terengganu
Pulau Pinang
Perak
Kelantan
Terengganu
Kuala Kangsar
Beruas
Teluk Bakong
Kg. Gajah
Strait of Melaka
Pahang
South China Sea
Jerantut
Dusun Pinang
N
Temerloh
Pekan
Selangor
Negeri Sembilan
Melaka
Merlimau
Segamat
Pagoh
Johor
Kota Tinggi
Johor Lama
Johor Bahru

Batu Aceh

0   100km

Early Islamic coins

Ever since coins were invented in the first millennium BCE, they have been recognized as guarantees of payment to their owners. Rulers of countries and cities have used coins to make known and celebrate their power and achievements. Coins of the Islamic tradition differ from those of the Western world, which often bear a ruler's portrait, because Islam prohibits anthropomorphic designs.

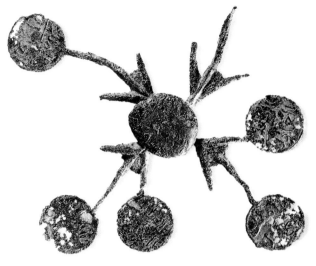

This 'sun-ray'-shaped coin tree of Terengganu, bearing the Arabic inscription 'Kali Malik Al Adil', or Reign of the Just Ruler, was made by the 'lost wax' process whereby molten tin was poured into the clay mould melting the wax. Before the discovery of these coin trees in the Riau Islands, coins were thought to be individually cast.

The Kijang coin

Unique to Kelantan, gold *kupang* depicting the *kijang*, or barking deer, were issued from 1400 onwards. They bear no dates, but coin historians tell their age by the different types of kijang depicted. 'Malik Al Adil' (The Just King) is inscribed in Jawi calligraphy on the reverse (see below).

A stylized version of the Kijang coin was adopted by Bank Negara Malaysia as its official logo in 1964.

Coins as historical markers

Islamic coins provide clear historical evidence about many aspects of Islamic economics, administration, society and civilization. The items usually included on Islamic coins are the name and rank of a leader or leaders, some religious material, the place where the coin was minted, and the date. This custom has resulted in lengthy and extended inscriptions. An additional item is the standard Friday exhortation, whereby the imam, who leads the congregation in prayer at the mosque, mentions the names of the ruler and his family in the sermon and prays for their prosperity. In other words, these inscriptions on the coins are like messages informing the public who the rulers were, when and where they reigned, and what their beliefs were. In addition, Islamic coins convey information about their makers. The inscriptions used illustrate the evolution of language, while the patterns reflect the level and style of their makers' artistic ability.

Islamic gold coins were introduced to the Malay Peninsula by Muslim traders from Pasai in northern Sumatra. When Melaka became Muslim, these coins were used as the first currency. Later, gold and tin coins were minted. The earliest indigenous coin discovered to date was issued in Melaka during the reign of Sultan Muzaffar Shah (1445–59). However, earlier issues could have been made. The surface of this coin is much eroded, but the embossed wording is still legible. On the obverse side is written 'Muzaffar Shah al-Sultan', while on the reverse is 'Nasir al-dunia Wa'l-Din' (Helper of the World and of the Religion). This inscription is in an Arabic script which relies on vertical strokes for prominence, and is set in a circular border which contrasts with the uneven edge.

Many more coins were produced during the reign of the next ruler, Sultan Mansur Shah (1459–77), who formalized his position in the dynastic line by minting his name and title on the obverse side, 'Mansur Shah bin Muzaffar Shah al-Sultan', while on the reverse he stamped the title of his predecessor, 'Nasir al-dunia Wa'l-din'. Like the first Melaka coin, this issue has hardly any embellishment. Later, however, during the reign of the ruler Sultan Mahmud Shah (1488–1530), the former title was dropped and 'al-Adil' (The Just) was substituted.

Another early coin from the Melaka sultanate is from the brief reign of Sultan Ahmad, the son of Sultan Mahmud Shah, who ruled Melaka for a few months after his father's abdication. Sultan Ahmad took an active part in the desperate defence of Melaka during the final assault by the Portuguese in 1511. However, during the retreat in the jungles east of Melaka, he was apparently murdered on the orders of his father for allegedly being ill-mannered. An indication of Ahmad's nonchalant attitude towards the institution

The evolution of Islamic coins

1445–1459 CE

The earliest known indigenous Islamic coin, a *duit casha* (tin coin), was issued during Sultan Muzaffar Shah's reign (1445–59).
OBVERSE: 'Sultan Muzaffar Shah'
REVERSE: 'Helper of the World and of the Religion (Islam)

1527/8–1564 CE

The first coins minted in Johor were octagonal gold *kupang* issued during the reign of Sultan Alauddin Riayat Shah II (1527/8–64).
OBVERSE: 'Sultan Alauddin'
REVERSE: 'Khalifatul Mu'minin' (Ruler of the Faithful)

1623–1677 CE

The first known silver quarter *penjuru* issued in Johor during the reign of Sultan Abdul Jalil Shah III (1623–77).
OBVERSE: 'Sultan Abdul Jalil Shah'
REVERSE: 'Khalifatul Mu'minin' (Ruler of the Faithful)

The *pohon pitis*, or coin tree from Kelantan (below), was cast in a brass mould (right) similar to those the Chinese used for copper coinage. Coins were broken off the 'tree' and the branches were melted down for reuse.

of the sultanate is indicated by the plebeian 'Ahmad bin Mahmud' (Ahmad son of Mahmud) on the obverse, and on the reverse 'Al-sultan al-Adil'. His father's name was his only claim to legitimacy, while the epithet of 'The Just Sultan' was by then an accepted formula in Melaka numismatics.

Islamic inscriptions

The majority of Malay coins, whether of gold or tin-alloy, were inscribed in Arabic or Jawi, and sometimes both, with various names, legends and titles. Many of these referred to the Muslim religion and frequently included the Islamic title *khalifah*, or 'successor'. This tradition began when the Prophet Muhammad died and the new leader of Islam, Abu Bakar, was styled Khalifah Rasul Allah, 'Successor to the Messenger (or Prophet) of God'. In due course, the second Caliph, Omar, called himself Khalifah Khalifah Rasul Allah, 'Successor to the Successor of the Prophet of God', but thereafter, the title was shortened to a single Khalifah, or even to a simple Khalifah Allah. A second title taken by each Caliph was Amir-al-Mumin'in, 'Commander of the Faithful (of the religion of Islam)'.

Production methods

Most of the gold coins first minted in the Malay Peninsula were made by cutting metal discs, or octagonal planchets, from sheets of beaten gold and then striking them individually between pairs of inscribed dies. The resultant coins were later trimmed around the edges until roughly the correct

weight was achieved. Variations from the true standard are not surprising, because before the accuracy of weights and measures was controlled by law, the counterweights by which the amount of metal was checked often consisted of selected seed weights. The type used was the *biji saga*, or seed of *Abrus amaculatus*, 24 of which were the equivalent of one mace. The weight of a mace (or *mas*) of gold was the equivalent of about 40 grains or 2.6 grams, and that of a *kupang* about 10 grains or 0.65 grams of gold.

Coin distribution

In Johor, believed to be the first Malay state to issue Islamic gold coins, both the mas and the kupang were minted, but in Patani and Kelantan only the small denomination was coined, the mas being used solely as a unit of account. The first Johor ruler to issue gold coins was Sultan Alauddin Riayat Shah II (1527/8–64) who also issued a tin coin known as a *katun*. In addition, silver coins were also produced in Johor and comprised two denominations known as the *penjuru* and the quarter penjuru; two penjuru were equal to one kupang.

Kedah began producing its own state coinage in the 17th century. The earliest known coin, issued by Sultan Rijaluddin Muhammad Shah (1625–51), was made of tin. During the reign of Sultan Muhammad Jiwa Zainal Abidin Shah II (1710–73) silver coins in three denominations—the one *rial*, half *rial* and quarter *rial*—were produced.

Gold coins known as *kijang*, which depict the barking deer of this name, are believed to have been issued in Kelantan since 1400. These coins were minted for use in Kelantan and Patani and are only of the kupang denomination.

Coin trees, known as *pohon pitis*, were also made in Kelantan. The coins were used as currency while the branches were re-smelted for the next casting.

During the course of the 16th century, Johor, Patani and the Sumatran state of Aceh all developed trade coinages, which in addition to being mutually interchangeable were also generally accepted throughout the remainder of the Malay Archipelago.

Tin money trees made in the form of fighting cocks perched on a series of joined rings are unique to Kedah and were first issued during the reign of Sultan Muhammad Jiwa Zainal Abidin Shah II (1710–73 CE).

These fragments of a half and quarter Arab *dirham* were found in a foundation deposit under a presumed temple in Kedah's Bujang Valley. The half dirham bears the Islamic date 234 Al Hijrah (848 CE), and was produced during the period of the Abbasid Caliph al-Mutawakil (847–61 CE). These coins provide evidence that early Arab traders frequented the entrepôt of Kedah.

1710–1773 CE

A silver one *rial* issued in Kedah during the reign of Sultan Muhammad Jiwa Zainal Abidin Shah II (1710–73). *OBVERSE:* 'Al-Sultan Muhammad Jiwa—Ruler under God the Merciful' *REVERSE:* 'State of Kedah the Abode of Peace Year AH 1154 (1741)'

1793–1808 CE

A gold kupang issued in Terengganu during the reign of Sultan Zainal Abidin Shah II (1793–1808). *OBVERSE:* 'Sultan Zainal Abidin Shah' *REVERSE:* 'Khalifatul Mu'minin' (Ruler of the Faithful)

A gold mas issued in Terengganu during the reign of Sultan Zainal Abidin Shah II (1793–1808). *OBVERSE:* 'Sultan Zainal Abidin Shah' *REVERSE:* 'Khalifatul Mu'minin'(Ruler of the Faithful)

Glossary

A

Age dating: Technique which estimates age by correlation with a similar time event.

Artefact dating: Technique which assesses archaeological periods from artefacts.

Aurea Chersonesus: Ancient Greek term meaning 'Golden Peninsula', believed to be the Malay Peninsula.

Australo-Melanesian: Also Australoid; racial group including Australian Aborigines and certain peoples of southern Asia and the Pacific islands.

Austroasiatic: Language superfamily consisting of Mon–Khmer and other Indian and Southeast Asian languages.

Austronesian: Also Malayo-Polynesian; relating to the peoples and language of the Malay Archipelago, central and southern Pacific.

Avalokitesvara: 'The Lord who looks down (in compassion)'; one of the most important Bodhisattvas of Buddhism.

B

Bajau Laut: Sea nomads from the Sulu Archipelago and eastern Sabah coasts.

Balang: Mythical tiger in Kelabit belief.

Bandar: Malay for 'town', formerly used for 'port'.

Bateq: Negrito subgroup.

Batu Aceh: Literally 'Aceh Stone'; carved Islamic gravestones believed to originate from Aceh, Sumatra.

Batu hidup: Literally 'living stones'; refers to megaliths in Melaka and Negeri Sembilan.

Belian: Sarawak ironwood.

Benzoin: Also 'gum benjamin'; tree resin used in perfumes.

Bidayuh: Sarawak ethnic group formerly known as Land Dayak.

Bifacial: Archaeological term for flints flaked on both sides.

Biji saga: *Abrus amaculatus*; small scarlet weighing beads.

Bodhisattva: Enlightened Being in Mahayana Buddhism.

Brahmana: Highest or priestly Hindu caste.

Bunga mas: Literally 'golden flowers'; small trees made of silver or gold used as tribute to Thai rulers.

C

Candi: Pre-Islamic permanent architecture, principally the religious shrine.

Candi Bukit Batu Pahat: 'The Temple on the Hill of Cut Stone'—the best known *candi*.

Celadon: Type of porcelain with a greyish-greenish glaze.

Cengal: Rainforest hardwood used in the construction of boats and dugouts.

Cist graves: Iron Age graves made of slabs of granite.

Cognatic: Descent traced through both maternal and paternal lines.

Cola: Tamil-controlled South Indian kingdom which attacked Malay ports in the 11th century.

D

Dammar: Tropical tree resins used for varnishes and lacquers.

Datu: Malay for 'headman'.

Derhaka: Treason against a Malay ruler.

Devaraja: Sanskrit term meaning 'god king'.

Dongson: Influential cultural style from North Vietnam (began c. 500 BCE) characterized by ornate bronze drums.

Duit casha: Indigenous tin coins.

Dvarapala: Guardian of a door or of a sacred place.

Dvipa: Sanskrit term attached to the names of the nine major units of Greater India—the world according to ancient Indians.

E

Extended burial: Burial where the body is placed in a supine position.

F

Fission track dating: Technique of dating mineral samples by comparing the fission tracks of their uranium nuclei before and after radiation.

Flake tool: Fragment removed by chipping or hammering from a larger stone; used as a stone tool.

Flexed burial: Burial where the body is in a foetal position.

Foraminifera: Order of marine protozoans.

G

Ganesa: Elephant-headed Hindu deity.

Garuda: Mythical bird and Visnu's mount.

Golden Khersonese: Ancient Greek term probably referring to the Malay Peninsula.

Guangzhou: Formerly Canton, China.

Gunung: Malay for 'mountain'.

Gunung-gunung: Mountain-shaped ornamentation on Malay rulers' thrones.

Gunungan: Fan-shaped figure symbolizing the 'tree of life' used in shadow-puppet plays.

H

Hadith: Teachings of Prophet Muhammad and his followers.

Haematite: Also red ochre; a mineral pigment used for cave painting and in burial rituals.

Hoabinhian: From Hoa Binh, North Vietnam; refers to a stone tool industry widely distributed in Southeast Asia between 14,000 and 4,000 years ago.

Holocene: Denoting the period of the last 10,000 years.

Homo erectus: Literally 'man walks erect'; fossils believed to be ancestral to modern humans.

I

In situ: In the natural or original position; used to describe archaeological findings.

Incremental dating: Dating technique using the study of tree rings and lichen.

Ipoh **tree**: Tree which produces a poisonous sap used on blowpipe darts.

Irau: Kelabit festival connected with burial rites.

J

Jaladwara: Spout on the outside of a temple enclosure where sacred liquids used to bathe an icon can be collected.

Jatakamala: Tales of the Buddha in his former existences before his final incarnation.

Jawi: Malay language written in Arabic script.

K

Kadazan: Largest indigenous ethnic group in Sabah.

Kala: Mythical Hindu animal.

Kalimah Shahadah: The Islamic declaration of the faith.

Katun: Early tin coin of Johor.

Kawi: Old Javanese script.

Kayan/Kenyah: Sarawak ethnic groups centred in the middle and upper reaches of the main rivers.

Kedatuan: Malay for 'kingdom'.

Kelabit: Sarawak ethnic group centred in the Kelabit Highlands.

Kendi: Spouted water vessel.

Keramat: Sacred place.

Khalifah: Islamic title meaning 'successor'.

Kijang: Malay for 'barking deer'; also a Kelantanese coin bearing an image of this animal.

Klirieng: Poles used for storing secondary burial jars in Sarawak.

Ksatria: Warrior-king caste of Hinduism.

Kupang: Early Malay Islamic coin equal to 10 grains of gold.

L

Lanceolate: Narrow and tapering to a point at each end; used to describe stone knife points.

Laterite: Insoluble oxide deposits formed by weathering of rocks in tropical regions.

Lingam: Hindu phallic image of the god Siva.

Lukut sekala: Ancient beads prized by the Kelabit of Sarawak.

M

Mahayana: 'Literally 'Greater Vehicle'; schools of Buddhism which espouse belief in other enlightened beings besides the Buddha.

Makam: Grave or tomb.

Mandala: Administrative districts controlled by Srivijaya.

Mandapa: Open-sided hall with a roof supported on pillars.

Mas: Indigenous Islamic coin equal to 40 grains of gold.

Masjid: 'Mosque' in Malay.

Masuk Melayu: Literally 'become Malay'; used to described a convert to Islam.

Megalithic: Literally 'great stone'; pertaining to large, irregularly shaped stones used as monuments.

Mesolithic: Period in Europe between the Palaeolithic and the Neolithic characterized by the appearance of hafted flint tools.

Minangkabau: Matrilineal society originating from Sumatra.

Molong: Resource preservation concept used by nomadic Penan.

Mount Meru: Sacred peak in Hindu–Buddhist cosmology.

Mudra: Hand gestures which characterize the transcendant Buddhas.

Mutisalah: Opaque red glass bead.

N

Nafiri: Royal Perak trumpet.

Naga: Serpent deities.

Nakhoda: Ship captain; derived from Arab–Persian sources.

Nandi: Sacred bull, the mount of the Hindu god Siva.

Negritos: Sometimes 'Semang'; Australo-Melanesian aborigines of Peninsular Malaysia.

Neolithic: Literally 'new stone age'; the period when farming began, characterized by polished stone tools and pottery.

O

Orang Asli: Literally 'original people'; denoting the aborigines of Peninsular Malaysia.

Orang kaya: Malay for 'rich person', formerly synonomous with 'noble'.

Orang Laut: Literally 'sea people'; Austronesian people, originally sea nomads, from the Strait of Melaka and the Riau Archipelago.

Orang Sungai: Ethnic group from southeastern Sabah.

Oxygen isotope records: Measurements of the amount of oxygen isotopes in materials used in determining past oceanic temperatures for dating purposes.

P

Palaeoenvironment: Term used to denote the external conditions of past ages.

Palaeo-lake: Extinct lake.

Palaeolithic: Literally 'old stone age'; the phase of technological development comprising the oldest man-made stone tools.

Palynology: Study of living and fossil pollen grains and plant spores.

Parang: Malay sharp-edged knife similar to a machete.

Pawang: Malay magician or shaman.

Penarikan: Portage between the Muar and Pahang rivers; derived from the Malay word for dragging or pulling boats.

Penjuru: Early Islamic silver coin produced in Johor.

Petroglyph: Prehistoric drawing or carving on rock.

Phytoliths: Silica bodies derived from plant cell structures.

Pleistocene: Epoch from 1.6 million years ago to about 10,000 years ago, also referred to as the Ice Age.

Pohon pitis: Tin coin trees cast in wooden moulds.

Postglacial period: Epoch beginning about 18,000 years ago, around the end of the Pleistocene or last Ice Age.

Prau: Malay sailing vessel.

Primogeniture: Right of the eldest child as the successor.

Protohistoric: Period in Malaysia from the end of the first century CE to the beginning of the 15th century when the historic period began with the emergence of Melaka.

Pulau: Malay for 'island'.

Punan/Penan: Hunter-gatherer ethnic group of Sarawak.

Q

Quaternary: Most recent period of geological time covering approximately the last 1.6 million years.

Qingbai: Formerly 'Ching pai'; type of ivory-coloured, glazed Chinese ceramics dating from the Song–Yuan dynasties.

R

Radiocarbon dating: Technique for determining the age of organic materials based on their radioactive carbon content.

Raja makhota: Malay for 'crown prince'.

Rami: Fibre obtained from a native plant used for making rope.

Relative dating: Archaeological method used to determine age by relating the dates of artefacts found together.

Rial: Early Islamic silver coin produced in Kedah, named after an Arab coin.

S

Salong: Burial hut used in Sarawak for storing jar burials.

Sape: Bornean four-stringed instrument.

Secondary burial: Reburial of cremated and burnt remains in receptacles such as jars and log coffins.

Semang: Former name for Negritos from Perak, Kedah and Pahang.

Senoi: Literally 'human being'; Orang Asli agriculturalists of upland Perak, Kelantan and Pahang.

Serambi: Malay for 'veranda'.

Singha-muka: 'Lion face'; a design thought to originate from 9th-century India.

Siva: Literally 'The Destroyer', one of the three main gods of the Hindu pantheon.

Snana-droni: Drain to catch sacred liquids used to bathe the main icon in a Hindu temple.

Speleothems: Secondary mineral deposits in stalagtites and stalagmites.

Sufi: An adherent of various mystical orders of Islam.

Sunda Continental Shelf: The sea bed surrounding Malaysia, Borneo, Sumatra, Java and other mainland Southeast Asian countries which ends at the continental slope.

Sundaland: The landmass enclosed by the Sunda Continental Shelf.

Sungai: Malay for 'river'.

Surau: Small Islamic prayer house.

Suvarnabhumi: Ancient Indian term meaning 'Land of Gold', probably the Malay Peninsula and the Malay Archipelago.

Suvarnadvipa: Ancient Indian term meaning 'Golden Island (or Peninsula)', probably Sumatra.

Syahbandar: Malay for 'harbourmaster'.

T

Tampang: Pyramid- or pagoda-shaped tin ingot.

'Tembeling knife': Fan-shaped Neolithic stone tool originally found in the Tembeling River region.

Tempayan: Malay for a large earthenware storage vessel.

Thermoluminescence: Phosphorescence of materials resulting from heating; used in archaeological dating.

Tufa: Soft, porous rock consisting of calcium carbonate deposits.

Tulang mawas: Literally 'apes' bones'; ancient, long-shafted metal tools of unknown use found in Peninsular Malaysia.

U

Usnisa: Cranial protuberance on Buddha images.

V

Vaisya: Hindu caste of artisans and traders.

Vaniaga: Class of traders from Srivijaya mentioned in a 7th-century Sumatran inscription.

Vimana: Enclosed sanctuary in a Hindu temple where the main icon is kept.

Visnu: One of the three main Hindu deities; in Sanskrit, literally 'the one who works everywhere'.

Y

Younger Dryas Stadial: Episode of climatic cooling from about 10,000 years ago which interrupted the general trend of postglacial climatic improvement.

Bibliography

Abbreviations

BIPPA   *Bulletin of the Indo-Pacific Prehistory Association*

BRM   *Bulletin of the Raffles Museum, Singapore*

FMJ   *Federation Museums Journal*

GSM   *Geological Society of Malaysia*

JAM   *Jurnal Arkeologi Malaysia*

JFMSM   *Journal of the Federated Malay States Museums*

JMBRAS   *Journal of the Malaysian Branch of the Royal Asiatic Society*

SMJ   *Sarawak Museum Journal*

SPAFA   *SEA Ministers of Education Organization Project for Archaeology and Fine Arts*

Adi Haji Taha (1983), 'Recent Archaeological Discoveries in Peninsular Malaysia, 1976–1982', *JMBRAS*, 56 (1): 47–63.

_____ (1985), 'The Re-excavation of the Rockshelter of Gua Cha, Ulu Kelantan, West Malaysia', *FMJ*, 30.

_____ (1987), 'Recent Archaeological Discoveries in Peninsular Malaysia, 1983–1985', *JMBRAS*, 60 (1): 27–44.

Adi Haji Taha and Abdul Jalil Othman (1982), 'The Excavation of the Megalithic Alignment at Kampung Ipoh, Tampin, Negeri Sembilan', *JMBRAS*, 55 (1).

Adi Haji Taha and Zulkifli Jaafar (1990), 'A Preliminary Report on Archaeological Research and Excavation at Gua Kelawar, Sungai Siput, Perak', *JAM*, 3: 111–24.

Andaya, Barbara Watson and Andaya, Leonard (1982), *A History of Malaysia*, Basingstoke and London: Macmillan.

Beekman, E. M. (ed., trans.) (1993), *The Poison Tree: Selected Writings of Rumphius on the Natural History of the Indies*, Kuala Lumpur: Oxford University Press.

Bellwood, Peter (1988), *Archaeological Research in South-*

Eastern Sabah, Kota Kinabalu: Sabah Museum Monograph 2.

_____ (1989), 'Archaeological Investigations at Bukit Tenggorak and Segarong, Southeastern Sabah', *BIPPA*, 9: 122–62.

_____ (1997), *Prehistory of the Indo-Malaysian Archipelago*, rev'd edn, Honolulu: University of Hawaii Press.

Biswas, B. (1973), 'Quaternary Changes in Sea-Level in the South China Sea', *GSM*, 6: 229–56.

Bock, Carl (1881), *The Head-Hunters of Borneo: A Narrative of Travel up the Mahakkam and down the Barrito; also Journeyings in Sumatra*, London: Sampson Low, Marston, Searle & Rivington.

Brown, C. C. (trans.) (1952), 'Sejarah Melayu or Malay Annals', *JMBRAS*, 25 (159).

Bulbeck, D. (1982), 'A Re-evaluation of Possible Evolutionary Processes in Southeast Asia since the Late Pleistocene', *BIPPA*, 3: 1–21.

Carey, Iskandar (1976), *Orang Asli: The Aboriginal Tribes of Peninsular Malaysia*, Kuala Lumpur: Oxford University Press.

Casparis, J. G. de (1980), 'Ahmat Majanu's Tombstone at Pengkalan Kempas and Its Kawi Inscription', *JMBRAS*, 53 (1): 1–22.

A Ceramic Legacy of Asia's Maritime Trade: Song Dynasty and Guandong Wares and other 11th to 19th Century Trade Ceramics Found on Tioman Island, Malaysia (1985), Kuala Lumpur: Southeast Asian Ceramic Society and Oxford University Press.

Chaudhiri, K. N. (1985), *Trade and Civilisation in the Indian Ocean: An Economic History from the Rise of Islam to 1750*, Cambridge: Cambridge University Press.

Chin, Lucas (1980), *Cultural Heritage of Sarawak*, Kuching: Sarawak Museum.

Christie, J. W. (1985), 'On Poni: The Santubong Sites of Sarawak', *SMJ*, 34 (55): 77–89.

Collings, H. D. (1937), 'Recent Finds of Iron Age Sites in Southern Perak and Selangor', *BRM*, Series B, 1 (2): 75–93.

Denton, Robert Knox et al. (1997), *Malaysia and the Original People: A Case Study of the Impact of Development on Indigenous Peoples*, Needham Heights, Mass.: Allyn & Bacon.

Dunn, F. L. (1964), 'Excavation at Gua Kechil, Pahang', *JMBRAS*, 37 (2): 87–124.

_____ (1975), 'Rainforest Collectors and Traders: A Study of Resource Utilisation in Modern and Ancient Malaya', *JMBRAS* Monograph No. 5.

Evans, I. H. N. (1927), *The Ethnology and Archaeology of the Malay Peninsula*, Cambridge: Cambridge University Press.

_____ (1928a), 'On Ancient Remains from Kuala Selinsing', *JFMSM*, 12: 139–44.

_____ (1928b), 'On Slab-built Graves in Perak', *JFMSM*, 12: 111–19.

_____ (1930), 'An Ancient Kitchen Midden in Province Wellesley', *JFMSM*, 15 (1): 15–18.

_____ (1931), 'Excavations at Nyong, Tembeling River', *JFMSM*, 15 (2): 51–62.

_____ (1932), 'Excavation at Tanjung Rawa, Kuala Selinsing', *JFMSM*, 15: 79–134.

_____ (1968), *The Negritos of Malaya*, London: Frank Cass.

Fatimi, S. Q. (1963), *Islam Comes to Malaysia*, Singapore: Malaysian Sociological Research Institute.

Gibson-Hill, C. A. (1952), 'Further Notes on the Old Boat Found at Pontian, in Southern Pahang', *JMBRAS*, 25 (1): 111–33.

Hall, Kenneth R. (1985), *Maritime Trade and State Development in Early Southeast Asia*, Honolulu: University of Hawai'i Press.

Harrisson, Barbara (1964),

'Recent Archaeological Discoveries in Malaysia, 1962–1963', *JMBRAS*, 37 (2): 192–200.

_____ (1967), 'A Classification of Stone Age Burials from Niah Great Cave, Sarawak', *SMJ*, 15: 126–99.

Harrisson, Tom (1958), 'A Living Megalith in Upland Borneo', *SMJ*, 8.

_____ (1971a), 'Niah Cave Double-spouted Vessels', *SMJ*, 19 (38–9): 367–73.

_____ (1971b), 'Prehistoric Double-spouted Vessels Excavated from Niah Caves, Borneo', *JMBRAS*, 44 (2): 35–78.

_____ (1973a), 'Newly Discovered Prehistoric Rock Carvings in Ulu Tomani, Sabah', *JMBRAS*, 46 (1): 141–3.

_____ (1973b), 'Megalithic Evidences in East Malaysia: An Introductory Summary', *JMBRAS*, 46 (1): 123–39.

Harrisson, Tom and Harrisson, Barbara (1968), 'Magala: A Series of Neolithic and Metal Age Burial Grottos at Sekaloh, Niah, Sarawak', *JMBRAS*, 41 (2): 154.

_____ (1969–70), *The Prehistory of Sabah*, Sabah Society Journal, 4.

Harrisson, Tom and O'Connor, S. J. (1967), 'The Tantric Shrine Excavated at Santubong', *SMJ*, 15 (30–1): 201–22.

_____ (1968), 'The Prehistoric Iron Industry in the Sarawak River Delta: Evidence by Association', *SMJ*, 16 (32–3): 1–54.

Harrisson, Tom and Peacock, B. A. V. (1965), 'Recent Archaeological Discoveries in Malaysia, 1964', *JMBRAS*, 38 (1): 244–55.

Ipoi Datan (1993), 'Archaeological Excavations at Gua Sireh (Serian) and Lubang Angin (Gunung Mulu National Park), Sarawak, Malaysia', *SMJ*, 45 (66).

Kamaludin bin Hassan (1989),

'Palynology of the Lowland Seberang Prai and Kuala Kurau Areas North-West Peninsular Malaysia', *GSM*, 23: 199–215.

Kamaludin bin Hassan et al. (1993), 'Radiocarbon and Thermoluminescence Dating of the Old Alluvium from a Coastal Site in Perak, Malaysia', *Sedimentary Geology*, 83: 199–210.

Kedit, Peter M. (1982), 'An Ecological Survey of the Penan', *SMJ*, 40 (61): 169–84.

Lamb, Alastair (1959), 'Recent Archaeological Work in Kedah, 1958', *JMBRAS*, 32 (1): 214–31.

_____ (1960), 'Report on the Excavation and Reconstruction of Chandi Bukit Batu Pahat, Central Kedah', *FMJ*, pp. 1–108.

_____ (1965), 'Some Observations on Stone and Glass Beads in Early South-east Asia', *JMBRAS*, 38 (2): 87–124.

Leong Sau Heng (1977), 'Ancient Finds from Kampong Jenderam Hilir', *Malaysia in History*, 20 (2): 38–47.

_____ (1990), 'A Tripod Pottery Complex in Peninsular Malaysia', in Ian Glover and Emily Glover (eds.), *Southeast Asian Archaeology 1986*, Oxford: BAR International Series 561: 65–75.

_____ (1991), 'Jenderam Hilir and the Mid-Holocene Prehistory of the West Coast Plain of Peninsular Malaysia', *BIPPA*, 10: 150–60.

_____ (1992), 'Recent Finds of More Slab-graves in the Bernam Valley, Peninsular Malaysia', *SPAFA* Journal, 2 (3): 4–8.

Linehan, W. (1951), 'Traces of a Bronze Age Culture Associated with Iron Age Implements in the Regions of Klang and the Tembeling, Malaya', *JMBRAS*, 24 (3): 1–80.

Loewenstein, Prince John (1956), 'The Origin of the Malayan Metal Age', *JMBRAS*, 29 (2): 1–84.

Mills, J.V. (1937), 'Malaya in the Wu-Pei-Chih Charts', *JMBRAS*, 15 (3): 1–48.

Mohd Kassim Haji Ali and Shaw, William (1970), *Malacca Coins*, Kuala Lumpur: Muzium Negara.

_____ (1971), *Coins of North Malaya*, Kuala Lumpur: Muzium Negara.

Nik Hassan Shuhaimi Nik Abd Rahman (1988), 'Arca Agama Buddha Purba Semenanjung Malaysia: Penelitian Ikonografi dan Kronologi serta Ertinya', *Jurnal Jebat*, 16: 15–30.

Nik Hassan Shuhaimi Nik Abd Rahman and Kamaruddin bin Zakaria (1993), 'Recent Archaeological Discoveries in Sungai Mas, Kuala Muda, Kedah', *JMBRAS*, 66 (2): 73–80.

Nik Hassan Shuhaimi Nik Abd Rahman, Mohd Kamaruzaman Abd Rahman and Mohd Yusof Abdullah (1990), 'Tapak Prasejarah Gua Bukit Ta'at, Hulu Terengganu', *JAM*, 3: 1–14.

Nik Hassan Shuhaimi Nik Abd Rahman and Othman Mohd Yatim (1990), *Antiquities of Bujang Valley*, Kuala Lumpur: Museum Association of Malaysia.

_____ (1994), *Beruas Kerajaan Melayu Kuno di Perak*, Kuala Lumpur: Persatuan Muzium Malaysia.

Noone, H. D. (1941), 'A Proposed Classification of Malayan Polished Stone Implements, *JFMSM*, 19 (2): 210–18.

Othman Mohd Yatim (1988), *Batu Aceh: Early Islamic Gravestones in Peninsular Malaysia*, Kuala Lumpur: Museum Association of Malaysia.

_____ (1989), *Warisan Kesenian Dalam Tamadum Islam*, Kuala Lumpur: Dewan Bahasa dan Pustaka.

_____ (1995), *Islamic Art*, Kuala Lumpur: Dewan Bahasa dan Pustaka.

Peacock, B. A.V (1964), 'Mahayana Buddhist Votive Tablets in Perlis', *JMBRAS*, 37 (2): 47–59.

_____ (1965), 'The Drum at Kampung Sungai Lang', *Malaya in History*, 10 (1): 3–15.

_____ (1966), 'Recent Archaeological Discoveries in Malaysia, 1965', *JMBRAS*, 39 (1): 201.

_____ (1974), 'Pillar Base Architecture in Ancient Kedah', *JMBRAS*, 47 (1): 66–86.

Perbadanan Muzium Negeri Kelantan (1986), *Kelantan Dalam Perskpektif Arkeologi: Satu Kumpulan Esei*, Kota Bharu.

Quaritch Wales, H. G. (1940), 'Archaeological Researches on Ancient Indian Colonization in Malaya', *JMBRAS*, 18 (1).

Quaritch Wales, H. G. and Quaritch Wales, Dorothy C. (1947), 'Further Work on Indian Sites in Malaya', *JMBRAS*, 20 (1): 1–11.

Sather, Clifford (1997), *The Bajau Laut: Adaptation, History, and Fate in a Maritime Fishing Society of South-eastern Sabah*, Kuala Lumpur: Oxford University Press.

Sheppard, Haji Mubin (1962), 'Megaliths in Malacca and Negeri Sembilan', *FMJ*, 6.

Sieveking, G. de G. (1954–5), 'Excavations at Gua Cha, Kelantan, 1954', *FMJ*, 1 & 2 (1): 75–138.

_____ (1956), 'The Iron Age Collections of Malaya', *JMBRAS*, 24 (2): 79–138.

_____ (1962), 'The Prehistoric Cemetery at Bukit Tengku Lembu, Perlis', *FMJ*, 7: 25–54.

Skeat, Walter William and Blagden, Charles Otto (1906), *Pagan Races of the Malay Peninsula*, London: Macmillan.

Sorensen, Per and Hatting, T. (1967), *Archaeological Excavations in Thailand*, Copenhagen: Munksgaard.

Stein Callenfells, P.V. van (1927), 'The Pengkalan Kempas Inscription', *JFMSM*, 12 (4): 107–10.

_____ (1936), 'An Excavation of Three Kitchen Middens at Guak Kepah, Province Wellesley, Straits Settlement', *BRM*, Series B: 27–37.

Sutlive, V. H. Jr. (ed.) (1993), *Change and Development in Borneo*, Kuching: Borneo Research Council, and Virginia: College of William & Mary.

Syed Muhammad Naguib Al-Atas (1970), *The Correct Date of the Terengganu Inscription*, Kuala Lumpur: Museum Department.

Theseira, O. A. (1976), 'Preliminary Report of Archaeological Sites along the Tembeling River, Pahang', *FMJ*, 21: 37.

Tibbetts, G. R. (1957), 'Early Muslim Traders in South-East Asia', *JMBRAS*, 30 (1): 1–45.

_____ (1979), *A Study of the Arabic Texts Containing Material on South-East Asia*, Leiden: E. J. Brill.

Treloar, F. E. (1978), 'Chemical Analysis of Iron, Iron Slag and Pottery Remains of the Prehistoric Iron Industry of the Sarawak River Delta', *SMJ*, 26 (47): 125–33.

Tweedie, M. W. F. (1940), 'Report on Excavations in Kelantan', *JMBRAS*, 18 (2).

_____ (1953), 'The Stone Age in Malaya', *JMBRAS*, 26 (2).

Wheatley, Paul (1961), *The Golden Khersonese: Studies in the Historical Geography of the Malay Peninsula Before A.D. 1500*, Kuala Lumpur: University of Malaya Press.

Wilkinson, R. J. (1939), 'The Bernam Slab-Graves', *JMBRAS*, 27 (1): 134–43.

Wolters, O. W. (1979), 'Studying Srivijaya', *JMBRAS*, 52 (2): 1–32.

Zakaria Ali (1994), *Islamic Art in Southeast Asia 830 AD–1570 AD*, Kuala Lumpur: Dewan Bahasa dan Pustaka.

Zuraina Majid (1982), 'The West Mouth, Niah, in the Prehistory of Southeast Asia', *SMJ*, 31 (52).

_____ (1988–9), 'Kota Tampan, Perak: The Geological and Archaeological Evidence for a Late Pleistocene Site', *JMBRAS*, 61 (2): 123–34.

_____ (1991), *Prasejarah Malaysia: Sudahkah Zaman Gelap Menjadi Cerah?*, Penang: Universiti Sains Malaysia.

_____ (1997), 'Archaeology of Bukit Jawa', *JMBRAS*, 70 (2): 49–52.

Zuraina Majid (ed.) (1994), *The Excavation of Gua Gunung Runtuh and the Discovery of the Perak Man in Malaysia*, Kuala Lumpur: Department of Museums and Antiquity Malaysia.

Index

Picture Credits

Antiques of the Orient, pp. 26–7, 'Upas Tree'; pp. 62–3, 'Malaye Proas', 'Indiae Orientalis', 'Pekan'; p. 119, 'Palembang'; p. 122, 'Singapore'; p. 123, 'Malacca'. **Anuar bin Abdul Rahim**, p. 48, rice; p. 52, dolmen, jar, burial hut; p. 58, pole erection; p. 59, burial pole. **Arkib Negara Malaysia**, p. 98, bathing ceremony. **Asian Civilisations Museum/National Heritage Board, Singapore**, p. 105, Buddha. **Bellwood, Peter**, p. 15, Tingkayu; p. 23, Madai, Hagop Bilo, Agop Atas dig, burial; p. 24, Tingkayu lake bed, lanceolates, dig; p. 27, Baturong Caves; p. 61, menhir and field workers. **British Library**, p. 84 and pp. 124–5, Idrisi's 'Map of the World' 1154; p. 110, *Sejarah Melayu*. **Chai Kah Yune**, p. 6, ring; p. 38, ape-man; p. 40, Batu Patung, Batu Narit; p. 41, Ulu Tomani; p. 49, casket and contents; p. 51, Angkor Wat mural; p. 54, Perak Man; p. 55, Gua Cha burial; p. 56, boat burial; p. 60, stone seat; p. 71, pot; p. 74, Arab ship; p. 77, shards; p. 79, belt; p. 81, temple, relic box lid; p. 85, Sinbad; p. 89, mountain money; p. 96, Buddha; p. 98, armlets and mouthpiece. **Chang, Tommy**, pp. 14–15, Mt Kinabalu; p. 47, Bajau Laut; pp. 88–9, jars. **Cheong Hoi Chan**, pp. 94–5, Candi Bukit Batu Pahat; p. 109, Buddha. **Dew, Stephen**, p. 65, old map; p. 66, old map; p. 73, Wubeizhi Chart; p. 74, old map; p. 78, old map; pp. 82–3, Faxian map and Wubeizhi Chart; p. 118, old map; p. 120, Cola map. **Dumarçay, Jacques**, p. 77, boat. **Elias-Moore, Kerry**, p. 19, Kota Tampan; p. 69, Chi tu; pp. 106–7, Bujang Valley; p. 114, port kingdom; p. 129, discovery scene. **Ipoi Datan**, p. 4, drawing; p. 20, Lubang Angin; p. 27, Penan; p. 40, spiral engraving. **Ishak Hashim**, pp. 132–3, tombstone diagram. **Jabatan Muzium dan Antikuiti Malaysia**, p. 6, Tunku Abdul Rahman; p. 7, bell discovery; p. 8, axe; p. 10, painting, excavation; p. 12, fossil, archaeologist; p. 17, Gua Peraling, tools; p. 18, Kota Tampan; p. 19, tools; p. 20, bones, excavation; p. 22, Negritos, burials, shards; p. 23, Gua Senyum, Gua Cha, Gua Taat, Gua Cawan; p. 24, Kota Tampan; p. 26, girl;

p. 30, bark cloth beater, stone tool; p. 31, stone tools on map, adze; p. 38, iron tools; p. 41, Pengkalan Kempas; p. 42, Gua Tambun; p. 44, fish trap, tree cutter, burial; p. 46, Negritos; p. 48, Gua Cha, rice, raft; p. 49, black knife; p. 50, stone tools, Kota Gelanggi; p. 59, jar and beads; p. 66, votive tablets; p. 67, Bukit Cawas, marker, iron tools, Gua Taat, Tasek Cini, Gua Tapa; p. 68, Gua Cawan; p. 71, cowries, burial; pp. 72–3, all pottery; p. 90, Site 50 and Site 11; p. 100, votive tablet, Gua Cawas; p. 103, inscriptions; p. 105, pottery; p. 108, tin mine; p. 114, reconstruction; p. 128, inscriptions. **Jabatan Muzium dan Antikuiti Malaysia/Kamaruddin bin Zakaria**, p. 35, Sg. Mas beads; p. 51, beads; p. 67 shards; p. 78, student; p. 83, researchers; p. 85, shards, researchers; p. 90, researchers; p. 106, Site 32; p. 117, shards. **Jabatan Penyiasatan Kajibumi Malaysia/Kamaludin bin Hassan**, p. 12, augering, core; p. 13, resins, Pantai Mine; p. 14, foraminifer; p. 15, satellite image; p. 16, rock; p. 18, mangroves; p. 70, dwellings, geologists, satellite image; p. 71, man; p. 79, Kuala Selinsing. **Khang, Peter**, p. 13, radiometric dating. **Kompleks Sejarah Kota Ngah Ibrahim, Perak/Radin Mohd Noh Saleh**, p. 6, bead; p. 8, stone tool, pot; p. 10, axe; p. 11, adze, vessel; p. 14, tool; p. 18, pot; p. 24, pebble tools; p. 25, bangle; p. 29, ring, adze; p. 45, beater; p. 63, necklace; p. 91, beads; p. 114, beads and pot; p. 116, beads and shells; p. 117, glass and bone objects; p. 140, tool. **Lau, Dennis**, p. 21, Penan. **Lee Sin Bee**, p. 30, flake making; p. 34, drilling beads; p. 57, transporting stones; p. 76, 3-part economy; p. 87, trade products of Southeast Asia; p. 109, sacred symbols. **Leong Sau Heng**, p. 20, tripod vessel, tripod legs; p. 25, tripod legs, vessel, fern spore; p. 57, cist graves and grave goods. **Manguin, Pierre-Yves**, p. 118, stone Ganesa; p. 119, Buddha image. **Miksic, John**, p. 83, Xingjiao Pagoda; p. 98, royal dais; p. 123, gold armlet. **Money Museum Bank Negara Malaysia**, p. 8, elephant money; p. 88,

beads; p. 89, animal money, ingots; p. 93, *bunga mas*; p. 125, Kijang coin; pp. 134–5, coin trees and coins. **Muzium Arkeologi Lembah Bujang/Radin Mohd Noh Saleh**, p. 8, votive tablet; p. 34, Bujang beads; p. 66, Buddha; p. 67, vessel; p. 74, glass; p. 75, stone; p. 77, reliquaries; p. 80, Nandi and Ganesa; p. 82, Hariti, jar; p. 83, Buddha head, shards; p. 85, stem, glass; p. 93, brick; p. 96, votive tablet; p. 97, guardian, Buddha; p. 101, shards, vase; p. 102, bronze; p. 117, pot; p. 121, lingam; reliquaries and objects; p. 138, beads. **Muzium Budaya Melaka**, p. 101, throne room scene. **Muzium Negara Collection/Tara Sosrowardoyo**, p. 6, 'money tree'; p. 36, bell; p. 96, figurine. **Muzium Negeri Pahang Darul Makmur/Radin Mohd Noh Saleh**, p. 7, pot, gravestone; p. 8, metal tool; p. 49, Tembeling knife; p. 50, shells, bowl; p. 51, iron tools; p. 63, jarlet; p. 74, urn; p. 75, ceramics; p. 86, ceramics, old boat; pp. 90–1, Buddha; pp. 114–15, bronze, bowl; p. 122, ceramics. **Muzium Seni Asia/Radin Mohd Noh Saleh**, p. 84, plate. **National Museum of Jakarta/Tara Sosrowardoyo**, p. 119, Telaga Batu. **Picture Library**: Lee Choong Min, Maurice, p. 47, Punan; Loh Swee Tatt, p. 44, drummers; Pan Poiw Kan, p. 18, Lake Toba; Geoffrey Smith, p. 118, Palembang; Cees Van Leeuwen, p. 26, Negrito; Yap Kok Sun, p. 20, p. 23, Niah. **Radin Mohd Noh Saleh**, p. 8, bricks; p. 9, gravestone; p. 16, Pantai Sri Tujuh; p. 24, Lake Chenderoh; pp. 28–9, megaliths; p. 41, Pengkalan Kempas; p. 49, megaliths, Bujang Valley; p. 53, cist grave, burial pole, megalith; p. 58, carvings, burial pole; p. 60, stone avenues, megaliths; p. 61, *ibu* megalith; p. 64, Cerok To'kun, Sg Mas stone, canal; p. 65, Buddhagupta Stone; p. 72, Pulau Tioman, Nenek si-Muka; p. 74, pillar mount; p. 75; lintel; p. 79, Muda River, Narathiwat, Kelantan River; p. 80, Site 50; p. 81, deity stand, cruciform; p. 84, Gunung Jerai; p. 90, Candi Bukit Batu Pahat, Site 19; pp. 92–3, cist grave, megaliths, boat dragon, 'tree of life', Gunung Jerai, Candi Bukit Batu Pahat; p. 94, spout,

Candi Bukit Batu Pahat; p. 95, Site 50, Site 21 and Site 19; p. 99, Candi Bukit Batu Pahat, puppets; p. 102, Site 50; p. 103, 'oath stone'; p. 104, Candi Bukit Batu Pahat; p. 106, Candi Bukit Batu Pahat; p. 107, Site 50 and Site 19; pp. 110–11, Beruas and gravestones; p. 112, Gunung Santubong, Batu Gambar; p. 116, museum and mounts; p. 117, Sg Mas; p. 120, pedestal, lintel; p. 121, Site 50; pp. 124–5, gravestones, megalith, inscriptions; pp. 126–7, all gravestones and details; p. 130, megalith; p. 131, standing stone; pp. 132–133, all gravestones. **Rossi, Guido**, p. 122, Muara Takus. **Sabah Museum**, p. 31, Sabah stone tools. **Sarawak Museum**, p. 6, Niah; p. 10, Gua Hitam; pp. 28–9, paintings, Niah dig; p. 31, Niah stone tools; p. 32, double-spout, baby carrier, urn, shards; p. 34, Sarawak beads; p. 35, bead hat, woman, single beads, necklaces; p. 40, Batu Gambar, Sungai Jaong engravings; p. 43, Gua Hitam and Gua Sireh; p. 53, baby carrier, amulet; p. 54, skull, Tom Harrisson; p. 55, earthenware; p. 56, Gua Hitam boat coffins, cave paintings; p. 61, dolmen, Tom Harrisson; p. 75, Buddha image; p. 88, skullcap; p. 112, Buddha; p. 113, barter trade, ceramics, relic box and relics, Bongkissam shrine; p. 114, trade products; p. 136, pottery. **Singapore History Museum of the National Heritage Board, Singapore**, pp. 122–3, monolith. **Tan Hong Yew**, p. 36, bronze celts; p. 37, belt toggles, Dongson drums; p. 39, cist grave, iron implements; p. 50, bronze drum; p. 52, cist grave, bronze drum, megaliths, coffin stands, Gua Cha burial; p. 59, log coffins; p. 88, bronze cannon, ox cannon; p. 100, Malay polity; p. 102, Terengganu Stone; p. 103, Minye Tujuh tombstone; p. 108, 4-armed Avalokitesvara, p. 109, 8-armed Avalokitesvara; p. 110, tin ingots; p. 129, Terengganu Stone; p. 130, 15th-century tomb; p. 131, Pengkalan Kempas megaliths; p. 135, Arab coin. **Yeap Kok Chien**, p. 32, potter's wheel, p. 33, reconstructed vessel. **Yu-Chee Chong Fine Art, London**, p. 87, 'Kora-kora from Gebe'.